Alabama High School Graduation Test in Science
Chart of Standards

<table>
<tr><td colspan="5">Passing the Alabama High School Graduation Test in Science
Chart of Standards
The following chart correlates each question on the Diagnostic Test, Practice Test 1, and Practice Test 2 to the Science HSGT Biology Core Standards published by the Alabama Department of Education. These test questions are also correlated with chapters in the Alabama High School Graduation Test in Science.</td></tr>
</table>

Competency Standards	Chapter Number	Diagnostic Test Questions	Practice Test 1 Questions	Practice Test 2 Questions
1 Select appropriate laboratory glassware, balances, time measuring equipment and optical instrument to conduct an experiment	1	48	42, 52	
1a Describing the steps of the scientific method	1	47, 60		1, 5, 7, 57
1b Comparing controls, dependent variables, and independent variables	1		23, 36	73
1c Identifying safe laboratory procedures when handling chemicals and using Bunsen burners and laboratory glassware	1	43, 50	19	

Competency Standards	Chapter Number	Diagnostic Test Questions	Practice Test 1 Questions	Practice Test 2 Questions
1d Using appropriate SI units for measuring length, volume, and mass	1	72	9	28
2 Describe cell processes necessary for achieving homeostasis, including active and passive transport, osmosis, diffusion, exocytosis, and endocytosis	2	1, 74	21, 24	33, 71, 75
2a Identifying functions of carbohydrates, lipids, proteins, and nucleic acids in cellular activities	3	26	80	78
2b Comparing the reaction of plant and animal cells in isotonic, hypotonic, and hypertonic solutions	2	49	5, 49	
2c Explaining how surface area, cell size, temperature, light, and pH affect cellular activities	2	38		
2d Applying the concept of fluid pressure to biological systems	2	78		8

Competency Standards	Chapter Number	Diagnostic Test Questions	Practice Test 1 Questions	Practice Test 2 Questions
3 Identify reactants and products associated with photosynthesis and cellular respiration and the purposes of these two processes	3	15, 21, 39, 44, 54, 77	15, 20, 31, 47, 55, 85	15, 16, 65, 81, 84, 88
4 Describe similarities and differences of cell organelles, using diagrams and tables	2	4, 10	2, 22, 25, 46, 78, 80	3, 66, 74
4a Identifying scientists who contributed to the cell theory	2			
4b Distinguishing between prokaryotic and eukaryotic cells	2	36		
4c Identifying various technologies used to observe cells	2			
5 Identify cells, tissues, organs, organ systems, organisms, populations, communities, and ecosystems as levels of organization in the biosphere	2, 8	75, 81, 83, 89	28, 38, 44, 63, 65	41, 50, 60, 77, 82, 90
5a Recognizing that cells differentiate to perform specific functions	2, 4			

Competency Standards	Chapter Number	Diagnostic Test Questions	Practice Test 1 Questions	Practice Test 2 Questions
6 Describe the roles of mitotic and meiotic divisions during reproduction, growth, and repair of cells	4	6, 73	34, 51, 81	18, 26, 59
6a Comparing sperm and egg formation in terms of ploidy	4	31, 51, 53	51	42, 61
6b Comparing sexual and asexual reproduction	4	18	3, 17, 30, 33	34

Competency Standards	Chapter Number	Diagnostic Test Questions	Practice Test 1 Questions	Practice Test 2 Questions
7 Apply Mendel's law to determine phenotypic and genotypic probabilities of offspring	5	30	11, 68	45, 86
7a Defining important genetic terms, including dihybrid cross, monohybrid cross, phenotype, genotype, homozygous, heterozygous, dominant trait, recessive trait, incomplete dominance, co-dominance, and allele	5	35, 90	12, 62, 79	10, 36, 89
7b Interpreting inheritance patterns shown in graphs and charts	5	55	68, 79	86
7c Calculating genotypic and phenotypic percentages and ratios using a Punnett square	5	33, 79	68, 87	10, 86, 87
8 Identify the structure and function of DNA, RNA, and protein	4	13, 17, 82	56, 69	6, 83, 85
8a Explaining relationships among DNA, genes, and chromosomes	5		69	85
8b Listing significant contributions of biotechnology to society, including agricultural and medical practices	5		86	44
8c Relating normal patterns of genetic inheritance to genetic variation	4, 5		73	
8d Relating ways chance, mutagens, and genetic engineering increase diversity	5	27, 29, 68		40
8e Relating genetic disorders and disease to patterns of genetic inheritance	5		32, 61	

Competency Standards	Chapter Number	Diagnostic Test Questions	Practice Test 1 Questions	Practice Test 2 Questions
9 Differentiate between the previous five-kingdom and current six-kingdom classification systems	6		66	
9a Sequencing taxa from most inclusive to least inclusive in the classification of living things	6	59, 71	8, 58	24
9b Identifying organisms using a dichotomous key	6		58	23
9c Identifying ways in which organisms from the Monera, Protista, and Fungi kingdoms are beneficial and harmful	6			80
9d Justifying the grouping of viruses in a category separate from living things	6	52		
9e Writing scientific names accurately by using binomial nomenclature	6			24
10 Distinguish between monocots and dicots, angiosperms and gymnosperms, and vascular and nonvascular plants	6	22, 62, 70	45, 60, 67	27, 29, 31, 52
10a Describing the histology of roots, stems, leaves, and flowers	6	16, 66	16, 60, 67, 72	31, 63
10b Recognizing chemical and physical adaptations of plants	7	65	67	37

Competency Standards	Chapter Number	Diagnostic Test Questions	Practice Test 1 Questions	Practice Test 2 Questions
11 Classify animals according to type of skeletal structure, method of fertilization and reproduction, body symmetry, body coverings, and locomotion	6	7, 8, 11, 34, 37, 42, 85	33, 54, 59, 74, 76, 84	9, 38, 48, 62, 76
12 Describe protective adaptations of animals, including mimicry, camouflage, beak type, migration, and hibernation.	7	23, 76	6, 27, 50, 88	39, 47, 51
12a Identifying ways in which the theory of evolution explains the nature and diversity of organisms	7	20	29, 89	4, 49, 51, 54
12b Describing natural selection, survival of the fittest, geographic isolation, and fossil record	7	19, 24	89	4, 49
13 Trace the flow of energy as it decreases through the trophic levels from producers to the quaternary level in food chains, food webs, and energy pyramids	8	28, 32, 41, 56, 61	13, 18, 40, 53	11, 14, 32, 46, 72
13a Describing the interdependence of biotic and abiotic factors in an ecosystem	8	14, 84	41	20
13b Contrasting autotrophs and heterotrophs	8		10	14
13c Describing the niche of decomposers	8		39	14
13d Using the ten percent law to explain the decreasing availability of energy through the trophic levels	8	2		

Competency Standards	Chapter Number	Diagnostic Test Questions	Practice Test 1 Questions	Practice Test 2 Questions
14 Trace biogeochemical cycles through the environment, including water, carbon, oxygen, and nitrogen.	8	9, 57, 64	14, 35, 37, 43, 57	13, 19, 35, 67
14a Relating natural disasters, climate changes, nonnative species, and human activity to the dynamic equilibrium of ecosystems	9	40, 87	4, 43	55
14b Describing the process of ecological succession	8			30
15 Identify biomes based on environmental factors and native organisms.	8	3, 25, 45, 67, 80, 88	1, 7, 26, 77, 83, 90	14, 22, 43, 64,69
16 Identify density-dependent and density-independent limiting factors that affect populations in an ecosystem	8	5, 46, 58, 69, 86	48, 64, 70, 71, 75	12, 21, 56, 58, 68
16a Discriminating among symbiotic relationships, including mutualism, commensalism, and parasitism	8	12	41	79

1. A	11. C	21. D	31. A	41. A	51. B	61. C	71. A	81. D
2. C	12. B	22. B	32. A	42. D	52. D	62 . D	72. A	82. B
3. A	13. B	23. A	33. A	43. B	53. D	63. A	73. A	83. A
4. B	14. A	24. C	34. D	44. A	54. D	64. A	74. C	84. B
5. D	15. B	25. A	35. B	45. B	55. A	65. C	75. A	85. A
6. B	16. A	26. B	36. D	46. B	56. A	66. C	76. B	86. B
7. B	17. A	27. D	37. B	47. D	57. C	67. D	77. A	87. D
8. B	18. D	28. C	38. A	48. A	58. D	68. A	78. A	88. C
9. A	19. B	29. A	39. A	49. A	59. B	69. B	79. B	89. D
10. C	20. B	30. C	40. C	50. B	60. B	70. A	80. B	90. A

CHAPTER 1: CELLS and CELLULAR TRANSPORT
Section Review 1: Safety Procedures in the Laboratory
Page 28
A. Responses will vary.
B.
1. B   2. A   3. C   4. D   5. C
C.
1. Kara and Mitch should also have heat resistant gloves or tongs to handle the hot beaker. (Either gloves or tongs would be correct.)
2. The equipment most likely needed are an apron and safety goggles.
3. Students should list at least two of the following: When working with an open flame, goggles and gloves should be worn, and a fire extinguisher should be available.

Activity
Page 31 (center)
Petri dish - culture microbes
microscope - examine microscopic (tiny) objects
Erlenmeyer flask - mix liquids
hot plate - heat substances
eyedropper - measure small volumes of liquid
spring scale - measure force
graduated cylinder - measure volume
tripod - hold glassware aloft
wire gauze - goes on top of tripod
meter stick - measures length
triple-beam balance - measures mass
pan balance - measures mass
beaker - measures volume of liquid or mix volumes of liquids
apron - protects the clothing of the wearer against hazardous chemicals
watch glass - mix, manipulate small amounts of matter (solids or liquids)
fume hood - removes hazardous fumes from the lab
thermometer - measures thermal temperature

Bunsen burner - heats substances
test tube - mix and manipulate small quantities of matter (solid or liquid)
goggles - protects the eyes of the wearer against harmful chemicals

Section Review 2: Equipment
Page 31 (bottom)
A. Responses will vary
B.
1. B   2. D   3. D   4. C

Practice Exercise 1: Unit Conversions
Page 33

1. 0.035 g	2. 6,000 m	3. 0.0215 L	4. 0.49 cm	5. 5,350,000 mL
6. 0.0000321 kg	7. 17,500 mL	8. 0.0042 kg	9. 41,700 cg	10. 205.7 cm
11. 20.723 m	12. 3 L	13. 5,060 mg	14. 0.1058 cL	15. 0.5643 kg

Practice Exercise 2: Drawing Conclusion
Page 40 (top)
Stars are changing in relationship to their position to Earth.

Section Review 3: Designing and Conducting an Experiment
Pages 40 (bottom) – 42 (top)
A. Responses will vary
B.
1. B   2. D   3. A   4. C   5. B   6. C   7. A
C.

1. *Responses may vary.* Example: What is causing the bubbles on the rock?

2. *Responses may vary.* Examples: 1) The acid is reacting with the limestone rock. 2) The acid in the vinegar is creating a chemical reaction with something in limestone.

3. *Responses may vary.* Carbon dioxide dissolved in a liquid will escape when the liquid is heated.

4. The experimental groups are group 1 and 2 because they are designed to test the variable components of the hypothesis, music affects the growth of plants.

5. An experiment should test one variable at a time so there is no confusion as to which variable affected any change in the outcome of the experiment.

6. *Responses may vary, but should include temperature and a way to measure volume either directly or indirectly.* Example: Allen should measure the temperature of the air and record it in the data table. He can assume that the outside air temperature is the same as the temperature inside the balloon. He could then submerge the balloon into ice water, wait for the temperature of the air in the balloon to reach the temperature of the water, and record the temperature of the water. Allen could then measure the circumference of the balloon at both temperatures and record the circumferences in the data table. The circumference could then be used to calculate the volume.

Challenge Activity - Marita
Page 42 (bottom)
1. B
2. in a fume head
3. 60g
4. It has become vapor.

Chapter 1 Review
Pages 43 – 46

1. D	9. A	17. A
2. B	10. A	18. C
3. A	11. D	19. A
4. C	12. A	20. C
5. B	13. C	21. B
6. B	14. B	22. A
7. D	15. A	23. D
8. A	16. B	

CHAPTER 2 CELLS AND CELLULAR TRANSPORT
Section Review 1: Characteristics of life
Page 49

A. Responses will vary.

B.

1. All living things must consist of cells, show sensitivity to stimuli, grow, maintain homeostasis, reproduce, metabolize food to produce energy and adapt to their environment.

2. One could debate the following:
   - fire reproduces and grows (it spreads);
   - it shows sensitivity, tries to maintain homeostasis and adapts (it will respond to changes in terrain it is burning); and
   - it metabolizes (uses oxygen to "feed" itself).

(Really, though, a fire performs none of these operation in the sense that they are intended.) However, one cannot debate that fire is not made of cells. The flames of a fire are nothing more than thermal energy made visible as light energy.

Activity
Page 55

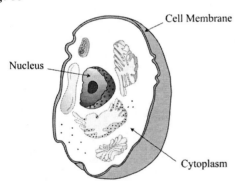

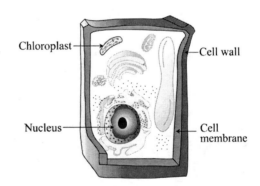

Section Review 2: Cells
Page 56

A. Responses will vary.

B.

1. D   2. A   3. B   4. D   5. D

C.

1. Any acceptable answer. Examples:
   - Granulation tissue is composed of granules that the body uses to temporarily replace the actual tissue missing from a wound.
   - The liver, an organ that processes and cleans the blood.
   - The circulatory system, which is comprised of blood; blood vessels, arteries and capillaries; the heart; and lymph nodes. The circulatory system is many organs that work in concert to perform the specific function of circulating blood and lymph.

2. Prokaryotic cells have genetic material stored in a central location, but it is not corralled by a membrane. In fact, non of its organelles are membrane–bound organelles, such as the nucleus. Prokaryotic cells are also smaller that eukaryotic cells.

3

3. Have fun with this. The vacuole is the cafeteria, the cell membrane is the security employed by the school, the ribosomes are the teachers, etc.

Section Review 3: The Cell Membrane and Cellular Transport
Pages 62 – 63
A. Responses will vary.
B.
1. B　　2. B　　3. B　　4. B　　5. D
C.
1. The process of plasmolysis causes a plant's leaves to wilt. Plasmolysis occurs when a plant is placed in a solution that has a lower solute concentration than the concentration in the cells of the plant. It causes the water inside the plant cell to move outside the cell. As a result, the plant cell shrinks away from the cell wall and wilts.
2. Diffusion and active transport move substances in opposite directions. Active transport moves dissolved substances from an area of lower concentration to an area of higher concentration by use of stored energy. Diffusion is the spontaneous movement of substances from an area of higher concentration to an area of lower concentration. Diffusion does not require energy.
3. When dried beans are soaked overnight, they absorb water through the process of osmosis, which causes the beans to swell.
4. Exocytosis is the removal of a substance out of a cell by using active transport. Endocytosis is the taking in of material into the cell by active transport.
5. A celery stalk will loose water and begin to wilt if it is placed in a hypertonic solution (a solution that has a higher solute concentrate).
D.

1.　isotonic　　　　2.　active　　　　3.　turgid, plasmolysis

Chapter 2 Review
Pages 64 – 66

1. B	3. B	5. A	7. D	9. B	11. B	13. B	15. D	17. C	19. C
2. C	4. D	6. C	8. C	10. A	12. B	14. B	16. B	18. D	20. C

CHAPTER 3: CHEMISTRY of LIFE
Section Review 1: Chemistry of the Cell
Pages 71 – 72
A. Responses will vary.
B.
1. B　　2. D　　3. C　　4. B
C.
1. Living things use six elements found in the earth's crust to comprise all living tissue.
2. Sulfur, phosphorous, oxygen, nitrogen, carbon, hydrogen.
3. Carbon forms extremely stable bonding arrangements that are the basis of all organic life.
D.

1.　Carbon or hydrogen　　2.　Polypeptides　　　　3.　DNA or RNA

Section Review 2: Cellular Energy
Page 77
A. Responses will vary.
B.

1.　A　　　　　2.　A　　　　　3.　B　　　　　4.　B

C.

1. When ADP gains a phosphate group, it becomes ATP and vice versa.

2. ATP provides cells with energy.

3. Enzymes lower activation energy in cellular reactions, helping cells increase the rate of chemical reactions.

Section Review 3: Obtaining Cellular Energy
Pages 82 – 84 (top)

A. Responses will vary.

B.

1. C   2. D   3. C   4. C   5. D   6. B   7. B

C.

1. Both are ways in which the cell converts energy from an available resource. Aerobic respiration occurs in the presence of oxygen. Anaerobic respiration occurs in the absence of oxygen.

2. Both alcoholic and lactic acid fermentation are forms of anaerobic respiration. Alcoholic fermentation produces ethanol and is used by yeasts and bacteria. Humans utilize this reaction to make breads and alcoholic drinks. Lactic acid fermentation occurs inside animal cells and some bacteria. During this process, lactose is converted into lactic acid. This process is used to create yogurts and cheese.

3. Photosynthesis ($6CO_2+6H_2O= C_3H_{12}O_6+6O_2$)
   Cellular respiration ($6O_2+C_3+H_{12}O_6=6CO_2+6H_2O$)

D.

1. P	3. B	5. R	7. R	9. B	11. P	13. B
2. R	4. R	6. P	8. P	10. R	12. P	14. P

Activity
Page 84 (bottom)

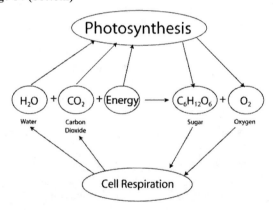

Chapter 3 Review
Pages 85 – 86

1. C	3. C	5. C	7. A	9. A	11. C	13. C	15. A	17. A
2. D	4. C	6. C	8. B	10. D	12. B	14. D	16. B	18. D

CHAPTER 4: NUCLEIC ACIDS and CELL DIVISION

Activity
Page 88
1. UAACGAGGUUUG
2. AAUGCGCCAUUU
3. GAGUGAGCCCUA
4. GUAUGACCGAUA
5. CGAAAGCCUUAA

Section Review 1: DNA, RNA and Protein Synthesis
Page 91
A. Responses will vary.
B.
1. A   2. B   3. D   4. C   5. C
C.
1. Translation is the process of taking the Codon, which corresponds to a particular amino acid, and creating a chain of amino acids.
2. Deoxyribose is the type of sugar found in DNA. Ribose is the sugar found in RNA.
3. Proteins are made of chains of polypeptides. Polypeptides are composed of chains of amino acids.
4. The DNA bases that pair up are adenine and thymine, guanine and cytosine.The RNA bases that pair up are adenine and uracil, guanine and cytosine.
5. The sequence of the DNA molecule contains gene segments that serve as the template for the creation of mRNA, which in turn codes for the amino acids that form a protein.

Section Review 2: Reproduction of Cells
Pages 95 – 96
A. Responses may vary.
B.

1. C	2. A	3. C	4. D	5. B	6. B	7. D

C.
1. The process of meiosis creates the sperm and ova. The sperm and ova unite during sexual reproduction. Without meiosis, gametes would not exist so sexual reproduction could not take place.
2. Pollen is the male gamete for pine trees. A gamete is formed by meiosis and only has half the number of chromosomes as a somatic cell.
3. Mitosis results in a diploid number of chromosomes in the new cell. Meiosis results in a haploid number of chromosomes in new cells.
4. During mitosis, the replicated chromosomes which were attached by the centromere are separated and travel to opposite ends of the poles. During meiosis, each homologue moves away from its partner toward opposite poles of the cell. At this point, independent random assortment occurs. The chromosomes from both parents mix together, and half from each parent move to the poles.

Section Review 3: Reproduction, Fertilization and Cell Differentiation.
Page 97
A. Responses may vary.
B.

1. C	2. A	3. C	4. A	5. B
6. A	7. B	8. B	9. A	10. C

Chapter 4 Review
Pages 98 – 100

1. C	5. A	9. B	13. A	17. C	21. B	25. A	29. A
2. C	6. C	10. C	14. B	18. C	22. A	26. B	30. B
3. C	7. C	11. A	15. B	19. B	23. C	27. D	
4. C	8. D	12. C	16. D	20. B	24. D	28. A	

CHAPTER 5: GENETICS, HEREDITY AND BIOTECHNOLOGY
Activity
Page 103

1.

	G	g
G	GG	Gg
G	GG	Gg

2.

	j	j
J	Jj	Jj
j	jj	jj

3.

	P	P
p	Pp	Pp
p	Pp	Pp

Section Review 1: Genetics
Page 105
A. Responses may vary.
B.

1. C	2. A	3. C	4. C	5. A

C.

1. To pass on a recessive trait to offspring, both parents have to be carriers of the recessive gene. Since only one in twenty people carry this gene, the chance of both parents having the gene is slim. If both parents are indeed carriers of the gene, there is only a 25% chance that the offspring will have the disease.
2. Phenotype is the physical expression of inherited traits such as eye color. Genotype is the combination of alleles inherited from the parents.
3. If an individual inherits two of the same alleles, either dominant or recessive, the genotype is homozygous. If an individual inherits one dominant allele and one recessive allele, the genotype is heterozygous. Both a homozygous and heterozygous individual may have the same phenotype (physical expression of the trait).
4. Genes specifically determine hereditary characteristics in an individual. More specifically, the order of the amino acid sequence within the genes.

Activity
Page 107

red and blue spots	yellow and blue spots	red and white spots
purple	green	pink
green and red spots	brown and white spots	violet and black spots
brown	tan	indigo

Section Review 2: Modes of Inheritance
Pages 108 – 109
A. Responses may vary.
B.

1. B   2. C   3. D   4. B

C. Short Answers
1.

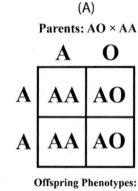

(A)
Parents: AO × AA

Offspring Phenotypes:
100% Type A, _____ Type B,
_____ Type AB, _____ Type O

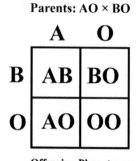

(B)
Parents: BO × AB

Offspring Phenotypes:
25% Type A, 50% Type B,
25% Type AB, _____ Type O

(C)
Parents: AO × BO

Offspring Phenotypes:
25% Type A, 25% Type B,
25% Type AB, 25% Type O

2.

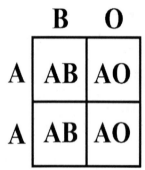

Section Review 3: Mutations
Pages 111 – 112
A. Responses may vary
B.

1. A   2. C   3. D

Section Review 4: Biotechnology
Pages 117 – 118 (top)
A. Responses may vary.
B.

1. B   2. A   3. A   4. C   5. B

C.

1. Answer may vary. Positive aspects may include allowing a childless couple to have a child, creating tissues for transplantation, creating proteins, helping patients with Alzheimer's and Parkinson's. Negative aspects include the use of a lot of embryos; possible creation of unhealthy individuals, possible creating genetically engineered children.

2. Answers may vary, but should include some of the following. Genetically modified crops can be beneficial to farmers in several ways: by producing higher quality food products and/or productive food plants; producing plants that are pest, herbicide, and rot resistant; precluding plants that can be grown in a greater variety of environmental conditions; producing food that can be

grown to contain specific vitamins and nutrients; and producing plants that require the use of fewer chemicals. Genetically modified plants can be harmful to farmers in several ways: causing food allergies in customers; cross pollination of modified foods into wild plants; increasing the cost of seeds; and requiring the same or more of traditional chemicals during production.

3. Answers may vary. Accept reasonable responses such as: cloning–allowing childless couple to have children, uses lots of embryos; gene therapy — cures diseases, little know about.

Activity
Page 118 (bottom)

The genetic marker for the known bear sample matches perfectly with Sample C. Based on these results, you can say with some certainty that Clarence killed a bear. No, Clarence is NOT innocent. He is very guilty based on the PCR results.

Chapter 5 Review
Pages 119 – 120
A. Choose the Best Answer
1. C   2. A   3. A   4. D   5. C   6. D   7. C
B.

8. Purple flowers are the dominant trait, and white flowers are the recessive trait.

9. Three of four will be purple, and one of four will be white; or 75% purple and 25% white.

10. Both parents have genotypes that have one gene for purple flowers and one gene for white flowers (Aa). The phenotype of both parents is for purple flowers.

11. Students should list two of the following: Products created by recombinant DNA technology are insecticide–resistant crops, rot–resistant tomatoes, bovine growth hormones for increased milk production, the vaccine for Hepatitis B, human insulin, human growth hormone, TPA, interferon, and monoclonal antibodies.

12. Students should give at least two of the following: Genetically modified plants which are herbicide and insecticide–resistant can be harmful to the environment because they are more heavily sprayed with chemicals that do not kill the plants but destroy the habitats of beneficial insects and negatively impact the ecosystem. Genetic pollution occurs through cross–pollination and occurs when pollen from genetically modified plants is carried by wind, birds, and insects to other areas or farms that do not want to grow genetically modified plants. Genetically modified seeds do not produce fertile offspring so the farmer must purchase seeds from a supplier for each crop. Milk produced by cows taking rBGH have higher incidences of infection and are then given antibiotics. The antibiotics, pus, and extra fat produced as side effects of the RBGH and antibiotics are passed along to humans that drink the milk. Other hormones can also be stimulated by rBGH. These other hormones can cause higher incidences of cancer.

13. The biomolecule that has the greatest amount of uncompensated negative charge that is also small (the one in the lower left of the diagram).

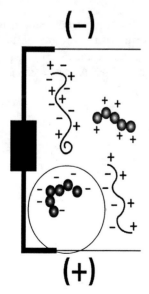

CHAPTER 6: TAXONOMY
Section Review 1: Biological Classification
Pages 126 – 127
A. Responses may vary.
B.

1. C	2. B	3. D	4. C	5. A	6. C	7. B

C.

1. Morphology (physical structure); DNA make up; life cycle (reproduction); metabolism; growth pattern and response to environment.
2. (a) does not account for changes over time. (b) variation exists within a species, (c) difficulty confirming breeding.
3. Responses may vary. Positive effects of bacteria for humans: Some bacteria help prevent harmful bacteria from forming colonies on skin and in the digestive tract. They are used in the food industry to make cheese, vinegar, and yogurt. They decompose dead matter and process raw sewage removing harmful bacteria. Negative effects of bacteria: Some bacteria cause disease by reproducing and damaging tissue or releasing toxins that interfere with cellular functions.

Section Review 2: Protists
Pages 128 – 129
A. Responses will vary
B.

1. A	2. C	3. C	4. D	5. A

C.

1. Euglenas are both autotrophic and heterotrophic. They live in fresh water, move around with a flagellum, and have no cell wall. They have an eyespot that responds to light.
2. All algae can make their own food (they are autotrophic) while protozoa must feed on food they find (the are heterotrophic)

Section Review 3: Fungi
Pages 130 – 131
A. Responses may vary
B.

1. C	2. B	3. A

C.

1. Fungi grow on and cause irritation to skin, hair, nails, and mucus membranes.Fungal spores can be inhaled causing infections in lungs and other organs, resulting in permanent damage.
2. Fungi forms a symbiotic relationship with algae or cyanobacteria called lichens. The fungi provides the protection and structure and the algae or cyanobacteria provides the food through photosynthesis. The lichens break down rocks and dead trees. Fungi forms a symbiotic relationship with the roots of vascular plants called mycorrhizae. The fungi penetrate the roots of the plant and extend into the soil. It is thought that the fungi convert minerals in the soil into a usable form of plants and that the fungi increase water uptake for the plant.

Section Review 4: The Plant Kingdom
Pages 135 – 136
A. Responses may vary.
B.

1. C	2. B	3. D	4. C	5. B
6. C	7. C	8. C	9. B	10. A

C.

1. Deciduous trees have falling leaves every year. Evergreen trees do not drop leaves every year.
2. Roots anchor plants, absorb water and minerals, and store food.

   Stems support leaves and reproductive parts; protect transport system

   Leaves make food.

   Flowers produce seeds and pollen.
3. Gymnosperms — seeds are on the outside of the plant; usually on the cone.

   Angiosperms — seeds are enclosed within a fruit.
4. To transport water and nutrients throughout the plant.
5. Because water is needed to soften the seed coat causing it to swell — spring rains provide the necessary water. Increase in sunlight is needed to encourage leaves and stems to grow upward. Increase in temperature is needed to protect frost sensitive plant tissues.
6. The plant may not survive because it would not be able to photosynthesize and had probably used up its food stores in the winter.
7. It depends on the arrangement of flowers. If the plant has clusters of five flowers, you could not be sure. If it has flowers arranged in fours or threes, then you could classify it as a dicot or monocot, respectively.

Section Review 5: The Invertebrates
Page 146
A. Responses will vary.

B.

1. B   2. D   3. C   4. B   5. C

C.

1. Earthworm casts (waste products) provide nutrients for the soil and also help aerate the soil.
2. Trichina, person contracts trichinosis by eating undercooked pork. Illness can be avoided by thoroughly cooking pork.
3. Complete metamorphosis- egg → larva → pupa → adult

   Incomplete metamorphosis egg → nymph → adult

Larva and nymph are similar because they don't look exactly like the adult, they eat a lot, and they molt often.

The larva and nymph are different because the nymph looks similar to the adult where the larva look nothing like the adult.

Section Review 6: The Vertebrates
Page 151
A. Responses will vary.

B.

1. C   2. A   3. B   4. B   5. B   6. B

Using a Dichotomous Key
Page 152 (bottom) – 153
Animals pictured in the dichotomous key: Koala, Bottle-nose dolphin, spider, starfish, roly poly (Wood louse), humpback whale, tuna, jellyfish, kangaroo.

Chapter 6 Review
Pages 154 – 156

1. D	5. A	9. C	13. A	17. A	21. B	25. D	29. A	33. A
2. A	6. D	10. A	14. D	18. C	22. C	26. D	30. B	
3. C	7. C	11. C	15. A	19. D	23. B	27. D	31. C	
4. B	8. B	12. A	16. C	20. B	24. C	28. B	32. A	

CHAPTER 7: EVOLUTION

Section Review 1: Biological Classification
Pages 160 – 161
A. Responses may vary.
B.
1. C   2. C   3. A   4. B   5. A
C. Short Answers
1. biodiversity and ecosystem diversity
2. adaptation and extinction
3. Both cells and viruses contain genetic material, and use proteins. Cells are considered life because they can metabolize and reproduce independently, adapt, and show sensitivity to environmental changes. Viruses cannot reproduce unless they are inside another organism, viruses cannot show sensitivity to environmental changes.

Section Review 2: Fossils and the Fossil Record
Pages 163 – 164
A. Responses may vary.
B.
1. A   2. C   3. B   4. B   5. D
C.
1. Relative dating places rocks in the order that they were formed. Absolute dating uses the rate of radioactive decay of isotopes to determine how many years have passed since a geologic event occurred.
2. Uranium–238 has a half–life too long to be useful in determining the age of a mummy. Carbon–14 would be more useful for determining the age of a mummy because of the shorter half–life and because every living organism absorbs carbon–14 until it dies.
3. Starting with 10,000 of parent isotope having a half–life of 10 million years, and after the third half–life, there would be 1,250 atoms of the parent isotope present. 30 million years will have passed since the magma cooled.
4. Scientists estimate that the fossil record only represents about 0.1% of all organisms that have lived or currently live on Earth. This low percentage is a result of two factors. First, organisms with hard body parts are more likely to fossilize than soft–bodied organisms. Second, fossils are more likely to form if the organism is quickly buried after death. If these two conditions are not met, then a fossils of the organism will most likely not be able to form.

Section Review 3: Development of Evolutionary Thought
Page 167
A. Responses may vary.
B.
1. C   2. A
C.
1. Those animals that are the most fit, or the best able to live in their environment, will survive and pass their genes on to many offspring.
2. Yes, you could observe the micro evolutionary changes in the genetic makeup of the populations; you could also see how the organisms interact with one another to work successfully within the ecosystem. You could also make changes to the ecosystem and observe the genetic drift that occurs along with any other changes.

Section Review 4: Mechanisms and Pattern of Evolution
Pages 172 – 173
A. Responses may vary.
B.
1. A   2. D   3. C
C.
1. Convergent evolution explains how two unrelated species can develop similar characteristics. The shark and the porpoise are examples of convergent evolution. Divergent evolution suggests that many species developed from a common ancestor. Penguins and vultures, both birds, have wings with the same basic form but different functions, one for swimming and one for flying.
2. Natural selection states that the organisms best suited to an environment are the ones most likely to survive and reproduce.

3. Allopatric speciation occurs when a population becomes geographically divided. Organisms can become physically isolated when a boundary such as an ocean, mountain, or lake divides a population. Two gene pools now exist in different environments, and after several years, the genetic differences become so great that new species are formed. Sympatric speciation exists when differences in habitat, sexual reproduction, niche, or heredity isolate members of a population from one another. For example, several frog species live in the same area. One breeds in May, and the other breeds in July. These two species of frog are genetically isolated from each other because of their breeding patterns. Many rain forest orchids cannot interbreed because their flowers bloom at different times.

4. Variations found within a population are beneficial to organisms because it can keep the organisms from competing for the same resources. Variations also allow some organisms to survive in changing conditions.

Section Review 5: Animal Behavior
Page 178
A. Responses may vary.
B

  1. A   2. B   3. C   4. A

C. (L. or I)
1. I   2. L   3. L   4. I   5. I   6. L   7. L   8. L
D.
1. Students should list two of the following: Some plants use wind to disperse their seeds. Others use water–born means to disperse their seeds. Still others have seeds that adhere to animal fur and are dispersed in that manner

2. Animals use sound to broadcast their locations for mating, to deter predators, and to communicate and transfer information.

Chapter 7 Review
Pages 179 – 182

1. D	4. A	7. A	10. D	13. B	16. A	19. D
2. A	5. B	8. D	11. C	14. A	17. C	20. A
3. B	6. C	9. B	12. A	15. A	18. D	21. D

22. The webbing between the toes.

23. Bird foot A. Has large claws and hind toes. This bird is a climber, like a woodpecker. The hind toes keep it from falling backward.

24. Algae were one of the most important life forms to bring about a change in the earth's atmosphere. The amount of oxygen increased, and the amount of carbon dioxide decreased. Algae were the first organism capable of photosynthesis.

CHAPTER 8: INTERACTIONS IN THE ENVIRONMENT
Activity
Page 185
Responses will vary.

Section Review 1: Earth's Major Ecological Systems
Page 187 – 188
A. Responses may vary.
B.
1. D   2. D   3. B
C.
1. *Answers may vary.* Both marine and freshwater ecosystems involve water. Freshwater ecosystems have low salinity, and marine ecosystems have higher salinity. Both support a wide variety of life.

2. *Answers may vary.* Climate is important because it determines the type of plants found in an area. Plants cannot respond to rapidly changing environmental conditions and depend on climate predictability.

Section Review 2: Organization of Ecosystems

Page 189

A. Responses may vary.

B.

1. B

C.

Answer may vary. Accept reasonable responses such as: amount of sunlight, amount of rainfall, temperature, particle size of soil.

Section Review 3: Relationships among Organisms
Page 191

A. Responses may vary.

B.

1. A

C.

Both mutualism and parasitism involve two species interacting closely. In a mutualistic relationship, however, both benefit. In a parasitic relationship, only the parasite benefits; the host organism is harmed.

Section Review 4: Population Dynamics
Page 195

A. Responses may vary

B.

1. B   2. D   3. D   4. A

C.

1. *Answers may vary.* Carrying capacity is predominantly determined by environmental quality, including both biotic and abiotic conditions.

2. *Answers may vary.* Accept any reasonable response such as "There would not be enough space on earth for all the organisms."

Practice Exercise 1 Food Chains
Page 198 (top)

Responses may vary. Accept any reasonable response.

Activity
Page 199

Answers will vary. Accept any reasonable response.

Section Review 5: Food Chains and Food Webs
Pages 200 – 201

A. Responses may vary.

B.

1. C   2. C

C.

1. omnivores

2. saprophytes

D.

Responses will vary. Example answers:

1. Grass (producer) feeds rabbit; rabbit feeds fox; fox feeds wolf.

2. A food web consists of several food chains interacting with each other. for a complete food web, see Figure 8.22 on page 198.

Section Review 6: The Nutrient Cycles
Page 205

A. Responses may vary.

B. Multiple Choice

1. A   2. C   3. B   4. C

Chapter 8 Review
Pages 206 – 210

1. A	6. A	11. C	16. C	21. D	26. D
2. C	7. C	12. A	17. A	22. D	27. B
3. C	8. A	13. D	18. C	23. C	28. A
4. B	9. B	14. C	19. D	24. B	29. B
5. B	10. B	15. A	20. B	25. B	30. A

CHAPTER 9: ENVIRONMENTAL AWARENES
Section Review 1: Pollution
Page 214
A. Responses may vary.
B.
1. D   2. C   3. D
C.
1. *Answers may vary.* Natural pollution can occur form volcanoes, earthquakes, and landslides.
2. *Answers may vary.* Respiratory or cardiac.

Section 2 Review: Protecting the Environment
Pages 220 – 221
A. Responses may vary

B.
1. C   2. A   3. A   4. B   5. D   6. D   7. A
C.
Answer may vary but should address: to protect present and future resources.
Section Review 3: Alteration to the Environment
Pages 224 – 225
A. Responses may vary.
B.
1. D   2. C   3. B   4. A   5. A

6. A   7. A   8. C   9. A

C.
1. Answers may vary. Accept reasonable responses such as: recycling, biotechnology to control waste, or changing manufacturing
   techniques.
2. Yes.

Chapter 9 Review
Pages 226 – 228

1. C	3. D	5. B	7. A	9. B	11. B	13. A	15. A
2. A	4. C	6. B	8. C	10. B	12. A	14. B	16. B

Short Answers.
17. *Answers may vary.* Mineral resources could have been deposited in one area and, through the movement of the tectonic plates,
    the resources could have moved to other locations.

18. *Answers may vary.* Humans mainly function to deplete natural resources.
19. *Answers may vary.* Accept reasonable responses with proper explanations. The three main topics should include reducing populations; promoting education and improving socioeconomic levels; and redistributing resources.
20. *Answers may vary,* and could include: emission controls on cars, use of enzymes in biowaste, increased fuel efficiency, and emission filters in factories.

Post Test 1
Pages 229 – 246

1. C	11. C	21. A	31. C	41. B	51. A	61. C	71. B	81. C
2. C	12. D	22. B	32. D	42. D	52. C	62. A	72. C	82. B
3. C	13. C	23. A	33. B	43. C	53. A	63. C	73. C	83. D
4. C	14. D	24. A	34. D	44. D	54. A	64. A	74. A	84. B
5. D	15. B	25. B	35. B	45. C	55. B	65. B	75. B	85. C
6. D	16. D	26. C	36. A	46. B	56. A	66. C	76. B	86. B
7. D	17. D	27. C	37. B	47. A	57. B	67. B	77. C	87. A
8. D	18. B	28. A	38. B	48. B	58. C	68. D	78. A	88. C
9. C	19. A	29. A	39. C	49. A	59. A	69. A	79. A	89. C
10. B	20. D	30. C	40. A	50. B	60. D	70. A	80. B	90. A

Post Test 2
Pages 247 – 264

1. A	11. D	21. B	31. B	41. A	51. A	61. A	71. D	81. C
2. A	12. A	22. C	32. D	42. C	52. C	62. D	72. B	82. B
3. A	13. C	23. D	33. B	43. A	53. A	63. D	73. C	83. C
4. A	14. C	24. A	34. B	44. C	54. C	64. D	74. A	84. C
5. D	15. C	25. B	35. B	45. A	55. B	65. D	75. C	85. A
6. C	16. B	26. B	36. B	46. D	56. B	66. A	76. C	86. A
7. D	17. B	27. C	37. A	47. A	57. B	67. A	77. C	87. C
8. D	18. B	28. C	38. C	48. C	58. D	68. A	78. B	88. D
9. B	19. D	29. B	39. A	49. C	59. A	69. A	79. B	89. C
10. A	20. C	30. C	40. B	50. A	60. D	70. B	80. B	90. A

PASSING THE
ALABAMA HIGH SCHOOL
GRADUATION EXAM
IN SCIENCE

Based on Alabama
Course of Study: Science; Biology Core
REVISED January 2008

Michelle Gunter

American Book Company
PO Box 2638
Woodstock, GA 30188-1383
Toll-Free Phone: 1-888-264-5877   Toll-Free Fax: 1-866-827-3240
Web site: www.americanbookcompany.com

ACKNOWLEDGEMENTS

The authors would like to gratefully acknowledge the formatting and technical contributions of Becky Wright.

We also want to thank Mary Stoddard and Eric Field for their expertise in developing the graphics for this book.

We would also like to thank Phil Lausier for allowing us to use his photographs in this book.

This product/publication includes images from CorelDRAW 9 and 11 which are protected by the copyright laws of the United States, Canada, and elsewhere. Used under license.

Chapter 6   Taxonomy   121

Chapter 9   Environmental Awareness   211

Preface

The Alabama High School Graduation Exam will help students who are learning or reviewing material for the Alabama test that is now required for each gateway or benchmark course. **The materials in this book are based on the Alabama Course of Study: Science; Biology Core as published by the Alabama Department of Education.**

This book contains several sections. These sections are as follows: 1) General information about the book; 2) A Diagnostic Test and Evaluation Chart; 3) Domains/Chapters that teach the concepts and skills that improve readiness for Alabama HSGE in Science; 4) Two Practice/Post Tests. Answers to the tests and exercises are in a separate manual. The answer manual also contains a Chart of Standards for teachers to make a more precise diagnosis of student needs and assignments.

We welcome comments and suggestions about the book. Please contact us at

American Book Company PO Box 2638 Woodstock, GA 30188-1383	Toll Free: 1 (888) 264-5877 Phone: (770) 928-2834 Fax: (770) 928-7483 web site: www.americanbookcompany.com

About the Author

Michelle Gunter graduated from Kennesaw State University in Kennesaw, Georgia with a B.S. in Secondary Biology Education. She is a certified teacher in the field of Biology in the state of Georgia. She has three years experience in high school science classrooms. She has nine years experience in biology and biological systems. She has won awards for her research in the field of aquatic toxicology. Mrs. Gunter enjoys teaching students of all ages, the wonders of the natural world. Mrs. Gunter is currently pursuing her M.S. in Biology at Georgia State University.

Alabama HSGE in Science Diagnostic Test

1 Which of the following accurately illustrates active transport?   2

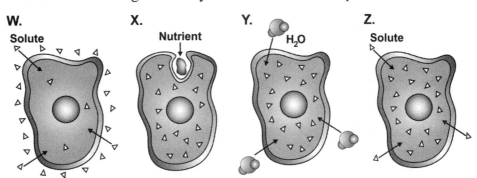

    A image Z

    B image W

    C image X

    D image Y

2 What is the main idea of the ten percent law?   13d

    A Only ten percent of life of the planet survives a mass extinction.

    B Only ten percent of life on the planet is considered a producer.

    C Only ten percent of energy is available to the next highest trophic level.

    D Only ten percent of energy is lost during the transition to the next trophic level.

3 Which terrestrial biome has the greatest diversity of both plants and animals?   15

    A rain forest

    B desert

    C marine

    D tundra

4 Which organelle is indicated by the arrow in the diagram below?   4

A ribosomes

B mitochondria

C nucleus

D nucleolus

5 Which student in the table below correctly identified the density dependent limiting factors?   16

Student	Flooding	Disease	Over-grazing	Dam building
A	X		X	
B		X		X
C	X			X
D		X	X	

    A   **B**   **C**   **D**

6 The correct order of the stages of meiosis I, as indicated in the diagram, is   6

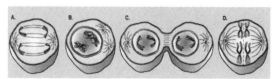

A a, b, c, d

B b, d, a, c

C c, a, b, d

D b, a, d, c

7 What type of organism is an earthworm?   11

A vertebrate

B invertebrate

C parasitic

D universal

8 Which of the following vertebrate classes contains organisms that undergo external fertilization?   11

A *Aves*

B *Osteichthyes*

C *Mammalia*

D *Reptilia*

9 Which of the following statements concerning physical and biological systems is correct?   14

A Matter recycles in a given system, while energy flows through it.

B Energy recycles in a given system, while matter flows through it.

C Matter is recycled in physical systems only, not in biological systems.

D Energy flows through biological systems only, not physical systems.

10 Examine the table. Determine which row describes a ribosome.   4

	Location	Function
A	surrounds entire cell	regulates materials that flow into or out of cells
B	double membraned organelle found in cytoplasm	stores DNA
C	free floating or attached to endoplasmic reticulum	produces proteins
D	free floating in cytoplasm	converts energy for use within cell

11 Which phylum is described by   11
the following characteristics?

- eukaryotic
- single celled
- chloroplasts filled with chlorophyll
- store their food in the form of oil
- golden brown pigment
- found in salt water
- are important in making toothpaste, detergents, paint removers, scouring powders, glass and road paint

A Euglenas

B Green Algae

C Golden Algae

D Brown Algae

12 Many types of interactions exist   16a
between species. Which of the
diagrams below represents
commensalism?

A W   B X   C Y   D Z

13 Which molecule carries   8
information from the DNA inside
the nucleus to the cytoplasm of the
cell?

A tRNA   C rRNA

B mRNA   D ATP

14 Grasses, trees, insects, squirrels   13a
and humans are all

A biotic factors in an ecosystem.

B abiotic factors in an ecosystem.

C unable to co-exist.

D living things that contain cell walls.

15 Photosynthesis does which of the following? 3

   A converts heat energy to light energy

   B converts light energy from the Sun to chemical energy

   C converts light energy from the Sun to heat energy

   D converts one form of light energy to another

16 In a leafy plant, gases exchange through the 10a

   A stomata.

   B veins.

   C stem.

   D roots.

17 The process shown in the diagram below 8

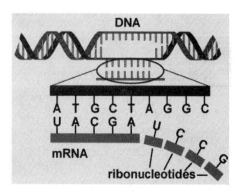

   A is transcription.

   B is the final process in the assembly of a protein.

   C is replication.

   D occurs on the surface of the ribosome.

18 Yolanda was examining active specimens of pond water under the microscope. She noticed several amoeba swimming around with smaller amoeba attached to them. Her teacher said the amoeba population was reproducing. What type of reproduction was Yolanda viewing? 6b

   A vegetative reproduction

   B sexual reproduction

   C spore formation

   D asexual reproduction

19 The peppered moth is often used as a case study to illustrate natural selection. The peppered moth comes in two speckled colorations: light colored and dark colored. The allele for dark colored moths is dominant, while the allele for light colored moths is recessive. In 1850s England, most of the peppered moth population was light in color and blended in with the trees that they commonly landed on, making it hard for birds and other predators to spot and capture them. Dark colored peppered moths were also present, but were fewer in number because they were more visible to predators. By the early 1900s, industrial air pollution had covered trees with soot, generally darkening their appearance. The dark colored moths now blended in with the trees more effectively than the light colored moths, were less easily spotted by predators, and correspondingly became greater in number than the light colored moths. Which of the following accurately represents the result of the environmental effect?

12b

A A smaller percentage of light colored moths survive to reproduce, shrinking the gene pool and causing mutations.

B More and more dark colored moths survive to reproduce, thus shifting the allele frequency towards the dark colored allele.

C Over time, light colored moths will become homozygous for the light allele and become extinct.

D Over time, birds will get used to eating the light colored moths and stop eating the dark colored moths.

20 The process by which many different species develop from a common ancestor is called

12a

    A natural selection.

    B divergent evolution.

    C convergent evolution.

    D a mutation.

21 Consider the reactions shown below. Which of the following statements is NOT true concerning these reactions?

3

$$6\,CO_2 + 6\,H_2O + \text{light energy} \rightarrow C_6H_{12}O_6 \text{ (glucose)} + 6\,O_2$$

$$C_6H_{12}O_6 \text{ (glucose)} + 6\,O_2 \rightarrow 6\,CO_2 + 6\,H_2O + \text{energy}$$

    A Photosynthesis converts solar energy into photochemical energy.

    B Respiration can be described as the oxidation of organic material.

    C Photosynthesis is an endothermic reaction, and respiration is an exothermic reaction.

    D Molecular oxygen is a reactant in photosynthesis and is a product of respiration.

22 Which of the following correctly describes the two main traits of Bryophytes?   10

    A contain tube-like structures for transporting water and nutrients and produces spores

    B spent part of their life as a gameto-phyte, part spent as a sporophyte and must have direct access to water

    C are anchored to the ground with roots and lack connective/trans-port tissues

    D spent entire life as a sporophyte where seeds are produced, con-tained in a thick seed coat, with tube-like structures for transporting water

23 The species name for the red drum, or channel bass, is   12
Sciaenops ocellatus. Sciaenops is Greek for a "perch-like marine fish" and *ocellatus* is Latin for "eye-like colored spot." Scientists believe that the spots may trick predators into attacking the spots toward the drum's tails instead of near their eyes, allowing the drum to escape. What type of adaptation does this represent?

    A physical

    B chemical

    C behavioral

    D all of the above

24 Charles Darwin originated the modern theory of evolution.   12b
Although he was not the first to propose that organisms changed over time, he was the first to propose a valid mechanism by which this happened. Central to his theory was the importance given to natural genetic variation within populations and its place in the context of natural selection. Which of the following statements most accurately describes Darwin's proposal on the nature of inherited variations?

    A Variations are only inherited if they have a positive effect in the previous generation.

    B Variations that have a negative effect are less likely to be passed from parent to offspring.

    C Inherited variations occur by chance, and have a variable degree of effect on the individual organism during its lifetime.

    D Inherited variations occur because of environmental conditions, and have a variable degree of effect on the individual organism during its lifetime.

25 One summer day, students all across America recorded the   15
temperature and precipitation amount in their area. The results are recorded in the table. Identify the student that lives in the tundra.

Student	A	B	C	D
Temperature in °C	-1	15	19	25
Precipitation in (cm)	4	10	2	12

26 The main function of carbohydrates within a cell is to   2a

   A compose the main structural components of the cell membrane.

   B provide cellular energy.

   C store cellular information.

   D provide energy storage within the cell.

27 Cri-du-chat syndrome is characterized in humans by an improperly developed larynx and a cry that sounds like that of a cat. Outward symptoms include misshapen ears, a rounded face and a small cranium. It is caused by a chromosome mutation known as deletion. If the upper portion of the diagram illustrates a normal chromosome, which of the following represents a chromosome that has undergone a deletion?   8d

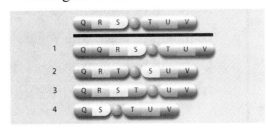

   A chromosome 1

   B chromosome 2

   C chromosome 3

   D chromosome 4

28 Consider an energy pyramid that has four trophic levels, as shown in the figure below. What is the correct ordering of the four organisms pictured from the lowest trophic level to the top trophic level?   13

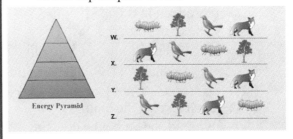

   A order W

   B order X

   C order Y

   D order Z

29 A normal DNA base sequence is shown below. Identify the complementary DNA sequence that has undergone an inversion mutation.   8d

       AAT TCG GGT CGA ATT

   A TTA AGC TCC GCT TAA

   B TTA AGC CCA GCT TAA

   C UUA UGC CCA GCU UAA

   D TTA AGC CC GCT AAT

30 In mice, brown hair is dominant to white. If we cross a heterozygous female with a heterozygous male, the phenotypic ratio will yield   7

   A 3 white:1 brown.

   B 1 brown: 2 tan: 1 white.

   C 3 brown: 1 white.

   D 4 brown.

31 Pollen grains produced by a particular pine tree contain 25 chromosomes. When the pollen grain comes into contact with a female embryo, the resulting seed contains 50 chromosomes. This type of reproduction is called   6a

  A sexual.　　　　**C** haploid.

  B asexual.　　　**D** abiotic.

32 Each level of the biomass pyramid shown below contains one of the following: carnivorous insects, trees, birds, or herbivorous insects. At what level will the herbivorous insects be found?   13

  A level B　　　**C** level C

  B level A　　　**D** level D

33 In some fruit flies the allele for having black eyes (B) is dominant to the allele for having red eyes (b). A scientist mated a batch of fruit flies with genotypes as shown in the Punnett Square below. What is the probability that the offspring will be born with red eyes?   7c

	B	b
B	BB	Bb
b	Bb	bb

  A 25%　　　　**C** 50%

  B 75%　　　　**D** 100%

34 The external characteristics of an arthropod include a feature which has a coxa, femur, tibia, tarsus, pads and claws. What external feature of the arthropod has these parts?   11

  A antennae　　　**C** thorax

  B wings　　　　**D** legs

35 A chicken has two kinds of genes that determine the color of its plumage; one lends the chicken a background color and the other modifies that background. Two common plumage genes are E and I. E is a gene coding for background color; it is often called "extended black." I is a modifying gene called dominant white; however, this gene is co-dominant to E. What color will a chicken with the gene combination EI be?   7a

  A It will be completely black.

  B It will be black with white spots.

  C It will be white with black spots.

  D It will be completely white.

36 When comparing the skin cells from a dog to bacterial cells, which observation would be false?   4b

  A The dog's skin cells lack a cell wall.

  B The bacterial cells lack membrane-bound organelles.

  C The bacterial cells are much smaller then dog's skin cells.

  D Bacterial cells have specialized communication pores in their nuclear envelope.

37 What do frogs, fish, apes and birds all have in common? ₁₁

    A legs

    B backbones

    C scales

    D four-chambered hearts

38 When the temperature increases, the rate of mitosis usually increases also. Based on this information, one can assume that in an aquatic ecosystem _{2c}

    A warm water would support a larger algal population.

    B cold water would support a larger algal population.

    C warm water would support the same amount of alga as cold water.

    D warm water alga would be more active than cold water alga.

Use the following diagram to answer question 39.

Plant Cell

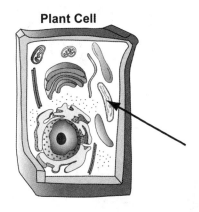

39 The organelle indicated in the diagram contains a pigment that captures the necessary sunlight for ₃

    A photosynthesis.

    B cellular respiration.

    C nutrient absorption.

    D cellular transport.

40 Which of the following statements correctly represents a negative impact of fossil fuel usage?   14a

   A The burning of fossil fuels disrupts the water cycle by adding hydrogen to the atmosphere.

   B Drilling for fossil fuels disrupts the carbon cycle by adding hydrogen to the atmosphere.

   C The burning of fossil fuels releases carbon, and thus carbon-based greenhouse gases, to the atmosphere in excess volume.

   D Mining for fossil fuels has irreversibly changed the ecological biomes of the Earth.

41 Urchins are considered a _____ to the snail and a _____ to the fish.   13

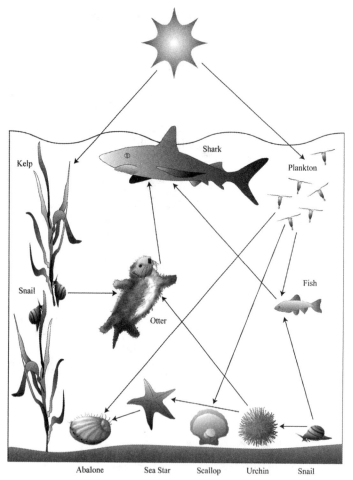

   A predator, competitor

   B competitor, predator

   C predator, predator

   D competitor, competitor

42 To learn how species are related, scientists can compare structures found in the species to find similarities. The skulls shown below are from four different animals. Which two animals are the most closely related?   11

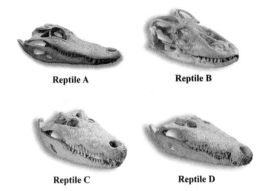

A reptiles A & B

B reptiles B & C

C reptiles A & D

D reptiles C & D

43 Sean was conducting a chemistry experiment that overheated and caught fire. Which safety rule would most likely have prevented this accident?   1c

A Wear safety goggles.

B Follow the teacher's instructions.

C Use tongs to handle hot glassware.

D Keep the work space clean and uncluttered.

44 Cellular respiration is to the mitochondria as photosynthesis is to the   3

A chloroplast.

B Golgi apparatus.

C cytoplasm.

D vacuole.

45 Examine the list of plant and animal types. Which group of plants and animals are characteristic of the desert biome?   15

	Plant Types
1	epiphytes, vines, tall broad leaved trees and orchids
2	lichen mosses, roots and conifers
3	grasses
4	shrubs, succulents, cacti

	Animal Types
1	insects, bats, birds, amphibians, monkeys, deer, pigs and jaguars
2	mice, rabbits, birds and bears
3	bison, antelope, deer and insects
4	mice, snakes, lizards, insects and birds

A plant type 1 and animal type 1

B plant type 4 and animal type 4

C plant type 3 and animal type 2

D plant type 2 and animal type 4

46 Which factor is density dependent for crows?   16

A tornados

B avian bird flu

C humans constructing new homes

D drought

47 Derek has taken the temperature reading for the month of September at 6:00 every evening. What is the best way to present the data?   1a

A a calendar

B a mathematical formula

C a written report

D a bar graph

48 In the lab, which piece of equipment would you use to measure 15 g of NaCl?   1

A equipment piece C, triple beam balance

B equipment piece A, graduated cylinder

C equipment piece B, beaker

D equipment piece D, meter stick

49 A freshwater plant is placed in a salt marsh. Predict the direction water will move across the plant's cell wall, and the effect of that movement on the plant. <small>2b</small>

  A Water would move out of the plant's cells, causing the plant to wilt.

  B Water would move into the plant's cells, causing the plant to wilt.

  C Water would move out of the plant's cells, causing the plant to swell.

  D Water would move into the plant's cells, causing the plant to swell.

50 You are going to perform an experiment where you test enzyme activity at various temperatures. You will be using chemicals, beakers, a thermometer and a hot plate. Which of the following guidelines will ensure safety during the experiment? <small>1c</small>

  A Tap the test tubes gently with the tip of your finger to test their temperature before picking them up, and point the mouth of the test tubes away from you.

  B Use gloves or tongs when handling the glassware, and follow instructions for safe disposal of chemicals.

  C Be sure to rinse all chemicals down the drain upon completion of the experiment, and then wash the sink thoroughly.

  D Since the mouths of test tubes are so small, there is no need to tie hair back, but wearing goggles is important because the contents of the test tubes could splash out.

51 If a human somatic cell contains 46 chromosomes, how many chromosomes would a human reproductive cell contain? <small>6a</small>

  A 46   **B** 23   **C** 92   **D** 12

52 A new disease is discovered in a population of marsupial mammals living in the rainforest of Papua, New Guinea. This disease is caused by a segment of DNA surrounded by a protein coat. This disease is passed directly from one animal to another and cannot reproduce in the environment. In which kingdom should this disease be classified? <small>9d</small>

  A Eubacteria

  B Archaebacteria

  C Protista

  D This disease is a virus and should not be classified into any kingdom.

53 During meiosis <small>6a</small>

  A two diploid cells are formed.

  B two identical haploid cells are formed.

  C four identical diploid cells are formed.

  D four haploid cells are formed.

54 The process in which a plant makes food from water and carbon dioxide, using energy from the Sun, is known as <small>3</small>

  A respiration.

  B absorption.

  C reproduction.

  D photosynthesis.

The pedigree below shows the occurrence of a certain genetic disorder in three generations of a canine family. Use the pedigree to answer question 55.

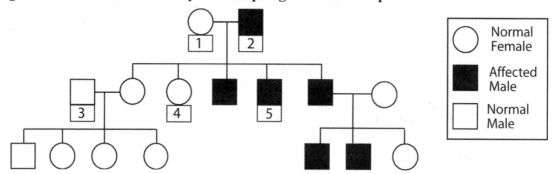

55 What is most likely the inheritance pattern for the disorder shown in this pedigree?

   7b

  A sex-linked

  B co-dominant

  C dominant

  D recessive

56 Consider the food web shown below. Which of the following organisms represents the trophic level where the least amount of energy is present?

   13

  A mountain lion

  B deer

  C mouse

  D tree

57 The carbon cycle, nitrogen cycle and water cycle are all part of

   14

  A the energy cycle.

  B the energy pyramid.

  C the nutrient cycle.

  D autotrophs.

58 Which statement below best describes a density-independent limiting factor?

   16

  A An ebola outbreak kills 25 million African fruit bats.

  B Starvation kills 22% of deer in Alabama.

  C The Ungoro lion pride kills a rival pride to take over the territory.

  D A hurricane strikes the Gulf Coast.

59 *Crotalus adamanteus* and *Crotalus horridus* are organisms that belong to the same   9a

A population.   C species.

B genus.   D chromosome.

60 Stefan observes goldfish in a tank with a light above it. The goldfish seem to be more active when the tank is bright than when it is dim. Going one step further, he asks himself, how does the color of light affect goldfish activity? If he were to do an experiment with several different colors of light above the tank, which of the following would be the best hypothesis?   1a

A Do goldfish like red light or green light?

B Goldfish are more active in white light than in green or red light.

C Goldfish live in green and red light.

D Light changes will kill goldfish.

61 Most soil is formed   13

A overnight from the weathering process.

B directly from volcanic eruptions.

C from the breakdown of organisms.

D spontaneously in the environment.

62 Susie picked flowers for her science class. She found some beautiful purple flowers with yellow stems in the center of the blossom. Her science teacher told her the yellow stems were part of the male reproductive structure of the plant. The name of this structure in the plant is   10

A stigmas.   C pistils.

B sepals.   D stamen.

63 An organism that lives on land, cannot move and makes all of its food from sunlight is a   13

A producer.

B primary consumer.

C secondary consumer.

D decomposer.

64 Which cycle of matter does the illustration best represent?   14

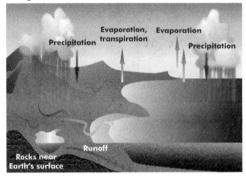

A the water cycle

B the carbon cycle

C the nitrogen cycle

D the phosphorus cycle

65 Plants' roots grow toward Earth in response to gravity, while stems and leaves grow away from Earth. What is the name of this phenomenon?   10b

A nastic movement

B blooming pattern

C geotropism

D photoperiodism

66 In vascular plants, vessels called _____ transport water and minerals from roots to the rest of the plant   10a

A cuticle   C xylem.

B stomata.   D phloem.

67 Study the graph and determine the biome represented by the data set. 15

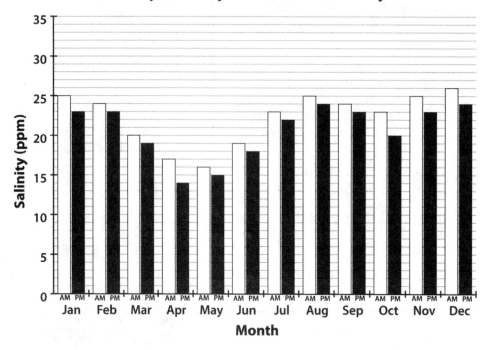

Monthly Salinity Levels for an Ecosystem

A desert   **C** freshwater

B marine   **D** estuary

Use the following information to help you answer question 68.

Severe combined immunodeficiency (SCID) is the collective name for a group of congenital disorders characterized by little or no immune response. Affected individuals have white blood cells that are unable to defend the body from viruses, bacteria and fungi. All forms of SCID are inherited, and both parents must be carriers for the offspring to have the disease.

68 Sequencing a gene that aids in   8d
DNA repair led researchers to
the discovery that SCID patients were
missing 5 base pairs on that gene. This
description indicates that SCID is

A a genetic mutation resulting from a recessive trait.

B an example of co-dominance.

C a chromosomal mutation resulting from a deletion mutation.

D an example of incomplete dominance.

69 Which statement best explains why drought affects all populations equally? 16

A Because drought is a density dependent limiting factor, large population are more at risk because they have more individuals to support.

B Because drought is a density independent limiting factor, all populations large or small suffer with lack of water sources.

C Because drought is a density dependent limiting factor, only small populations that have limited genetic variability are at risk.

D Because drought is a density independent limiting factor, larger populations pass the disease between individuals at a faster rate than smaller populations.

70 The type of plant that has stem vascular bundles located in a ring and flower parts in multiples of four or five is a 10

A dicot.

B monocot.

C monotreme.

D gymnosperm.

The diagram below shows the classification of four organisms.

Common Name	Heartworm	Hookworm	Tapeworm	Roundworm
Organism	1	2	3	4
Class	Secernentea	Secernentea	Secernentea	Secernentea
Order	Spirurida	Spirurida	Ascaridida	Spirurida
Family	Filariidae	Uncinariidae	Ascarididae	Filariidae
Genus	*Dirofilaria*	*Necator*	*Ascaris*	*Loa*

71 According to the diagram, which two organisms are the most related? 9a

A 1 and 4   C 2 and 4

B 1 and 2   D 2 and 3

72 Bob put a liter of gas in his lawn mower. How many milliliters would this equal? 1d

A 1,000 milliliters

B 100 milliliters

C 10,000 milliliters

D 1,000,000 milliliters

73 Which process of cell division results in progeny with half the chromosomes of the parent cells? 6

A meiosis   C mitosis

B replication   D fertilization

74 A pouch of syrup is placed in a container of water. The pouch is permeable to water, but impermeable to syrup. The movement of water across the membrane is the result of 2

A combustion.   C osmosis.

B diffusion.   D plasmolysis.

75 Which level of biological organization is shown in the picture? 5

A population

B cell

C organism

D biosphere

76 Upon hatching from the egg, sea turtles are attracted to the brightest light in the night sky, usually provided by the moon. This light guides the baby turtles out to sea. The attraction to light is considered a 12

A learned behavior.

B innate behavior.

C diurnal behavior.

D nocturnal behavior.

77 Robert started a small business growing bean sprouts for a local restaurant. He discovered the bean sprouts needed extra oxygen and gave off heat energy. What process caused the bean sprouts to use oxygen and produce heat? 3

A respiration

B diffusion

C photosynthesis

D evaporation

78 The wilting of most plants is caused by 2d

A a reduction in turgor pressure.

B an increase in turgor pressure.

C a reduction in blood pressure.

D slow rate of photosynthesis.

79 Tay-Sachs disease is a genetic disease caused by a recessive allele, found predominantly in those of Eastern European descent. Individuals affected with this disease accumulate fatty substances in the nerve cells of the brain. Although mostly observed in infants, a rare form of the disease affects people in their twenties and thirties. A woman affected with Tay-Sachs marries a man who is a carrier for this disease. What is the probability that their child will be affected with Tay-Sachs? 7c

A 25%

B 50%

C 75%

D 100%

80 Which student correctly compared the benthic zone to the intertidal zone?   15

Student	Benthic Zone	Intertidal Zone
A	• warm • low pressure • zero species diversity	• cold • high pressure • high species diversity
B	• little sunlight • high pressure • bacteria are producers	• high sunlight • low pressure • protists are producers
C	• high sunlight • cold • salty	• low sunlight • warm • freshwater
D	• low sunlight • low pressure • protists are producers	• high sunlight • high pressure • bacteria are producers

Study the image below.

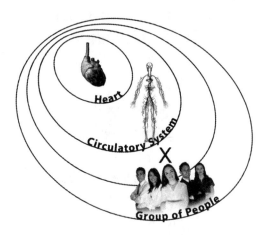

81 Which term belongs in the location of the X?   5

    A cell

    B organ system

    C ecosystem

    D organism

82 A liquor store is burglarized at twilight. After the police arrive, they find blood on the broken glass and send it to the laboratory for DNA analysis. A DNA analysis of the three suspects produces the fingerprints shown below. Which suspect was the burglar?   8

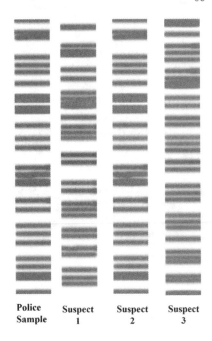

    A suspect 1

    B suspect 2

    C suspect 3

    D All suspects have some of the DNA markers from the police sample, so the test is inconclusive.

83 How would you organize the following list to show the correct order from simplest to most complex?   5

a. circulatory system

b. red & white blood cells, platelets & plasma

c. human being

d. heart

A b, d, a, c

B d, a, b, c

C c, a, d, b

D c, d, b, a

84 The biotic factors in a balanced food web are   13a

A producers and humus.

B producers, consumers and decomposers.

C light, water and rocks.

D large and small predators.

Use the classification key to answer number 85.

1. a. Fur is marked with stripes and spots……………... go to 2.

   b. Fur is primarily solid-colored…...……………. go to 3.

2. a. Dwells primarily in trees………....................…… *Leopardus wiedii* (margay)

   b. Dwells primarily on the ground…...................…… *Leopardus pardalis* (ocelot)

3. a. Ears and tail are tipped with short, black fur …... *Puma concolor* (puma)

   b. Ears are tufted with long, black fur …................. *Caracal caracal* (caracal)

85 According to the dichotomous key, to which genus and species does this cat   11
     belong?

   A *Caracal caracal*

   B *Leopardus pardalis*

   C *Puma concolor*

   D *Leopardus wiedii*

86 The Giant Moa was a large flightless bird found only in New Zealand. It was larger than an ostrich, standing up to 3 meters (10 ft) high and weighing up to 280 kg (600 lbs). Until the arrival of humans on the island, the moa's main predator was Haast's Eagle. In fact, the Haast Eagle's main prey was the Giant Moa. This eagle species was the largest ever recorded, having a wingspan of up to 3 meters (10 ft) and weighting up to 30 lbs. When Maori tribesmen settled New Zealand in the 1100s, they began to aggressively hunt the Giant Moa. By the late 1400s, all species of moa were extinct. What most likely happened to the population of Haast's Eagle following the extinction of the moa?

From Public Library of Science

16

A The Haast's Eagle found a new prey source, humans.

B The Haast's Eagle soon went extinct.

C The Haast's Eagle developed a symbiotic relationship with humans.

D The Haast's Eagle evolved into a ground dwelling bird.

87 The use of windmills to produce power is encouraged by many environmental proponents and by the U.S. government, which subsidizes this power technology at a comparatively high rate. Windmills produce a great deal of clean energy. Also, their use does not cause pollution or deplete any natural resource. Wind power is an example of   14a

A a non-renewable resource.

B a renewable resource.

C a sustainable practice.

D both B and C.

88 Which biome has extreme temperature fluctuations, little rain, plants like sagebrush and mesquite, and animals like scorpions, lizards and birds?   15

A grassland   C desert

B rain forest   D tundra

89 A swarm of locusts destroys crops in Africa. What level of biological organization is a swarm an example of?   5

A ecosystem   C habitat

B community   D population

90 A landscaper crossed a short juniper with another short juniper. She noticed that 73% of the offspring junipers were short and 27% were tall. These results indicate that the allele for shortness is   7a

A dominant.   C co-dominant.

B recessive.   D incompletely dominant.

EVALUATION CHART FOR ALABAMA HIGH SCHOOL GRADUATION EXAM

Directions: On the following chart, circle the question numbers that you answered incorrectly, and evaluate the results. These questions are based on the Alabama Course of Study: Science; Biology Core. Then turn to the appropriate topics (listed by chapters), read the explanations, and complete the exercises. Review other chapters as needed. Finally, complete the practice test(s) to assess your progress and further prepare you for the *Alabama High School Graduation Exam*.

*Note: Some question numbers will appear under multiple chapters because those questions require demonstration of multiple skills.

Chapters	Diagnostic Test Question
1. Safety, Equipment, Measurement & Scientific Method	43, 47, 48, 50, 60, 72
2. Cells and Cellular Transport	1, 4, 10, 36, 38, 44, 49, 74, 78, 83
3. Chemistry of Life	15, 21, 26, 39, 54, 77
4. Nucleic Acids and Cell Division	6, 13, 17, 18, 31, 51, 53, 73
5. Genetics, Heredity, and Biotechnology	27, 29, 30, 33, 35, 55, 68, 79, 82, 90
6. Taxonomy	7, 8, 11, 16, 22, 34, 37, 52, 59, 62, 66, 70, 71, 85
7. Evolution	19, 20, 23, 24, 42, 65, 76
8. Interactions in the Environment	2, 3, 5, 9, 12, 14, 25, 28, 32, 41, 45, 46, 56, 57, 58, 61, 63, 64, 67, 69, 75, 80, 81, 84, 86, 88, 89
9. Environmental Awareness	40, 87

Chapter 1
Safety, Equipment, Measurement &
Scientific Method

1	Select appropriate laboratory glassware, balances, time measuring equipment and optical instrument to conduct an experiment.
1a	Describing the steps of the scientific method.
1b	Comparing controls, dependent variables, and independent variables.
1c	Identify safe laboratory procedures when handling chemicals and using Bunsen burners and laboratory glassware.
1d	Using appropriate SI units for measuring length, volume, and mass.

SAFETY PROCEDURES IN THE LABORATORY

Safety procedures are set up to protect you and others from injury. Before working in the laboratory, fully read all of the directions for the experiment. Laboratory accidents can be easily avoided if safety procedures are followed. Be sure that you wear appropriate clothing for the lab and remove any dangling jewelry. Know where all safety equipment, including eyewash and fire extinguishers, are located. Decide what personal protective equipment — like aprons, goggles or gloves — are necessary. If there is an accident, spill or breakage in the laboratory, report it to your instructor immediately.

Glassware Safety

- Never use broken or chipped glassware. Dispose of broken or chipped glassware in a container specified by your teacher.
- Never heat glassware that is not thoroughly dry.
- Never pick up any glassware unless you are sure it is not hot. Remember, hot glass looks the same as cold glass.
- If glassware is hot, use heat-resistant gloves or use tongs.
- Do not put hot glassware in cold water or on any other cold surface.

Sharp Instrument Safety

- Always use single edged razors.
- Handle any sharp instrument with extreme care.
- Never cut any material toward you. Always cut away from you. Immediately notify your teacher if your skin is cut.
- Dispose of used or ruined sharp instruments in a container specified by your teacher.

Fire and Heat Safety

- Never use an open flame without wearing safety goggles.
- Never heat anything (particularly chemicals) unless instructed to do so.
- Never heat anything in a closed container.
- When using a Bunsen burner to heat a substance in a test tube, move the test tube in and out of the flame. Never leave the test tube directly in the flame.
- Never reach across a flame.
- Always use a clamp, tongs or heat-resistant gloves to handle hot objects.

Animal Safety

- Do not cause pain, discomfort or injury to a live animal.
- Follow your teacher's directions when handling animals.
- Wash your hands thoroughly after handling animals or their cages.

Electrical Safety

- Never use a long extension cord to plug in an electrical device.
- Do not plug too many appliances into one socket.
- Never touch an electrical appliance or outlet with wet hands.

Chemical Safety

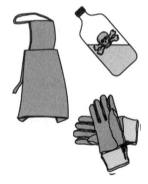

- Always wear a safety apron and protective gloves when handling chemicals to protect yourself from chemical spills. If a chemical contacts your skin, rinse immediately and notify your instructor or seek emergency care.
- Never smell any chemical directly from its container.
- Always use your hand to waft some of the odors from the top of the container toward your nose and only when instructed to do so.
- Use proper ventilation in the lab through use of a chemical fume hood.
- Keep all lids closed when chemicals are not in use.
- Dispose of all chemicals as instructed by your teacher.

Eye and Face Safety

- Wear safety goggles when handling chemicals.
- When you are heating a test tube or bottle, always point it away from you and others.
- Remember chemicals can splash or boil out of a heated test tube.
- If a chemical comes in contact with your eyes, use the eyewash fountain immediately and seek emergency care.

Proper Dress

- Wear long-sleeved blouses, shirts and pants rather than shorts.
- Tie back long hair to prevent it from coming into contact with chemicals or an open flame.
- Wear shoes without open ends.
- Remove or tie back any dangling jewelry or loose clothing to prevent getting caught on any equipment.

Official Safety Information

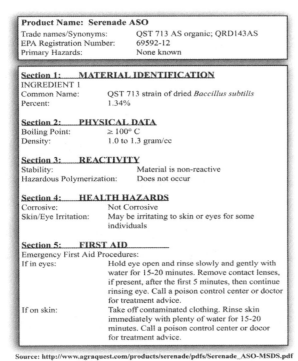

Source: http://www.agraquest.com/products/serenade/pdfs/Serenade_ASO-MSDS.pdf

Figure 1.1 Example of an MSDS

Through the Department of Labor, the United States Government runs the **Occupational Safety and Health Administration**, also called **OSHA**. The goal of OSHA is to protect the health and safety of America's workers. OSHA has many regulations regarding workplace safety and procedure. Alabama, through an approved plan with the U.S. Department of Labor, administers its own occupational health and safety program, which protects workers in both private and public sectors. The Web site for Alabama's state OSHA program is http://www.alalabor.state.al.us. The national OSHA web site is http://www.osha.gov.

Manufacturers of chemicals are required to produce, update and maintain a safety data sheet for each chemical they produce. This document is called a **material safety data sheet** or **MSDS**. An MSDS lists information on chemical structure, chemical appearance, chemical properties and personal safety. It also contains information on safe storage and disposal of chemicals.

Read and understand all MSDS sheets for chemicals used in the lab.

MSDS sheets can be found on the internet. Some revelant Web sites are http://www.scorecard.org/chemical-profiles and http://msds.ehs.cornell.edu/msdssrch.asp.

Section Review 1: Safety Procedures in the Laboratory

A. List several rules for ensuring the various safety concerns below are met.

glassware	animal	chemical	sharp
fire and heat	electrical	eye and face	instrument

B. Multiple Choice

1. How should you pick up a piece of hot glassware?

    A. with bare hands   C. with the sleeve of your shirt

    B. with heat-resistant gloves   D. with a spatula

2. How should you hold a test tube containing a chemical?

    A. pointed away from your face   C. held right up to your nose

    B. pointed at your eye   D. very close to your partner's face

3. You should report a cut in your skin, glass breakage or a chemical spill

    A. after the problem is handled.   C. immediately.

    B. never.   D. after you write down what happened.

4. Why shouldn't you wear dangling jewelry and baggy clothing to the laboratory?

    A. The baggier the clothes, the more chemical fumes are absorbed.

    B. The metal in the jewelry changes the expected reaction.

    C. Lab coats don't fit over baggy clothes.

    D. Jewelry and clothing could get caught on equipment, and clothes can catch on fire.

5. When you are done with an experiment, how should you dispose of any chemicals used?

    A. Mix them all up in a waste container and dump them in the trash.

    B. Pour them all down the sink.

    C. Follow the instructions given to properly dispose of the particular chemical(s).

    D. Mix the chemicals in a flask and heat the mixture until it evaporates into the air.

C. Short Answer

1. Kara and Mitch are partners in physical science lab. Their class is conducting an experiment on supersaturated solutions. Kara and Mitch put on safety goggles and safety aprons, and read the experiment's directions. The experiment directs them to add sugar to water in a beaker, heat the beaker with the solution on a hot plate add more sugar to the solution, remove the beaker with the solution from the hot plate and allow the solution to cool undisturbed. What additional safety equipment will Kara and Mitch need to use for this experiment?

2. Mr. Ohm's physical science class is making soap. The students will be using sodium hydroxide, which is a potent chemical. Which types of safety equipment will the class most likely need?

3. Name two pieces of safety equipment that should be used or made available when working with an open flame.

EQUIPMENT AND MATERIALS

Laboratory equipment and materials are tools or devices used in scientific investigations. Each article in the lab has a specific purpose. If you don't know the purpose of a piece of equipment, ask your teacher. Instruments are used to enhance the ability of our senses to observe.

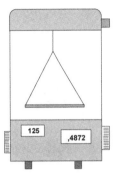

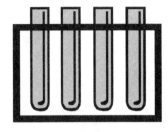

An **Erlenmeyer flask** is used to measure liquid and helps prevent liquids from splashing or giving off noxious fumes.

Test tubes are used to mix, measure, or heat liquids. Test tubes are not usually marked with measurements, so they are only used to make approximate measurements.

A **mechanical pan balance** is used to accurately determine mass to the nearest ten thousandth of a gram.

Graduated cylinders are "graduated" or marked with a scale for measurement. They are used to accurately measure liquid volume.

An **eyedropper** is used to dispense small measures of a liquid.

A **Bunsen burner** is a source of gas heat.

A **watch glass** is a holding container.

Thermometers measure temperature.

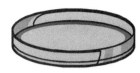

A **petri dish** is used to culture (grow) bacteria and other microorganisms.

Tongs are used to grasp heated material.

A **hot plate** is a source of electric heat.

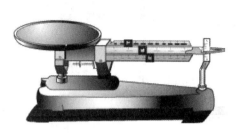

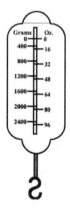

A **triple-beam balance** is used to determine the mass of heavier materials to the nearest gram.

A **spring scale** is used to determine force.

Beakers are used to mix, measure, or heat liquids, but they are not designed for accurate measurement.

A **telescope** enables us to see objects too far away to be seen with the unaided eye.

A **meter stick** measures length or width.

A chemical **fume hood** is used to contain and safely remove hazardous gases from the laboratory.

Wire gauze usually goes on top of a tripod to hold the glassware being heated.

A **microscope** enables us to see very small objects or organisms too small to see with the unaided eye.

A **tripod** holds glassware above a Bunsen burner.

Activity

Define the correct usage of the following tools. If the tool is designed to measure something, indicate which parameter it is designed to measure (length, volume, etc.). If the tool is designed to protect the wearer, indicate what it protects against.

Petri dish	eyedropper	wire gauze	beaker	thermometer
microscope	spring scale	meter stick	apron	Bunsen burner
Erlenmeyer flask	graduated cylinder	triple-beam balance	watch glass	test tube
hot plate	tripod	pan balance	fume hood	goggles

Section Review 2: Equipment

1. Which of the following is used as a source of heat in the laboratory?

    A. thermometer   B. Bunsen burner   C. thermostat   D. gasoline

2. Which has specific markings for measurement and is used to accurately measure liquid volume?

    A. test tubes   B. beakers   C. ruler   D. graduated cylinders

3. Which of the following are pieces of equipment used to measure liquids and are built to prevent spilling?

    A. Petri dish   B. beaker   C. funnel   D. Erlenmeyer flask

4. If you were instructed to heat something on the Bunsen burner, you would need to set your container on a _____ to hold your container over the burner.

    A. watch glass   C. a piece of wire gauze held by a tripod

    B. hotplate   D. Petri dish

SCIENTIFIC MEASUREMENT

In order to describe the world around them, scientists often take measurements that quantify a certain phenomenon. However, there is uncertainty with every measurement. This uncertainty can arise from several sources including poor measuring devices or improper use of the measuring device (i.e., human error). Scientists can express the uncertainty of their measurements by using the proper amount of significant figures. Scientists must also include a unit with their measurements, otherwise the numbers have no meaning. The following sections discuss scientific units, significant figures and scientific notation in more detail.

INTRODUCTION TO SI UNITS

The **SI units** of measurement are used throughout the world when performing calculations related to scientific investigations. It stands for *Le Système International d'Unites* and was established in France about 200 years ago. SI units were adapted from the metric system, and the base units are the meter, to measure length; the gram, to measure mass; and the second, to measure time. In addition, volume, density and temperature are frequent measurements in the laboratory.

The **English system**, also called the **U.S. Customary System**, of measurement is used in the United States. In this system, the foot is the standard length, the pound is the standard weight, and the second is the standard for time. Although you are probably more familiar with the English system, the SI units are used in the scientific community and throughout the world. Therefore, SI units will be the standard system of measurement used in this book. Some units and conversions are listed in Table 1.1 below.

Table 1.1 Unit Conversions

Length			Area		
12 in (inches)	=	1 ft (foot)	144 sq. in (square inches)	=	1 sq. ft (foot)
3 ft (feet)	=	1 yd (yard)	9 sq. ft (feet)	=	1 sq. yd (yard)
5,280 ft (feet)	=	1 mi (mile)	4,840 sq. yd (yards)	=	1 ac or A (acre)
Capacity (liquid)			640 ac	=	1 sq. mi (mile)
16 fl oz (fluid ounces)	=	1 pt (pint)	**Mass**		
2 pt (pints)	=	1 qt (quart)	16 oz (ounces)	=	1 lb (pound)
4 qt (quarts)	=	1 gal (gallon)	2,000 lb (pounds)	=	1 tn or T (ton)
Conversions from SI to U.S. Customary Units					
2.54 cm (centimeter)	=	1 in (inch)	0.453 kg (kilograms)	=	1 lb (pound)
1 m (meter)	=	3.281 ft (feet)	1°C (Celsius)	=	33.8°F (Fahrenheit)
1 km (kilometer)	=	0.6214 mi			

UNIT CONVERSIONS

The units in the metric system are defined in multiples of 10 from the standard unit. The metric prefixes indicate which multiple of 10 — 10, 100 or 1,000 — the standard unit should be multiplied or divided by. To convert from one unit to another in the metric system, you multiply and divide. Multiply when changing from a greater unit to a smaller one; divide (or rather, multiply by a fraction) when changing from a smaller unit to a larger one. The chart below is set up to help you know how far and which direction to move a decimal point when making conversions from one unit to another.

Example 1:

2 L = 2000 mL

List or visualize the metric prefixes to figure out how many places to move the decimal point.

$$2.000\,L = 2000\ mL$$

k　　h　　da　　u　　d　　c　　m

To convert the 2 L to mL, move the decimal point three places to the right, which is equivalent to multiplying by 1000. You will need to add three zeros.

Example 2:

5.25 cm = 0.0525 m

To convert from centimeters to meters, you need to move the decimal point two spaces to the left.

$$005.25\ cm = 0.0525\ m$$

k　　h　　da　　u　　d　　c　　m

So, to convert 5.25 cm to m, move the decimal point two spaces to the left, which is equivalent to dividing by 100. Again, you need to add a zero.

Prefix	kilo (k)	hecto (h)	deka (da)	**Base Unit**	deci (d)	centi (c)	milli (m)
Abbreviation	km	hm	dam	**meter**	dm	cm	mm
	kL	hL	daL	**Liter**	dL	cL	mL
	kg	hg	dag	**gram**	dg	cg	mg
Multiplication Factor	1000	100	10	**1**	0.1	0.01	0.001

You may see some abbreviations that are unfamiliar to you. In the science lab, and in most real-life applications, kilo-, centi- and milli- will be the abbreviations that you most often encounter. However, all these units are correct, and some of the lesser-known ones are even common in particular industries. The hectometer, for instance, is a commonly used unit in agriculture and forestry.

Practice Exercise 1: Unit Conversions

Convert the following measurements to the specified units.

1.　35 mg = _____ g　　6. 32.1 mg = _____ kg　11.　72.3 cm = _____ m

2.　6 km = _____ m　　7. 17.5 L = _____ mL　12. 0.003 kL = _____ L

3. 21.5 mL = _____ L　　8.　4.2 g = _____ kg　13.　5.06 g = _____ mg

4. 4.9 mm = _____ cm　9.0.417 kg = _____ cg　14. 1.058 mL = _____ cL

5. 5.35 kL = _____ mL　10. 2.057 m = _____ cm　15.　564.3 g = _____ kg

STANDARD SI MEASUREMENTS

The standard SI unit of measurement to determine **length** is **meter (m)**. To better visualize a meter, it is helpful to know that 1 meter is equal to 3.28 feet. Length measures the distance from one point to another and can be used to determine a person's height in meters, the distance between your home and your school in kilometers, the length of an almond in centimeters, or the thickness of a dime in millimeters. A ruler (used to measure feet) or **meter stick** (used to measure meters) is commonly used to measure length. Figure 1.2 measures an almond using a metric ruler (used to measure cm and mm).

This almond measures about 2 cm in length.

Figure 1.2 Metric Ruler

Mass is the measure of the amount of matter in an object. Its standard SI measurement unit is the **kilogram (kg)** and the tool of measurement is the balance. One kilogram is equal to 2.2 pounds (on Earth). The masses of medicine, a rock, and a person, can be determined using milligrams, grams, and kilograms, respectively.

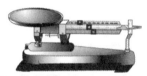

Figure 1.3 Triple-beam Balance

The terms *mass and weight* are sometimes used interchangeably, but they are <u>not</u> the same. Mass is a property of the object itself. **Weight** is the measurement of the gravitational force that attracts an object to the Earth. The SI unit for weight is the **newton (N)**, and in the English system of measurement, weight is given in pounds (lbs.) or ounces (oz.). Weight varies depending on the amount of gravitational force. On Earth, a person might weigh 130 pounds, but on the moon, which has a lower gravitational force, the same person would weigh 1/6th of that amount. Scientists use mass when conducting and reporting experiments because it is a property of matter that is unaffected by gravity.

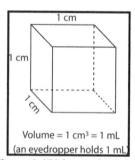

Figure 1.4 Volume of a Cube

Volume is the amount of space occupied by an object. Volume is determined in different ways depending on the shape (i.e. cube, sphere, irregular) and state of matter (i.e. solid, liquid, gas) of the object. For a regularly shaped object, like a cube, volume is determined by multiplying the length times the height times the width of the object $(V = l \times h \times w)$. The units used for volume are **cubic centimeters (cm^3** or **cc)** or **milliliters (mL)**. Figure 1.4 shows this relationship. One cubic centimeter is equal to one milliliter, which is equal to one thousandth of a liter.

A **graduated cylinder** is used to measure the volume of liquids. When liquids are placed in a graduated cylinder, a meniscus will form. A **meniscus** is the curve of liquid at its surface. The meniscus generally curves downward but can also curve upward depending on the liquid. Most menisci curve downwards, but a few curve up, depending on the liquid. To read the volume of the liquid, you must be at eye level with the meniscus and measure from the bottom of the curve of the meniscus if it curves downward or the top of the meniscus if it curves upward. Figure 1.5 shows how to read a meniscus that curves downward.

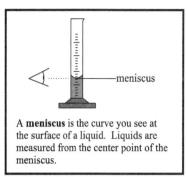

A **meniscus** is the curve you see at the surface of a liquid. Liquids are measured from the center point of the meniscus.

Figure 1.5 Graduated Cylinder

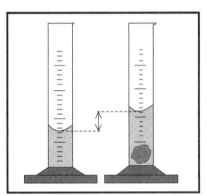

Figure 1.6 Water Displacement Method

To determine volume of irregularly shaped objects, the **water displacement** method is used. To measure volume by water displacement, place an amount of water in a container and determine its volume. Then add the object. When the object is placed in the container of water, the water level will rise. Measure the volume again. To determine the volume of the object, simply subtract the first volume measurement from the second.

Density (D) is the mass (m) of an object divided by its volume (V), $(D = m/V)$. The standard SI unit for density is **kg/m^3**, but it is also commonly expressed in units of grams per cubic centimeter (g/cm^3). Density is a characteristic material property; thus, the density of two objects of the same material is always the same even if the objects have different masses. For example, a gold ring and a gold brick both have the same density, because they are both made of gold. However, because the gold brick contains more matter than the gold ring, it has a greater mass.

Density explains why some things float and other things sink. A rock at the bottom of a stream is denser than water, so it sinks to the bottom, whereas a piece of wood is less dense than the water, so it floats. If an object sinks, it is denser than the liquid it is placed in. If an object floats, it is less dense than the liquid it is placed in.

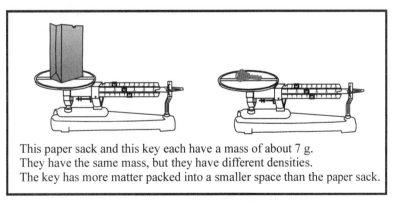

This paper sack and this key each have a mass of about 7 g.
They have the same mass, but they have different densities.
The key has more matter packed into a smaller space than the paper sack.

Figure 1.7 Mass - Density Relationship

Temperature measures how hot or cold something is. All measurements for temperature are taken in degrees. In the metric system, **Celsius** is used. The SI unit for temperature is **Kelvin**, and the English unit is **Fahrenheit**. To convert from one unit to another, use the following formulas:

$$C = \frac{(F - 32)}{1.8} \qquad F = 1.8\,C + 32 \qquad C = K - 273.15 \qquad K = C + 273.15$$

C is degrees Celsius; F is degrees Fahrenheit; K is Kelvin.

Figure 1.8 Temperature Conversion Formulas

DESIGNING AND CONDUCTING AN EXPERIMENT

Science is the observation, identification, description and explanation of phenomena (occurrences in the world around us). The Latin root for the word "science" is *scientia*, meaning knowledge. Through the study of science, we ask questions, develop hypotheses (educated guesses), and design and carry out experiments to gain a better understanding of the universe. The **scientific method** is a procedure for studying nature. It consists of several steps listed in Table 1.2 below and shown in Figure 1.8. Each of these steps will be discussed in detail in this section.

Table 1.2 Steps in the Scientific Method

1. Make an observation:	Observe birds in flight.
2. Ask questions:	How do birds fly?
3. Form the hypothesis:	The wing designs of birds catch the air differently.
4. Set up an experiment:	Make and fly different designs of paper airplanes to test the hypothesis.
5. Collect the data:	Take notes on flight patterns of paper airplanes. Create a data table on how each airplane flew.
6. Draw a conclusion:	The size and shape of the wing gives lift to the bird.
7. Make a prediction:	Wing designs are dependent on the size of the bird.

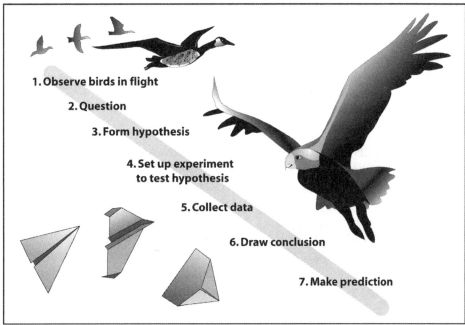

Figure 1.9 Steps in the Scientific Method

MAKING OBSERVATIONS AND DEFINING THE PROBLEM

Scientists believe all natural phenomena in the universe have logical, verifiable explanations. A **natural phenomenon** is something occurring in nature that we experience through our senses. The **scientific process** is used to research and explain natural phenomena.

The basic steps in the scientific process begin by observing and experimenting with the things around us. Observations are made by using the **five senses** (sight, touch, smell, sound and taste) to obtain information. Examples of observations include watching a bird build a nest, listening to the bird's call and touching

Figure 1.10 Observable Bird Behaviors

the nest's material. All these observations help describe or explain the bird's behavior. Making observations may lead to identifying problems as well. For example, you might observe that pigeons are making nests on the tops of city buildings. You might also observe the problem that pigeon droppings are damaging shingles and defacing city property, as well as possibly spreading disease.

ASKING QUESTIONS

Asking appropriate questions is the second step in solving a problem. By asking questions, we seek logical explanations for what we observe and find ways to solve problems.

We observe birds in flight. There are large and small birds. Some flap their wings quickly while others seem to hardly move their wings at all. The question we might ask is, "How do birds fly?"

We can also ask other questions. "What is the effect of sunlight on green plants?" "Does water temperature affect the oxygen intake of goldfish?" "Will aspirin help cut roses last longer?"

FORMING THE HYPOTHESIS

Everything we experience takes place in an ordered universe. As our knowledge of the universe grows, we recognize patterns. After observing these patterns and asking questions, we can form an opinion about how or why something happens.

A **hypothesis** is a statement that gives the best possible response to the question and should be based on already known facts. It is an educated guess. For example, the question might be "What is the effect of sunlight on green plants?" The hypothesis might be "Green plants need sunlight to grow."

The hypothesis can be developed by using inductive reasoning. **Inductive reasoning** is the ability of a scientist to draw from knowledge and experience to make a general explanation. For example, large amounts of petrified wood (stony, fossilized wood) are found in the desert area of a southwestern state. By using inductive reasoning, it is reasonable to assume that at one time large forests grew in that desert.

SETTING UP THE EXPERIMENT

A **scientific experiment** should give accurate and measurable results. An experiment should be designed to collect information to either prove or disprove the hypothesis. To gather meaningful data, the experiment must be set up to examine only one condition (or **variable**) at a time.

To test the hypothesis, the experiment should have two components: a control group and one or more experimental groups. The **control group** is the part of the experiment that is designed without changing any of the variables. This helps to support the hypothesis. The **experimental groups** are designed to test components of the hypothesis and to indicate changes which might invalidate the hypothesis. Through observations and measurements of the different groups, information is collected and recorded. When the data from the experimental groups are compared to the data from the control group, the scientist can calculate how much the variables affected the investigation.

Assume the hypothesis is that radish seeds will sprout fastest in a dark environment. Five sets of eight radish seeds are wrapped in a moist towel and placed in Petri dishes. They are called group A. Another five sets of eight radish seeds are wrapped in a moist towel and placed in Petri dishes. They are called group B. Another five sets of eight radish seeds are wrapped in a moist towel and placed in Petri dishes. They are called group C. The seeds are placed under different conditions and the number of seedlings in each group that germinate are counted after four days.

Table 1.3 Conditions (and Variables) for Radish Seed Experiment

Group	Temperature	Light	Moist
A	23° C	full	yes
B	23° C	partial	yes
C	23° C	none	yes

There are three types of variables seen in an experiment:

1. **independent variable** - the factors that are changed or manipulated during the experiment. They are the ones that the experiment is trying to test. In this experiment, the independent variable is the presence or absence of light. As the chart shows, this is the only variable that has been changed.

2. **dependent variable** - it is usually the factor that the experimenter is measuring or counting. The dependent variable is the one that changes in response to the independent variable. In this experiment, the dependent variable is the number of radish seeds that germinated.

3. **control variable** - all the other factors in the experiment. These are things that you attempt to control such as temperature, amount of moisture present, type of light bulb or length of time the experiment ran. These are all considered control variables and are kept constant.

COLLECTING DATA

Data is gathered from the observations and measurements taken during a scientific experiment. The observations from the experiment must be recorded. If the data collected are organized in a logical manner, they can be more easily analyzed to determine the results of the experiment.

Data could include time intervals, temperatures and metric units of mass, length and volume. A table is a good way to organize data. **Qualitative data** is information that cannot be assigned a numerical value. It is often collected using the five senses. Examples of qualitative data can include shades of color, texture, taste or smell. **Quantitative data** is anything that can be expressed as a number, that is, it can be quantified. Quantitative data can include lengths, weights, masses, volumes, time or anything else expressed as a number. Both qualitative and quantitative data can be organized in a data table.

Table 1.4 below shows data collected from an experiment on the effects of light on sprouting radish seeds. The experimenter collected data on the number of seeds that sprouted over several days.

Control: Temperature, moisture level, type of radish used.

Variable: Amount of light provided to seeds.

Table 1.4 Number of Radish Seeds Sprouted over Seven Days.

Days after planting	1	2	3	4	5	6	7
Number of seeds sprouted in full light		1	2	2	3		
Number of seeds sprouted in partial light			1	2	2	3	
Number of seeds sprouted in the dark						1	1

DRAWING CONCLUSIONS

A **conclusion** is a judgement or inference based on observation and experimentation. It is drawn from the results of the experiment. The **results** are the end product of an experiment. The analytical method of investigation is an examination of parts of an experiment to seek reliable information that will support or reject the hypothesis. To really know the true outcome of an experiment, it must be performed many times. Through the analysis of results obtained from all experiments, a summary or conclusion can be determined.

Table 1.4 above shows the number of radish seed sprouted in different amounts of light. From this table, we can conclude that seeds sprout the fastest in full light and seeds sprout the slowest in the dark.

Practice Exercise 2:

Drawing Conclusions

Scientists have given us a diagram of the Big Dipper in the north sky as it looked 100,000 years ago. We know how it looks now. Scientists have also suggested what the Big Dipper will look like 100,000 years in the future. Study the diagrams to the right

If the earth has not changed its position in the sky, then some change must have happened to explain the way the Big Dipper has changed its appearance. What conclusion can you draw about the apparent differences in the Big Dipper's shape over time?

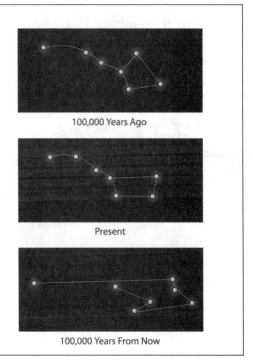

100,000 Years Ago

Present

100,000 Years From Now

Section Review 3: Designing and Conducting an Experiment

A. Terms

science	hypothesis	control group	dependent variable
scientific method	inductive reasoning	experimental group	qualitative data
natural phenomenon	variable	independent variable	quantitative data

B. Multiple Choice

1. The ability to draw from previous knowledge and experience to make an explanation is

   A. a problem.

   B. inductive reasoning.

   C. a reasonable explanation.

   D. processing.

2. Something occurring in nature that is experienced through our senses is

    A. asking a question.
    C. defining a problem.

    B. inductive reasoning.
    D. a natural phenomenon.

3. An educated guess is a/an

    A. hypothesis.
    B. puzzle.
    C. answer.
    D. reason.

4. The situation in an experiment where no variables are changed is the

    A. experimental group.
    C. control group.

    B. hypothesis.
    D. natural phenomenon.

5. The group designed with a variable to test or invalidate the hypothesis is called the

    A. control group.
    C. question.

    B. experimental group.
    D. experiment setup.

6. Both qualitative and quantitative data collected during an experiment can be organized in a

    A. group.
    B. variable.
    C. table.
    D. question.

Use this information to answer question 7.

A nutritional supplement manufacturer conducted an experiment to determine how creatine supplements affect muscle growth in body builders. One hundred body builders were divided into four equal groups. All groups were given the same diet and the same strict workout schedule. Group 1 was given a placebo sugar pill for 4 weeks. Group 2 was given 5 grams of creatine 2 times a day for 4 weeks. Group 3 was given 5 grams of creatine 4 times a day for 4 weeks. Group 4 was given 5 grams of creatine 4 times a day for the first 2 weeks and then 5 grams 2 times a week for the second 2 weeks.

7. Which group was used as the control group?

    A. Group 1
    B. Group 2
    C. Group 3
    D. Group 4

C. Short Answer

1. Judy went to a picnic at the lake. A jar of dill pickles fell off the table and broke on a rock. When she cleaned up the spill, she noticed small foaming bubbles on the rock. What scientific questions might she ask?

2. When Judy went to clean up the spilled pickles in question 1, she noticed a strong smell of vinegar. She learned in science class that vinegar is an acid. If the rock on which the pickles landed was a limestone rock, what hypothesis might she form?

3. Ryan noticed that his cola loses its carbonation as it warms. He knows that it is carbon dioxide that causes cola to fizz. Ryan decided to do a scientific experiment to research this phenomenon. Write a hypothesis for Ryan based on the knowledge and observation given.

4. The hypothesis of an experiment states: "Exposure to music changes the growth rate of plants." Three groups of plants are grown in the same conditions, and their growth rates are compared. Group 1 has plants that are exposed to heavy metal music for 3 hours per day. Group 2 is composed of plants that are exposed to love songs for 3 hours per day. Group 3 is not exposed to any music. Which of the groups discussed above is/are the experimental group(s) and why?

5. Why should an experiment test only one variable at a time?

6. Allen wants to know the relationship between the temperature of a gas and the volume of a gas. He used a spherical balloon filled with air to conduct his experiment. Explain how he should obtain the data and what measurements he should record in his data table.

Challenge Activity

Marita places a beaker containing chemical A on a triple beam balance. She records the mass. She adds chemical B to the beaker and records the mass. As the chemicals begin to react, fumes are produced, and mass is lost. Marita records the mass of the beaker every 10 seconds. Her results are shown below.

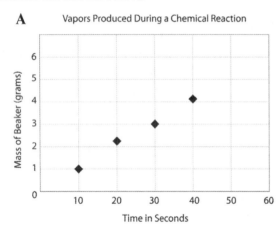

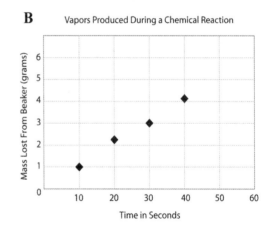

1. Which of these two graphs reflects the scenario outlined above?

2. Where should this experiment be performed?

3. Predict how many grams will be lost at the 60-second mark.

4. Where has the mass gone?

CHAPTER 1 REVIEW

Choose the best answer.

1. When trying to determine mass of a heavy object, use

   A. a spring scale.   C. a hot plate.

   B. a tripod.   D. a triple-beam balance.

2. What is the difference between mass and weight?

   A. There is no difference.

   B. Mass is the amount of matter in an object, and weight measures gravitational force
      that attracts an object to the earth.

   C. Weight is the amount of matter in an object, and mass measures gravitational
      force that attracts an object to the earth.

   D. The only difference is the type of tool used to make each measurement.

3. Kilograms are a unit of measurement for

   A. mass.   B. height.   C. volume.   D. size.

4. In the Kelvin temperature scale, water freezes at

   A. 0 K.   B. 180 K.   C. 273.15 K.   D. −273.15 K.

5. On a summer day, the outside temperature equals 86°F. What would be the equivalent
   temperature in degrees Celsius?

   A. 97°   B. 30°   C. 38°   D. 14°

6. Scientists across the world share information about their discoveries. Why is it
   important for scientists to use the same measurement system?

   A. copyright laws

   B. proof or evidence for comparison and understanding

   C. conforming to code

   D. to avoid repetition

7. Graduated cylinders are marked in units of

   A. grams.   B. meters.   C. millimeters.   D. milliliters.

8. Various safety rules apply in the laboratory. In order to protect your clothing, you should

   A. wear an apron.

   B. wear clothing treated with Teflon™.

   C. wear clothing treated with Scotchgard™.

   D. wear as many layers as possible.

9. In biology class, the students are asked to do an experiment that shows the effects of temperature on bacterial growth rates. Suggest two pieces of laboratory equipment needed for this experiment.

   A. Petri dish and thermometer

   B. Bunsen burner and tongs

   C. microscope and watch glass

   D. test tube and eye dropper

10. Reaching across a flame is

   A. never acceptable.

   B. always acceptable.

   C. sometimes acceptable.

   D. seldom acceptable.

11. Hot glass looks the same as

   A. hot coals.

   B. frosty glass.

   C. a piece of hot metal.

   D. cold glass.

12. You should report a chemical spill to your teacher

   A. immediately.

   B. after you've cleaned up the spill.

   C. only if you think the spill is dangerous.

   D. after you've finished the experiment so your results are not ruined.

13. Proper ventilation in the lab should be through the use of

   A. opening all the doors and windows.

   B. proper placement of box fans.

   C. a chemical fume hood.

   D. positioning near a central heating and air duct.

14. Keisha observes goldfish in an outdoor pond. The goldfish seem to be more active when the weather is warm than when it is cold. She asks herself, "How do temperature changes affect goldfish?" If she were to do an experiment, which of the following would be the best hypothesis?

   A. Do goldfish like warm water or cold water?

   B. Goldfish are more active in warm water than in cold water.

   C. Goldfish live in warm and cold water.

   D. Temperature changes will kill goldfish.

15. Four groups of rats are tested in a lab. Group 1 is given a special hormone for muscle growth. Group 2 is given a special multivitamin diet. Group 3 receives both the hormone treatment and the multivitamin diet. Group 4 does not receive any extra treatment or special diet. Which of the following groups is the control group for this experiment?

A. Group 4   B. Group 2   C. Group 3   D. Group 1

16. In a previous experiment, Josh determined that the growth of goldfish depends on the size of the container they are in. Now, Josh wants to know if the number of goldfish in a container affects the growth of goldfish. To conduct his experiment, he placed 10 goldfish in a 20 gallon aquarium, 5 goldfish in a 10 gallon aquarium, and 1 goldfish in a 1 gallon aquarium. All the goldfish received the same food in equal amounts. He recorded goldfish growth over a 10-week period. From his data, he concluded that the more goldfish in an aquarium, the larger they grow. Why was his conclusion not valid?

A. His data was skewed because he should have put the 10 goldfish in the 1 gallon aquarium and the 1 goldfish in the 20 gallon aquarium.

B. His data was not valid because he failed to control the size of the aquariums equally for all the groups.

C. His data was valid, but he should not make a conclusion based on just one experiment.

D. His new experiment assumed the validity of a past experiment.

17. Ryan noticed that his cola loses its carbonation as it warms. He knows that it is carbon dioxide that causes cola to fizz. Ryan decided to do a scientific experiment to research this phenomenon. What is Ryan's next step in the scientific method?

A. ask a question   C. make an observation

B. draw a conclusion   D. form a hypothesis

18. A conclusion is drawn based on

A. a hypothesis.   C. observation and experimentation.

B. textbook statistics.   D. an educated guess.

19. A control group must be established in a scientific experiment to

A. support the hypothesis.   C. talk about the hypothesis.

B. make the rules.   D. report mistakes.

20. A hypothesis is checked by

A. research.   C. experimentation.

B. guessing.   D. researching on the Internet.

Read the science experiment below, and then answer questions 21–23.

Problem: Some green bean plants grow in shaded areas while others grow in full sun.

Question: What would happen to a green bean plant if the amount of sunlight it received was altered?

Hypothesis: Green bean plants will grow better in full sunlight.

Set up an experiment with green bean plants to record their growth over a seven week period.

Materials: 6 small green bean plants of approximately the same size.

6 Styrofoam cups filled with potting soil and with a hole in the bottom of each.

10 mL of water for each plant once a week.

A metric ruler.

Directions: Transfer the bean plants to the Styrofoam cups. Water each plant only once a week. Measure each plant and record the height. Place plants A and B in complete darkness. Place plants C and D in full sunlight. Place plant E and plant F in partial sunlight.

Observations: Closely measure the rate of growth of the control group plants and the experimental groups. Take notes about the conditions of each plant and record the measurements on tables.

Record Data: Make a graph to show the growth rate for each plant. Plot their growth on a multiple line graph showing height and time.

Conclusion: What conclusion can be drawn about the growth of the plants in relationship to the amount of light they each received? Does the investigation support the hypothesis? Can a theory be stated about the effect light had on the green bean plants?

Prediction: Based on the theory that is stated, make a prediction about the behavior of green bean plants in the presence of full sunlight.

21. What was the variable in the experiment with the green bean plants?

   A. the type of potting soil used

   B. the amount of sunlight

   C. the size of the container

   D. how frequently the plant was watered

22. Which plants were the control group plants?

   A. the plants kept in darkness

   B. the plants kept in partial sunlight

   C. the plants kept in full sunlight

   D. there was not a control group

23. Which of the following factors were kept constant in order for the data to be valid?

   A. the type of plant used

   B. the size of the container used to grow the plants

   C. the amount of water given to each plant

   D. all of the above are control factors

Chapter 2
Cells and Cellular Transport

ALABAMA HSGT IN SCIENCE STANDARDS COVERED IN THIS CHAPTER INCLUDE:

2	Describe cell process necessary for achieving homeostasis, including active and passive transport, osmosis, diffusion, exocytosis, and endocytosis.
2b	Comparing the reaction of plant and animal cells in isotonic, hypotonic, and hypertonic solutions.
2c	Explaining how surface area, cell size, temperature, light and pH affect cellular activities.
2d	Applying the concept of fluid pressure to biological systems.
4	Describe similarities and differences of cell organelles, using diagrams and tables.
4a	Identifying scientists who contributed to the cell theory.
4b	Distinguishing between prokaryotic and eukaryotic cells.
4c	Identifying various technologies used to observe cells.
5	Identify cells, tissues, organs, organ systems, organisms, populations, communities, and ecosystems as levels of organization in the biosphere.
5a	Recognizing that cells differentiate to perform specific functions.

CHARACTERISTICS OF LIFE

All living things, also called **organisms**, share the following characteristics:

1. Cells

2. Sensitivity (response to stimuli)

3. Growth

4. Homeostasis (stable internal environment)

5. Reproduction

6. Metabolism (transformation and use of energy)

7. Adaptation

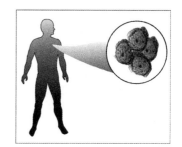

Figure 2.1 Cellular Makeup of Man

Characteristics of Organisms

Cells: Cells make up all living things. Cells can sometimes organize into complex structures. Multicellular organisms have many cells and unicellular organisms have only one cell.

Sensitivity: Organisms respond to stimuli in the environment. A **stimulus** is a change in the environment. **Responses** are reactions to stimuli in the environment. Examples of responses to stimuli include a plant that grows toward a light source or an animal that flees from a predator.

Growth: Organisms change over their lifetime. This growth may be characterized by an increase in size, the development of new physical structures or the refinement of reasoning or behavior.

Homeostasis: Organisms must maintain an internal environment that is suitable for life. Living things need the correct amount of fluids, salts, hormones and food sources in order to survive. **Homeostasis** is the ability of an organism to maintain a steady internal state regardless of external influence.

Reproduction: All living things must be able to reproduce. Organisms can reproduce sexually or asexually. **Sexual reproduction** occurs when two organisms create offspring, and **asexual reproduction** occurs when one organism is capable of creating offspring by itself.

Metabolism: Organisms must get energy from the environment. The processes of extracting energy from the environment, using that energy and disposing of waste by-products are all chemical reactions. **Metabolism** is the sum of all chemical reactions within a cell or organism.

Adaptation: Over time, organisms can become specially suited to a particular environment. Sea turtles have long, flipper-like legs and cannot easily walk on land; they have become **adapted** to living in the ocean. **Adaptations** occur slowly, over the course of many generations.

Living things also carry out life processes. These are the specific events that allow cells to grow, respond to stimuli, maintain homeostasis, reproduce, metabolize and adapt. Non-living things cannot carry out these processes. A list of life processes is given in Table 2.1.

Table 2.1 Life Processes

Life Process	Description
Nutrition	the use of nutrients by an organism.
Digestion	the process that breaks large food molecules into forms that can be used by the cell.
Absorption	the ability of a cell to take in nutrients, water, gases and other substances from its surroundings.
Transport	the movement of nutrients, water, gases and other substances into and out of the cell.
Biosynthesis	the cellular process of building new chemical compounds for the purpose of growth, repair and reproduction.
Secretion	the release of substances from a cell.
Respiration	the release of energy from chemical breakdown of compounds within the cell.
Excretion	the ability of the cell to rid itself of waste products.
Response	the ability of a cell to react to stimuli from its environment.
Reproduction	the process of fission in which one cell divides to form two identical new cells.
Photosynthesis	the cellular process in which a plant makes food from water and carbon dioxide, using energy from the sun.

Section Review 1: Characteristics of Life

A. Terms

stimulus   life   sexual reproduction

response   homeostasis   asexual reproduction

metabolism

B. Short Answer

1. List the seven characteristics all living things must show.

2. Based on what you know, how would you explain the fact that fire is not considered alive even though it grows and uses oxygen?

CELLS

CELL THEORY

The **cell** is the structural and functional unit of all organisms. Some cells can operate independently to carry out all of life's processes. Some cells function using many small structures called organelles, while other cells do not have organelles. **Organelles**, or "little organs," are small, specialized cellular subunits separated from the rest of the cell by a membrane. Organelles help a cell to move molecules, create and store energy, store information, and perform many other functions.

DISCOVERY OF THE CELL

In 1665, **Robert Hooke**, an English scientist, published his observations of thin slices of cork. Cork comes from the bark of trees. Hooke observed the remains of cell walls left in the cork. According to many accounts, the arrangement and box-like structure of the cells reminded him of the local monastery. The rooms that monks lived in were called cells, so Hooke coined the term "cell."

Another man associated with the discovery of the cell was **Antony Van Leeuwenhoek** (layu-wen-hook). He built and used over 500 microscopes which were made out of copper, brass and even gold tubing. He made the first recorded observations of bacteria.

The cell theory was developed through the efforts of several scientists, most notably **Theodor Schwann** (1810–1882), **Matthias Schleiden** (1804–1881), and **Rudolf Virchow** (1821–1902). Schwann worked with animal cells and Schleiden worked with plant cells. Together they cofounded the cell theory. The **cell theory** states that:

- all living things are made of cells.
- cells are the basic unit of all living things.
- all cells come from other living cells of the same kind.

Virchow's contribution to the cell theory stated that "all cells come from pre-existing cells."

Since many similarities exist among different kinds of cells, scientists believe, though they cannot be absolutely certain, that cells originated from a common ancestor. Scientists can study a small group of cells and apply the knowledge gained from those cells to all cells.

BASIC CELL STRUCTURE

The cell has three basic parts, as listed in Table 2.2.

Table 2.2 Parts of the Cell

Cell membrane	The cell membrane is the thin, flexible boundary surrounding the cell.
Cytoplasm	The cytoplasm is the watery, jelly-like part of the cell that contains salts, minerals, and the cell organelles.
Genetic material	The genetic material is the area of the cell where the DNA (deoxyribonucleic acid) is stored. It regulates all the cellular activities.

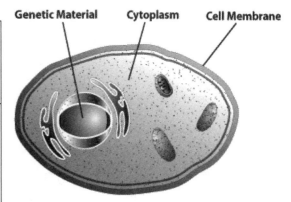

Figure 2.2 Parts of the Cell

TECHNOLOGY AND CELLS

The invention of the **compound light microscope** in the 1590s allowed scientists to view a limited number of cell structures. At that time only cell walls, cell membranes, nucleus, and vacuoles could be observed.

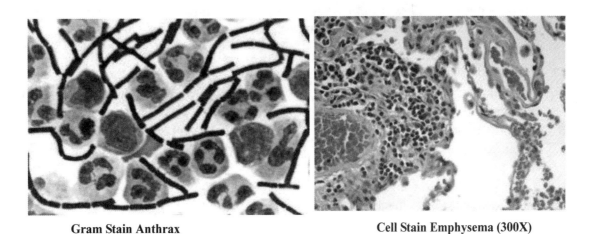

Gram Stain Anthrax   Cell Stain Emphysema (300X)

Figure 2.3 Images of cells from a compound light microscope

The compound microscope benefits from today's advances in lens making and machining that produce much higher magnification.

The invention of the **scanning election microscope** (SEM) in the 1920s allowed scientists to observe cells in greater detail. A scanning electron microscope has a resolution of between 1 nm and 20 nm. This allows scientists to observe many cellular organelles like the endoplasmic reticulum, Golgi apparatus and lysosome.

Figure 2.4 SEM image of an ant's head

Another recent invention, the **transmission electron microscope** (TEM), has allowed scientists to observe microscopic objects in even greater detail. A thin slice of the specimen is placed in the machine and a beam of electrons is used to take a picture of the object. This technique is useful for reconstructing 3-D cellular structures and locating the position of atoms within molecules.

CELLULAR ORGANIZATION

PROKARYOTIC VS. EUKARYOTIC CELLS

There are two basic types of cells: prokaryotic and eukaryotic. A **prokaryotic** (*pro-* before; *karyotic-* nucleus) cell does not have a true nucleus. Although the genetic material is usually contained in a central location, a membrane does not surround it. Furthermore, prokaryotic cells have no membrane-bound organelles. Bacteria are prokaryotic. See Figure 2.5 for a schematic drawing of a prokaryotic cell.

A **eukaryotic** (*eu-* true; *karyotic-* nucleus) cell has a nucleus surrounded by a nuclear membrane. It also has several membrane-bound organelles. Eukaryotic cells tend to be larger than prokaryotic cells. Plant and animal cells are both eukaryotic and, although similar in structure, contain unique cell parts. For instance, plant cells have a cell wall and chloroplasts, while animal cells have centrioles and some even have cilia and flagella. See Figures 2.6 and 2.7 for schematic drawings of eukaryotic cells including plant and animal cells. Table 2.5 lists definitions of the parts in eukaryotic cells.

TYPES OF CELLS

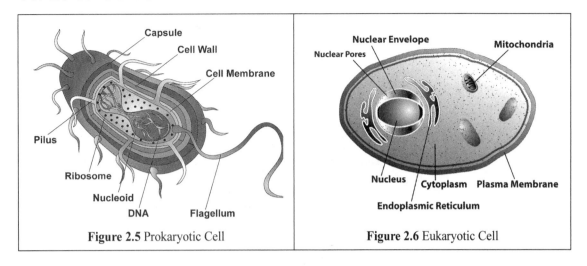

Figure 2.5 Prokaryotic Cell

Figure 2.6 Eukaryotic Cell

CELLULAR PARTS

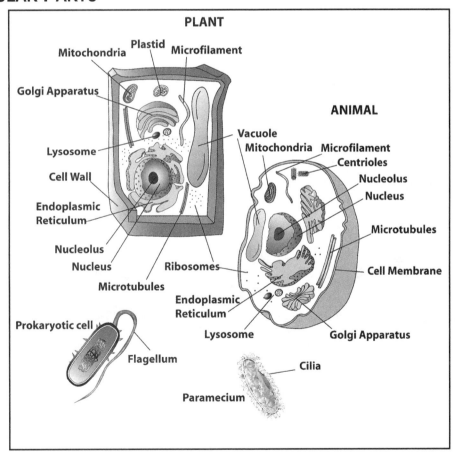

Figure 2.7 Specific Parts of the Cell

Table 2.3 Parts of the Eukaryotic Cell

Name	Description
Plastids (plant cells only)	Group of structures (chloroplasts, leukoplasts, chromoplasts) used in photosynthesis and product storage; have a double membrane and provide color and cellular energy
Vacuoles	Spherical storage sac for food and water
Golgi Apparatus	Flattened membrane sacs for synthesis, packaging, and distribution
Mitochondria	Rod-shaped double membranous structures where cellular respiration takes place
Endoplasmic Reticulum (ER)	Folded membranes having areas with and without ribosomes used for transport of RNA and proteins
Nucleus	Control center of the cell; location of hereditary information; surrounded by nuclear envelope
Ribosomes	Structures that manufacture proteins; found on endoplasmic reticulum and floating in the cytoplasm
Lysosomes	Spherical sac containing enzymes for digestive functions

Table 2.4 Other Important Cellular Parts

Name	Description
Cell Wall (plant cells, bacteria and fungi)	Rigid membrane around plant cell; provides shape and support
Cell Membrane	Membrane surrounding the cell that allows some molecules to pass through also called the phospholipid bilayer
Cytoplasm	Jelly-like substance in the cell around nucleus and organelles; site of many metabolic cycles and protein synthesis
Microfilaments & Microtubules	Fibers and tubes of protein that help move internal cell parts
Nucleolus	Dense body within the nucleus; site of ribosome production
Nuclear Envelope	Double membrane that surrounds the nucleus; fused at certain points to create nuclear pores; outer membrane is continuous with the ER
Centrioles (animal cell only)	Short tubes necessary for cell reproduction in some cells
Cilia (animal cell only)	Short, hair-like extensions on the surface of some cells used for movement and gathering food made mostly of microtubules
Flagella (animal cell only)	Long, whip-like extension on the surface of some cells used for movement made mostly of microtubules

Activity

Label the cell parts below.

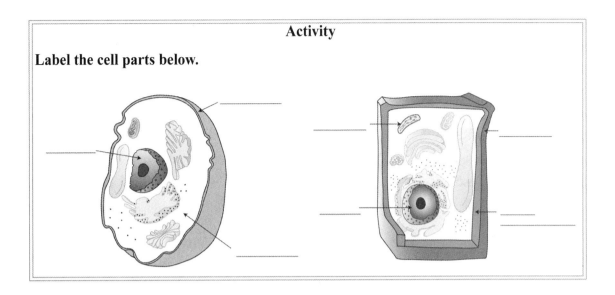

CELLULAR HIERARCHY

Some organisms are **unicellular** (single celled), like bacteria and amoebas. The single cell carries out all life functions. **Multicellular** organisms are composed of many cells that work together to carry out life processes. In multicellular organisms, the cells group together and divide the labor. **Tissues** are groups of cells that perform the same function. Several types of tissues group together to perform particular functions and are called **organs**.

An **organ system** is a group of organs working together for a particular function. The organ systems of multicellular organisms work together to carry out the life processes of the organism, with each system performing a

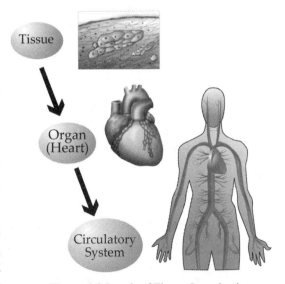

Figure 2.8 Levels of Tissue Organization

specific function. The organelles in unicellular organisms work like the organ systems of multicellular organisms. Each organelle has a specific function that helps to keep the one-celled organism alive.

Table 2.5 Examples of Cellular Hierarchy

Examples of Tissues	Examples of Organs	Examples of Organ Systems
cardiac tissue	heart	circulatory system
bone marrow	femur	skeletal system

Section Review 2: Cells

A. Terms

cell	Golgi bodies	cilia	ribosomes
organelles	mitochondria	flagella	centrioles
cell theory	microfilaments & microtubules	cytoplasm	lysosomes
prokaryotic		unicellular	vacuoles
eukaryotic	endoplasmic reticulum (ER)	multicellular	cell membrane
cell wall	nucleolus	tissue	organ system
plastids		organ	nucleus

B. Multiple Choice

1. The mitochondrion of a cell

   A. has only one membrane.

   B. has no membrane.

   C. is circular.

   D. is where cellular respiration occurs.

2. Ribosomes

   A. are the site of protein synthesis.

   B. are made by other ribosomes.

   C. have their own DNA.

   D. none of the above

3. A(n) _____ is a group of different tissues that work together to perform a certain function.

   A. organ system   B. organ   C. cell   D. organelle

4. Structures that support and give shape to plant cells are

   A. microbodies.   B. Golgi bodies.   C. nucleus.   D. cell walls.

5. Which of the following is part of the cell theory? All cells

   A. are eukaryotic.

   B. are prokaryotic.

   C. have nuclei.

   D. come from other cells.

C. Short Answer

1. List five more examples of tissues, organs, and organ systems not mentioned in the text.

2. Compare and contrast prokaryotic and eukaryotic cells.

3. Create an analogy comparing your school to the eukaryotic cell. Use all the cell parts and compare them to locations within your school.

SOLUTIONS

A **solution** is a liquid mixture of **solute** dissolved in **solvent**. Think of salt water, a solution in which salt (the solute) is dissolved in water (the solvent).

The interior of a cell is also a solution. The cytoplasm is a watery jelly-like substance (the solvent) that contains a variety of substances like salt and minerals (the solutes). Maintaining the concentration of solutes in the cytoplasm is critical to cell function — too much or too little of any component causes damage to the cell. This ideal balance of solutes within the cell is a state the cell strives to maintain through a variety of mechanisms. The process is referred to as maintaining **homeostasis**. Furthermore, cells maintain homeostasis by controlling internal temperature and pressure.

THE CELL MEMBRANE AND CELLULAR TRANSPORT

Hormones are chemical messengers that regulate some body functions in multicellular organisms. One function of hormones is to help maintain homeostasis. Other functions of hormones include the control of movement of oxygen into cells and the removal of carbon dioxide from cells, the maintenance of the internal temperature of an organism, and the regulation of fluids. Individual cells move fluids and nutrients in and out through the semi-permeable cell membrane. To maintain homeostasis, they can move these materials by either passive or active transport mechanisms.

CELL MEMBRANE

The main purpose of the cell membrane is to regulate the movement of materials into and out of the cell. The cell membrane is **semi-permeable**, or selectively permeable, meaning that only certain substances can go through.

The cell membrane is composed of a phospholipid bilayer as shown in Figure 2.9. Each phospholipid layer consists of **phosphate groups** (phosphorous bonded with oxygen) attached to two fatty acid (lipid) tails. The layers arrange themselves so that the phosphate heads are on the outer edges of the membrane, and the fatty acid tails compose the interior of the membrane. Globular proteins used for various functions, such as transporting substances through the membrane, are embedded in the cell membrane. The **phospholipids** are free to move around, allowing the membrane to stretch and change shape.

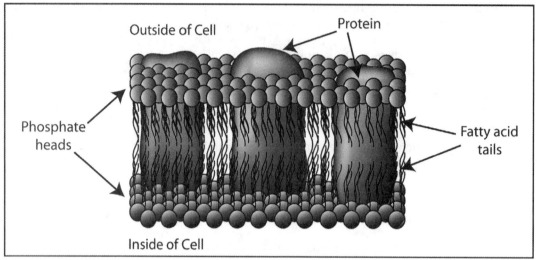

Figure 2.9 Phospholipid Bilayer

PASSIVE TRANSPORT

Passive transport is spontaneous and does not require energy. In passive transport, molecules move spontaneously through the cell membrane from areas of higher concentration to areas of lower concentration. They move with the **concentration gradient**. The three types of passive transport are diffusion facilitated diffusion, and osmosis.

Diffusion is the process by which substances move directly through the cell membrane as shown in Figure 2.10 on the below. **Facilitated diffusion** involves the help of a carrier protein to move a substance from one side of the cell wall to the other.

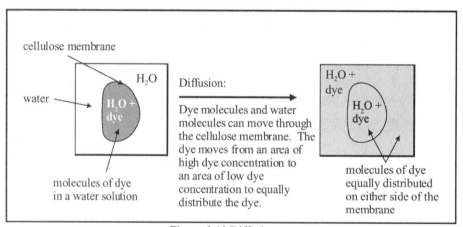

Figure 2.10 Diffusion

Osmosis is the movement of water from an area of high water concentration to an area of low water concentration through a semi-permeable membrane. Figure 2.11 shows a solution of water and starch inside a cellulose membrane. The cellulose membrane allows water to pass through, but the starch cannot. Since the starch cannot diffuse through the membrane, water moves into the membrane to dilute the starch. Think of osmosis as the diffusion of water.

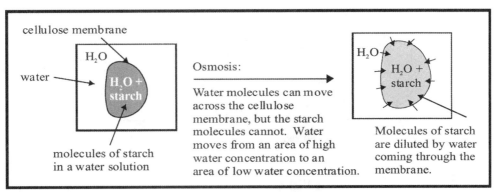

Figure 2.11 Osmosis

Osmosis can occur in either direction, depending on the concentration of dissolved material inside and outside the cell. Defining the solution concentrations *relative to one another* will predict the direction in which osmosis will occur. A **hypotonic** solution has the lower concentration of solute; this may be thought of as a higher concentration of water. A **hypertonic** solution has a higher concentration of dissolved solute, which may be thought of as a lower concentration of water. If the solute concentrate are the same inside and outside the cell membrane, the solutions are said to be **isotonic** to each other. Diffusion of water (osmosis) across a cell membrane always occurs from hypotonic to hypertonic. Three situations are possible:

a) The solution surrounding the cell membrane has a lower concentration of dissolved substances than the solution inside the cell membrane. Here, the solution outside the membrane is hypotonic with respect to the solution inside the cell membrane. The cell will experience a net gain of water and swell as in Figure 2.11.

b) The solution surrounding the cell membrane has a higher concentration of dissolved solute than the solution inside the cell membrane. In this case, the solution outside the membrane is hypertonic with respect to the solution inside the cell membrane. The cell will lose water to its surroundings causing it to shrink.

c) In the third case, the concentration of dissolved solutes is the same inside the cell as it is outside the cell. These solutions are said to be isotonic with respect to each other. There will be no net movement of water across the cell membrane. This is a state of equilibrium, which the cell often reaches only after a prior exchange of water across the membrane.

These situations are illustrated in Figure 2.12.

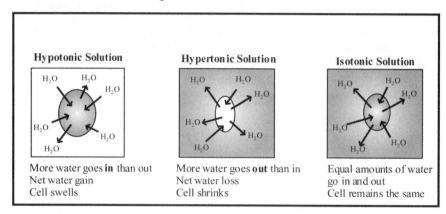

Figure 2.12 Possible Results of Osmosis

Placing plant cells in a hypertonic solution causes the plant cell membranes to shrink away from the cell wall. This process is called **plasmolysis**. Plasmolysis can result in plant cell death due to water loss. A wilted plant shows signs of plasmolysis. Placing a plant in a hypotonic solution has an opposite effect: the cell will swell until the cell wall allows no more expansion. The plant then becomes very stiff and turgid.

Kidney dialysis is an example of a medical procedure that involves diffusion. Another example is preserving food by salting, sugar curing or pickling. All of these examples are methods of drawing water out of cells through osmosis.

ACTIVE TRANSPORT

In some cases, the cell may need to move material across the cell membrane against the concentration gradient. To do so, the cell must expend energy. The movement of substances from an area of low concentration to an area of high concentration is called **active transport**. The movement is characterized by its directionality. **Exocytosis** is a form of active transport that removes materials from the cell. A sac stores the material to be removed from the cell, and then moves near the cell membrane. The cell membrane opens, and the substance is expelled from the cell. Waste materials, proteins and fats are examples of materials removed from the cell in this way.

Endocytosis, another form of active transport, brings materials into the cell without passing through the cell membrane. The membrane folds itself around the substance, creates a **vesicle** and brings the substance into the cell. Some unicellular organisms, such as an amoeba, obtain food this way.

Active transport allows certain organisms to survive in their environments. For instance, sea gulls can drink salt water because their cells remove excess salt from their bodies through active transport. However, freshwater fish are not able to remove excess salt from their cells and, therefore, would become dehydrated in a saltwater environment. Another example of active transport involves blood cells which use carrier proteins to transport molecules into the cell.

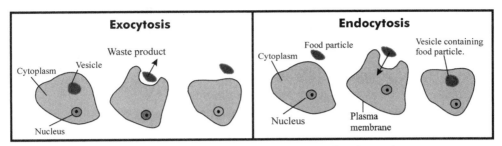

Figure 2.13 Schematic of Exocytosis and Endocytosis

MANY FACTORS AFFECT CELLULAR ACTIVITY

Cellular activity is affected by several factors. Cells cannot grow to extremely large sizes due to the ratio between cellular surface area and internal cell volume. For example, a cube with sides 1 cm long will have a volume (volume = (length of a side)^3) of 1 cm^3 and a surface area (surface area = (6 × length of a side^2) of 6 cm^2. A cube with sides equaling 10 cm long will have an internal volume of 1,000 cm^3 and a surface area of 600 cm^2. We can see that the cell has increased its volume by

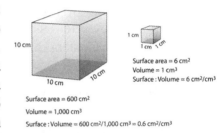

Surface area = 600 cm^2
Volume = 1,000 cm^3
Surface : Volume = 600 cm^2/1,000 cm^3 = 0.6 cm^2/cm^3

Surface area = 6 cm^2
Volume = 1 cm^3
Surface : Volume = 6 cm^2/cm^3

Figure 2.14 Surface Area to Volume Ratio

eight fold, but it has only increased its surface area by four fold. Cells depend on the transport of materials across membranes. A cell with a large internal volume cannot efficiently transport materials to the organelles that need them.

Cell organelles like the mitochondria and the chloroplast are considered highly active because they must trap and organize all the energy needed by the cell. These organelles have large amounts of surface area. This is achieved by having many folded membranes within the organelle. Similar to having a long winding workbench, the increased surface area provides the cell space to do work.

Environmental factors can also affect cellular activity. Cellular activity can be anything the cell does, like metabolism, reproduction, and movement. Most cells function best within a specific range of temperature, light and pH. Conditions too far above or below those ranges can hinder cell functions.

FLUID PRESSURE IN BIOLOGY

Fluids are liquids and gases. The physical properties of a fluid are determined by the interactions among its particles. Particle interactions include the interactions between atoms that form compounds, as well as the interactions between molecules. The collisions of the particles against the surface of the container cause the gas or liquid to exert pressure upon the container. **Pressure** is a force (push or pull) applied uniformly over an area. Some examples of how pressure affects plants and animals are listed on the next page.

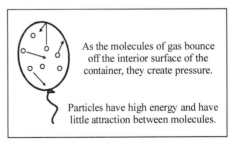

As the molecules of gas bounce off the interior surface of the container, they create pressure.

Particles have high energy and have little attraction between molecules.

Figure 2.15 Particle Motion in Gases

Blood is moved throughout the human body by pressure. **Blood pressure** is the pressure exerted by blood on the walls of blood vessels. The continuous cycle of the heart contracting and relaxing creates blood pressure, measured in millimeters of mercury (mm Hg).

In plants, pressure is important for several reasons. Plants must take up water from the surrounding environment through osmosis. Once a plant cell is filled with water, its vacuoles become swollen and large. The cell has a large amount of fluid inside, causing a higher pressure. The cell wall begins to exert pressure on the neighboring cell. The internal pressure inside the cell is called **turgor pressure**. This pressure is what allows terrestrial plants to stand upright. Plants also use atmospheric pressure, humidity and special tissues to move water up the stem or trunk to the top of the plant.

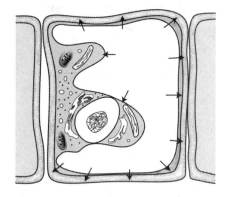

Figure 2.16 Turgor pressure from within the cell

The effect of pressure on gas solubility has important implications for scuba divers. Underwater, pressure increases rapidly with depth. High pressure allows more nitrogen than usual to dissolve into body tissues. If divers ascend too rapidly, the lower pressure causes the nitrogen gas to come out of solution, forming air bubbles in blood and body tissues. The bubbles result in a condition called "**the bends**," which can cause severe pain, dizziness, convulsion, blindness and paralysis. Divers must come up to the surface slowly to keep air bubbles from forming.

Section Review 3:   The Cell Membrane and Cellular Transport

A. Terms

hormones	diffusion	hypertonic	exocytosis
semi-permeable	facilitated diffusion	isotonic	endocytosis
passive transport		plasmolysis	vesicle
solute	osmosis	active transport	solvent
solution	hypotonic	homeostasis	

B. Multiple Choice

1. The movement of substances into and out of a cell without the use of energy is called

   A. active transport.

   B. passive transport.

   C. exocytosis.

   D. endocytosis.

2. The movement of water across a semi-permeable membrane from an area of high water concentration to an area of low water concentration is called

    A. active transport.   C. osmosis.

    B. diffusion.   D. hypotonic.

3. A type of membrane which allows only certain molecules to pass through is called

    A. permeable.   C. active.

    B. semi-permeable.   D. porous.

4. A cell placed in a solution shrinks by the process of osmosis. What kind of solution is outside the cell?

    A. hypotonic   B. hypertonic   C. active   D. isotonic

5. If the solution surrounding a cell has a lower concentration of solutes than inside the cell, water will move into the cell through osmosis, expanding the cell. What kind of solution is surrounding the cell?

    A. active   B. passive   C. hypertonic   D. hypotonic

C. Short Answer

1. What causes a plant's leaves to wilt?

2. How does active transport differ from diffusion?

3. Dried beans are soaked overnight in preparation for cooking. Explain the process affecting the beans. What will happen to the dried beans?

4. Differentiate between exocytosis and endocytosis.

5. A celery stalk is placed in a solution. It begins to wilt. What is a likely component of that solution?

D. Fill in the blanks

1. A cell which has no net gain or loss of water is in a(n) _____ solution.

2. The process of expending energy to move molecules across a membrane is _____ transport.

3. A plant cell that has swelled to its limits is referred to as _____; a shrunken plant cell has undergone _____.

CHAPTER 2 REVIEW

Choose the best answer.

CHAPTER
REVIEW

1. In order to be classified as living, an organism must have

    A. a heart and lungs.

    B. the ability to nourish itself, grow, and reproduce.

    C. the ability to photosynthesize and to eliminate waste products.

    D. a true nucleus and nuclear membrane.

2. _____ are the main products of a cell.

    A. Lipids   B. Amino acids   C. Proteins   D. Carbohydrates

3. A _____ is a type of cell that has a true nucleus.

    A. prokaryote   B. eukaryote   C. bacterium   D. virus

4. What is one of the functions of a plastid in the cell?

    A. digest food and break down wastes

    B. produce proteins

    C. carry on cellular respiration

    D. carry out photosynthesis and provide color

5. If a cell has a flagellum on its surface, it is

    A. an animal cell.   C. a isotonic cell.

    B. a plant cell.   D. a diseased cell.

6. If an animal cell is placed in distilled water, it will

    A. remain the same size.

    B. shrink.

    C. swell and eventually explode.

    D. swell, but stop when the cell wall prevents further expansion.

7. What will result if a plant cell is placed in distilled water?

    A. remain the same size

    B. shrink

    C. swell and eventually explode

    D. swell, but stop when the cell wall prevents further expansion

8. When you perspire on a hot, humid day, drinking water will restore _____ in your body.

    A. substances   B. oxygen   C. homeostasis   D. proteins

9. What are two structures found in plant cells that are not found in animal cells?

    A. mitochondria and ribosomes   C. cell membrane and centrioles

    B. cell wall and plastids   D. nucleolus and endoplasmic reticulum

10. Prokaryotic cells are lacking which cell part below?

    A. nucleus   C. cell membrane

    B. energy exchange   D. metabolism

11. When more water goes in through a cell membrane than out of it, the solution around the membrane is

    A. isotonic.   B. hypotonic.   C. permeable.   D. hypertonic.

12. Which organelle is the site of protein synthesis?

    A. plastid   B. ribosome   C. nucleolus   D. mitochondrion

13. What are groups of cells that perform the same function collectively known as?

    A. plastids   B. tissues   C. organs   D. molecules

14. Amoebas obtain food by wrapping the cell membrane around the food particle creating a vesicle. The food is then brought into the cell. What is this process called?

    A. exocytosis   B. endocytosis   C. osmosis   D. photosynthesis

Study the diagram. Use the information to answer question 15.

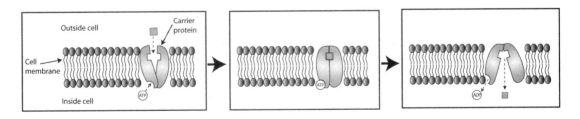

15. What process is shown in this diagram?

    A. osmosis   C. passive transport

    B. exocytosis   D. active transport

16. What is the cell part indicated by the arrow in the diagram called?

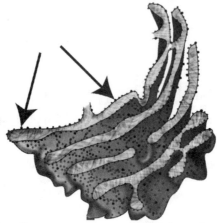

    A. nucleus   B. ribosome   C. chloroplast   D. mitochondria

17. Which example below describes an organ found in the human body?

    A. The function of this part is to provide active immunity against disease. This part actively seeks out and destroys pathogens found in the blood.

    B. The function of this part is to provide structure and support to the body. Muscles attach to all 205 pieces of this system allowing humans to move.

    C. The function of this part is to take oxygen into the blood stream. The cells and tissues that make up this body part are thin to allow oxygen to easily diffuse into the blood.

    D. The function of this part is to transport oxygen throughout the body's tissues. The characteristic hemoglobin molecule temporarily links to oxygen and carbon dioxide and is responsible for the coloration of the body part.

18. Which cell part is shown in the diagram?

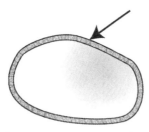

    A. cell wall   B. nucleus   C. chloroplast   D. cell membrane

19. Which cell part is double membrane and is responsible for converting solar energy into chemical energy?

    A. cell wall   B. cell membrane   C. chloroplast   D. mitochondria

20. Which example below is made of many cells working together?

    A. heart   B. skin   C. muscle   D. skeleton

Chapter 3
Chemistry of Life

ALABAMA HSGT IN SCIENCE STANDARDS COVERED IN THIS CHAPTER INCLUDE:

2a	Identifying functions of carbohydrates, lipids, proteins and nucleic acids in cellular activities.
3	Identify reactants and products associated with photosynthesis and cellular respiration and the purposes of these two processes.

All living things have in common several distinctive characteristics. As we have seen, the first among these is the existence of cells. Cells carry out the basic functions of life by organizing chemical features into a biological system. How is this done? Let us look at the basic chemistry and molecular components of a cell.

CHEMISTRY OF THE CELL

KEY ELEMENTS

An **element** is a type of matter composed of only one kind of atom which cannot be broken down to a simpler structure. There are six elements (listed in no particular order) commonly found in living cells: **sulfur, phosphorous, oxygen, nitrogen, carbon,** and **hydrogen** (easily remembered as

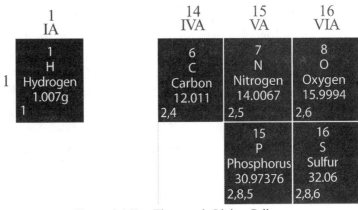

Figure 3.1 Key Elements in Living Cells

SPONCH). These elements make up 99% of all living tissue and combine to form the molecules that are the basis of cellular function. Carbon is especially important, because one carbon atom can make covalent bonds (bonds are discussed later in the chapter) with four other atoms, resulting in the formation of very stable and complex structures. Carbon is in all living things, even in the remains of living things. Molecules containing carbon are called

67

organic molecules, while those without carbon are called **inorganic molecules**. Water is the most important inorganic molecule for living things, and serves as the medium in which cellular reactions take place.

Those cellular reactions occur in great part between biological molecules often called **biomolecules**. The four primary classes of cellular biomolecules are carbohydrates, lipids, proteins and nucleic acids. Each of these is a **polymer** — that is, a long chain of small repeating units called **monomers**.

CARBOHYDRATES

Carbohydrates, often called sugars, are an energy source. Structurally, they are chains of carbon units with hydroxyl groups (-OH) attached. The simplest carbohydrates are monosaccharides. The ends of these sugars bond and unbond continuously, so that the straight chain and cyclic (ring-like) forms are in equilibrium. Figure 3.2 shows a Fischer diagram projection of glucose, a very common biomolecule. A Fischer projection depicts the straight chain form of a monosaccharide. Figure 3.3 shows a Hayworth representation of ribose, another common carbohydrate. A Hayworth representation indicates the structure of a cyclic monosaccharide.

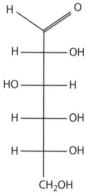

Figure 3.2
Fischer Diagram
of Glucose

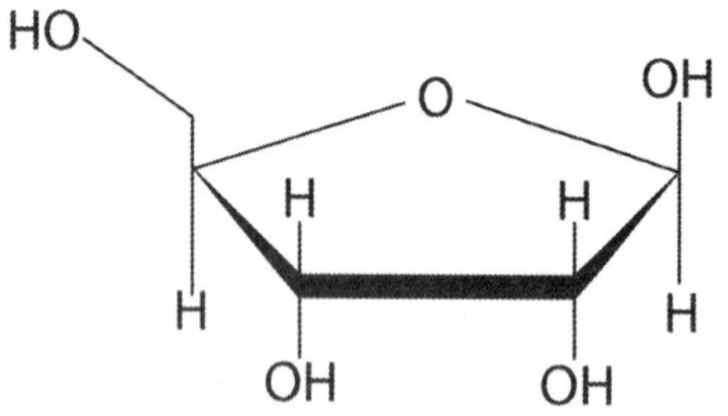

Figure 3.3 Hayworth Representation of Ribose

These monosaccharides may join together to form disaccharides (2), oligosaccharides (3 – 10) or polysaccharides (10+), depending on how many monosaccharides make up the polymeric carbohydrate. Disaccharides consist of two monosaccharide units. Common table sugar, or sucrose, is a disaccharide formed from the bound monosaccharides, fructose and glucose. Oligosaccharides are made up of 3 – 10 monosaccharide units. Polysaccharides consist of ten or more monosaccharide units. Oligosaccharides are sugars that are either being assembled or broken down, so there aren't any well-known common names for them. Complex carbohydrates such as starch and cellulose are classified as polysaccharides.

Lab Activity 1: Testing for Carbohydrates in Food

Biologists use Benedict's solution to test for sugar. Use grapes, egg white and butter. Place bits of the different foods in test tubes. Add ten drops of Benedict's solution to each test tube. Heat the contents of the tube gently for three minutes. Observe any color change.

- Brown means the food contains little or no sugar.
- Greenish-yellow means the food contains some sugar.
- Copper-orange means the food contains a lot of sugar.

Lab Activity 2: Testing for Starch

Iodine is useful in testing for the presence of starch. Use the same kind of food bits as Lab Activity 1. Place these bits of food on a paper towel. Put a drop of iodine on each bit of food. Observe any change in color.

- Reddish-brown means the food contains little or no starch.
- Yellow means the food contains some starch.
- Blue-black means the food contains a lot of starch.

LIPIDS

Lipids are fats, made up of chains of methylene ($-CH_2$) units. The chains may be long or short and may be straight or fused into rings (cyclic). They have several functions, but are most well known as fat molecules that store energy. They are also the structural components of the cell membrane. Several important lipids have names that you may recognize: waxes, steroids, fatty acids and triglycerides. The excess of triglycerides like the one pictured in Figure 3.4 is strongly linked to heart disease and stroke. It may not surprise you to know that butter is a triglyceride too.

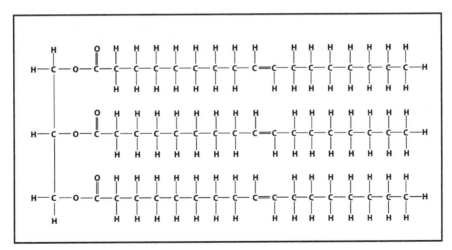

Figure 3.4 Lipid

Lab Activity 3: Testing for Fats in Food

Use a piece of brown paper bag to test for fat. Use the same kind of food bits as Lab Activity 2. Rub the brown paper with each bit of food. Wait for 10 minutes. Hold the paper up to the light.

- If no fat is present, the paper will appear opaque.
- If some fat is present, the paper will appear semi-translucent.
- If a lot of fat is present, the paper will appear translucent.

PROTEINS

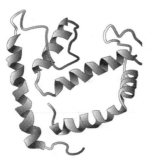

Figure 3.6 Protein

Proteins consist of long, linear chains of **polypeptides**. The polypeptide is itself a chain of **amino acid** monomers. There are 20 standard amino acids which combine to form every single protein needed by the human body; protein synthesis will be discussed in chapter 4. Figure 3.5 shows a polypeptide, while Figure 3.6 shows a protein which is a long polypeptide that folds into specific shapes and has a particular function Several polypeptides join together to form a protein.

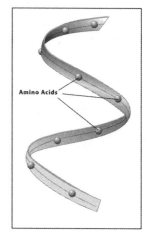

Figure 3.5 Polypeptide

There are many different types of proteins, which all have different biological functions. They include: structural proteins, regulatory proteins, contractile proteins, transport proteins, storage proteins, protective proteins, membrane proteins, toxins and enzymes. Despite the wide variation in function, shape and size, all proteins are made from the same 20 amino acids. Since mammals cannot make all 20 amino acids themselves, they must eat protein in order to maintain a healthy diet. Protein may be eaten in animal (meat) or vegetable (beans) form, but most organisms must have protein to survive.

NUCLEIC ACIDS

Nucleic acids are found in the nucleus of a cell. The nucleic acid polymer is made up of **nucleotide** monomers. The nucleotide monomer consists of a sugar, a phosphate group and a nitrogenous base. Nucleic acids are the backbone of the following genetic material:

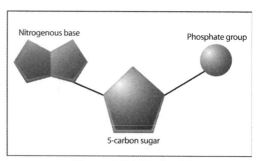

Figure 3.7 A Nucleotide

A. **DNA** (deoxyribonucleic acid) directs the activities of the cell and contains the sugar deoxyribose.

B. **RNA** (ribonucleic acid) is involved in protein synthesis and contains the sugar ribose.

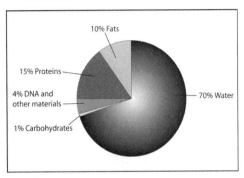

Figure 3.8 Composition of the Cell

Now that the biomolecules present in the cell have been introduced, can you guess which one makes up the bulk of a cell? Look at Figure 3.8. The bulk of a cell is not made up by a biomolecule — or even all the biomolecules put together! The bulk of the cell is made up of water.

Section Review 1: The Chemistry of the Cell

A. Terms

organic molecule	monomer	DNA	lipid	polymer
inorganic molecule	biomolecule	RNA	protein	polypeptide
nucleotide	nucleic acid	carbohydrate	amino acid	

B. Multiple Choice

1. Carbon chains are principal features of both carbohydrates and lipids. What is the primary difference between these two types of biomolecules?

    A. Lipids always have longer carbon chains than carbohydrates.

    B. Carbohydrates carry hydroxyl groups on their carbon backbone.

    C. Carbohydrates cannot form rings as lipids can.

    D. Lipids provide energy, but carbohydrates do not.

2. What molecules make up the bulk of a cell?

    A. carbohydrates

    B. lipids

    C. proteins

    D. water

3. Carbon is important to living things because

    A. it metabolizes easily, creating a quick energy source.

    B. it is abundant on the earth's surface.

    C. it can form four covalent bonds with other atoms.

    D. it has twelve protons and neutrons.

4. Nucleotides are to nucleic acids as amino acids are to

    A. DNA.   C. fats.

    B. polypeptides.   D. carbohydrates.

C. Short Answer

1. All living things have a common tie with the earth on which we live. Explain why this is true.

2. What are the six elements commonly found in living things?

3. Why is carbon important to living things?

D. Fill in the blanks

1. One element found in all living and dead organisms is _____.

2. Chains of amino acids are called _____.

3. _____ is an example of a nucleic acid.

CELLULAR ENERGY

The life processes of a cell are the end result of a series of chemical reactions. Each chemical reaction requires energy. In many cases, chemical reactions also require substances to speed up the time of the reaction. In the cell, energy comes in the form of a molecule called **ATP**, and the substances used to speed up reactions along are called **enzymes**.

THE ROLE OF BONDING IN ENERGY PRODUCTION

When chemical bonds are formed, energy is stored, and when chemical bonds are broken, energy is released. The stronger the bond, the more energy that will be released when the bond is broken.

Covalent bonding is present throughout many biomolecules. An **ionic bond** is the joining of two atoms based on their opposite electrical charges, which generate an electrostatic attraction. Covalent bonds generally occur between non-metallic elements, whereas metals tend to form ionic bonds.

A purely covalent bond is **nonpolar**, meaning that both atoms share electrons equally. Nonpolar bonding occurs between two atoms of the same element, like the carbon-carbon (C-C) bonds in an organic molecule or the H-H bond in hydrogen gas (H_2). When atoms of different elements bond covalently, they bring to the bond their different electron configurations. This has the effect of one atom pulling electrons toward it more strongly than the other. These bonds are called **polar** covalent

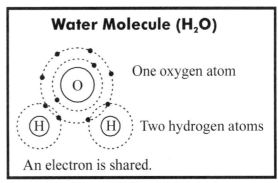

Figure 3.9 Water Molecule

bonds. Water is a good example of polar covalent bonding; two hydrogen atoms are bound to one oxygen atom to form the water molecule. The H-O bonds are polar because oxygen pulls electrons toward it and away from hydrogen. Polar covalent bonds are often said to have "ionic character."

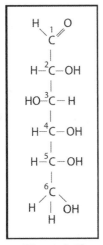

Figure 3.10 Bonding in Glucose

A glucose sugar molecule, which has the chemical formula of $C_6H_{12}O_6$, forms a molecule with 6 atoms of carbon, 12 atoms of hydrogen, and 6 atoms of oxygen as shown in the modified Fischer projection of Figure 3.10. The atoms of the molecule are held together by covalent bonds involving the sharing of electrons through the molecule.

Bond strength is a measure of the amount of energy required to break a bond. It depends on several factors, including the number of electrons shared (a single, double or triple bond), the identity of the atoms involved in the bond and the polarity of the bond. In general, the greater the polarity of a bond, the easier it is to break, and the lower the bond strength. Bond strength is important because it can be a source of energy. When bonds break, energy is either released or consumed (depending on the bond strength). Bond strength is measured in joules; the joule is the SI unit of energy. As an example, the average bond energy for the O-H bonds in water is about 459 kJ/mol.

Free energy, or energy available to do work, is stored in chemical bonds of molecules. When a muscle contracts, it converts the free energy from glucose into energy that can be used to shorten muscle cells. The movement of the muscle is work. Free energy is released by glucose when its chemical bonds are broken. The energy conversion is not completely efficient and much of the free energy is lost as heat. However, the energy conversions in living cells are significantly more efficient than most types of energy conversion. One reason is that the cell has a variety of ways to store energy (especially as ATP) and break down processes into small energy saving steps. For instance, mitochondria are useful in the conversion of glucose because they break the chemical reaction into smaller steps, allowing organisms to harness the greatest amount of energy possible. The whole process of breaking down glucose is known as **cellular respiration** and is better than 40% efficient at transferring the chemical energy of glucose into the more useful form of ATP. By contrast, only 25% of the energy released from a gasoline engine is converted to work.

ATP

ATP (adenosine triphosphate) is a molecule that serves as the chemical energy supply for all cells. Adenine, the sugar ribose, and three phosphates compose ATP. The covalent bonds between the phosphate groups contain a great deal of energy. The release of that energy occurs when the last phosphate in ATP breaks off, forming **ADP (adenosine diphosphate)** and P_i (an inorganic phosphate molecule).The bonding of ATP is shown in Figure 3.11.

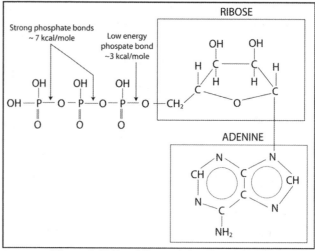

Figure 3.11 Bond Strength in ATP Molecule

After the ATP molecule breaks down, a free phosphate and an ADP are joined together to form a new ATP molecule. Each ATP molecule is recycled in this way 2000 – 3000 times a day in the human body. The energy released during each cycle drives cellular processes. Examples of cellular processes that require energy include heat production, muscle contractions, photosynthesis, cellular respiration, locomotion and DNA replication.

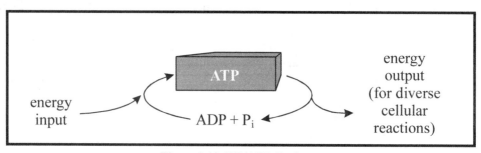

Figure 3.12 ATP/ADP Cycle

CATALYSTS AND ENZYMES

A **catalyst** is a substance that speeds up a chemical reaction without being chemically changed by the reaction. Catalysts decrease the amount of activation energy required for the reaction to occur. **Activation energy** is the amount of energy required in order for reactant molecules to begin a chemical reaction. When a molecule reaches its energy of activation, its chemical bonds are very weak and likely to break. Activation energy provides a barrier so that molecules will not spontaneously react with one

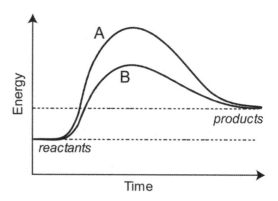

Figure 3.13 Effect of Catalysts on Activation Energy

another. Catalysts lower the activation energy for a reaction, allowing reactant molecules with less energy to process in the reaction. One example of an inorganic catalyst is nickel, which is used in the hydrogenation of vegetable oil to make margarine. The nickel is recovered; it is not used up, and it is not part of the final product.

Our bodies use catalysts called enzymes to break down food and convert it to energy. Every cellular activity is a result of many biochemical reactions that take place at a cellular level. Substances that speed these reactions are called enzymes. **Enzymes** are specific proteins that combine with other substances called **substrates**. There is one enzyme for one substrate, and they fit together like pieces of a puzzle. Metabolism cannot occur unless the energy of activation has been reached. These biological reactions would eventually take place on their own, but in the presence of enzymes, the reactions take place with some increases being a million times faster! Enzymes help to lower the energy of activation, making some chemical processes occur with greater frequency.

Some reactions use **cofactors** to help enzymes by transporting electrons, ions or atoms between substances. A **cofactor** is either a metal ion (a metal atom that has lost or gained electrons) or a coenzyme. A **coenzyme** is a non-protein molecule that activates the enzyme. Important cofactors in photosynthesis and cellular respiration are **NADP+** (nicotinamide adenine dinucleotide phosphate) and **NAD+** (nicotinamide adenine dinucleotide). These cofactors pick up free hydrogen ions and electrons and transport them so the next stage of the reaction can take place. We will not be addressing the specific movement of molecules and bonds in this text, but it is a good idea to have an idea of what these cofactors look like. Figure 3.14 shows the structure of the coenzyme NAD+.

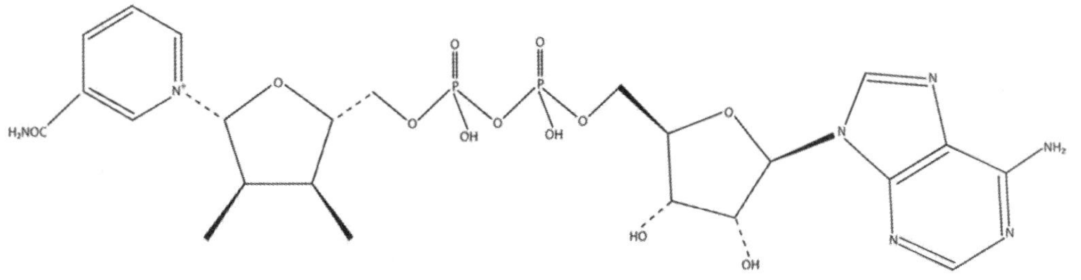

Figure 3.14 NAD+ (nicotinamide adenine dinucleotide)

Metabolic processes can occur without enzymes, though at biological temperatures metabolism would happen so slowly most that organisms would be unable to survive. Some enzyme failures result in disease or death of the organism.

Factors that influence the rate at which enzymes act include such things as temperature, pH and amount of substrate present. Most enzymes have an optimum temperature and pH. Their optimum temperature or pH is the range at which the enzyme functions best. Enzymes vary from one organism to another. Some bacteria have enzymes that have an optimum temperature of 70°C or higher; this temperature would destroy most human enzymes.

With a few exceptions, most enzymes have an optimum pH of between 6 and 8. Table 3.1 contains several enzymes and their optimal pH.

Table 3.1 pH for Optimum Activity

Enzyme	pH Optimum
Lipase – hydrolyzes glycerides (pancreas)	8.0
Lipse – hydrolyzes glycerides (stomach)	4.0 – 5.0
Pepsin – decomposition of proteins	1.5 – 1.6
Urease – hydrolysis of urea	7.0
Invertase – hydrolysis of sucrose	4.5
Maltase – hydrolysis of maltose to glucose	6.1 – 6.8
Amylase (pancreas) – hydrolysis of starch	6.7 – 7.0
Catalase – decomposition of hydrogen peroxide into water and oxygen	7.0

Recall that a pH of 7 is considered **neutral**. Water has a pH of about 7. Substances with a pH less than 7 are **acids** and substances with a pH greater than 7 are **bases**. One example of an enzyme is pepsin, an acidic enzyme found in the human stomach. Pepsin has an optimum pH of 1–2.

FOOD ENERGY

Organisms must use food to live. Organisms that obtain their food from other living things are called consumers. Consumers ingest food, digest the meal and then excrete waste. The food ingested by a consumer must be broken down into smaller molecules that the consumer can absorb and use. The proteins found in the food are broken down into amino acids and absorbed by the consumer. The consumer can then rearrange the amino acids into the appropriate form. For example, humans eat cow meat. The proteins contained in the cow meat are broken down and rearranged into human proteins. Through digestion, organisms can obtain energy, grow and carry out life's functions.

Section Review 2: Cellular Energy

A. Terms

ATP	catalyst	enzyme	coenzyme
ADP	activation energy	calorie	pepsin
covalent bond	molecule	cofactor	free energy
substrate	acid	p_i	base
			neutral

B. Multiple Choice

1. ATP stands for
   A. adenosine triphosphate.   C. a triphosphate.
   B. adenine triphosphate.   D. none of the above

2. Enzymes are
   A. catalysts used by living things.
   B. catalysts used in all reactions.
   C. chemicals used to increase activation energy.
   D. fats used by living things to help speed up chemical reactions.

3. Enzymes
   A. function at any temperature and pH.
   B. function at an optimum temperature and pH.
   C. increase the activation energy of a chemical reaction.
   D. aid in the formation of ATP.

4. Organic molecules most often form using
   A. ionic bonds.   C. polar ionic bonds.
   B. covalent bonds.   D. hydrogen bonds.

C. Short Answer

1. In your own words, describe the relationship between ATP and ADP.

2. What is the purpose of ATP?

3. Briefly describe the function of enzymes.

Obtaining Cellular Energy

Photosynthesis

Photosynthesis is the process of converting carbon dioxide, water and light energy into oxygen and high energy sugar molecules. The chemical equation representing this process is shown in Equation 3.1. Plants, algae and some bacteria can use the sugar molecules produced during photosynthesis to make **complex carbohydrates**, such as starch or cellulose, for food. The process of photosynthesis consists of two basic stages: **light-dependent reactions** and **light-independent reactions**. The light-independent reactions are also called the **Calvin cycle**.

$$6CO_2 + 6H_2O + light \rightarrow C_6H_{12}O_6(glucose) + 6O_2 \qquad \textbf{Equation 3.1}$$

Photosynthesis takes place inside an organelle called a **chloroplast**. A chloroplast is one of a group of organelles called plastids. **Plastids** engage in photosynthesis and store the resulting food. The chloroplast is a specific organelle with a double membrane that contains stacks of sac-like membranes called **thylakoids**. The thylakoid membrane contains within itself a green pigment called **chlorophyll**. **Pigments** are substances that absorb light. Light-dependent reactions take place inside the thylakoid membrane. Light-independent reactions take place in the **stroma**, which is the region just outside the thylakoid membrane. In the **light-dependent phase**, sunlight hits the leaf of the plant, where it is absorbed by the pigments in the leaf. There are several pigments in plant leaves, but the main one used in photosynthesis is chlorophyll, the green pigment. Chlorophyll is stored in the chloroplasts of the plant cell.

When light hits the chlorophyll, electrons absorb the energy, become excited and leave the chlorophyll molecule. Carrier molecules transport the electrons, which follow an electron transport chain. Electron acceptor molecules pick up the electrons in a series and pass them from one molecule to another. As this occurs, energy is released, and ATP is formed. The final electron acceptor is NADP+.

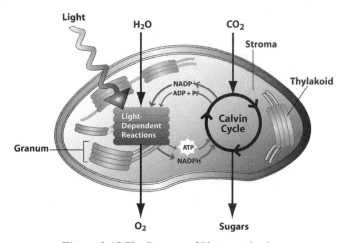

Figure 3.15 The Process of Photosynthesis

Splitting a molecule of water replaces the electrons released from the chlorophyll. These electrons, now available, combine with the NADP+ to form **NADPH**. The next stage of photosynthesis uses the NADPH, while oxygen leaves as an end product of the reaction.

The end products of the light-dependent reactions are ATP, oxygen and NADPH. The ATP and NADPH will be used in the light-independent reactions, and the oxygen will be released into the atmosphere.

The next phase, the **light-independent** or **carbon fixation reactions**, uses the ATP formed during the light-dependent reaction as an energy source. In this phase, carbon, from carbon dioxide, and NADPH are used to form **glucose**. To accomplish this, a five-carbon sugar uses a carbon atom from carbon dioxide to create a six-carbon sugar (a hexose). Glucose is the end result, after several conversions have taken place. The glucose can then be used as food to enter cellular respiration, or it can be converted to other carbohydrate products such as sucrose or starch.

CELLULAR RESPIRATION

Cellular respiration is the process of breaking down food molecules to release energy. Plants, algae, animals and some bacteria use cellular respiration to break down food molecules. There are two basic types of cellular respiration: aerobic and anaerobic. **Aerobic respiration** occurs in the presence of oxygen, and is represented by the chemical equation in Equation 3.2. The energy released through cellular respiration is used to create ATP. Cellular respiration occurs in three phases: **glycolysis**, **Krebs cycle**, and **electron transport**. The process starts with a molecule of glucose. The reactions of cellular respiration occur with the use of enzymes. Respiration is the primary means by which cells obtain usable energy.

$$C_6H_{12}O_6 + 6O_2 \rightarrow 6CO_2 + 6H_2O + \text{energy} \quad \text{Equation 3.2}$$

Glycolysis is the first phase in cellular respiration. This step occurs in the cytoplasm of the cell, and it can occur whether or not oxygen is present. In this phase, the glucose molecule (a 6-carbon sugar) is broken in half through a series of reactions. The energy released by breaking down the glucose is used to produce ATP. Additionally, some high-energy electrons are removed from the sugar during glycolysis. These electrons pass on to an electron carrier called **NAD⁺**, converting it to **NADH**. These electrons will later be used to create more energy.

In aerobic respiration, the 3-carbon sugars produced from glycolysis enter the **mitochondria** along with the oxygen. As the sugars enter the mitochondria, they convert to citric acid in phase two of cellular respiration. The **citric acid cycle**, or Krebs Cycle, is the cyclical process that breaks down the citric acid through a series of reactions. The citric acid cycle produces more ATP, as well as some **GTP** (a high-energy molecule similar to ATP). More high-energy electrons are released, forming NADH from NAD⁺.

The last phase of cellular respiration is the **electron transport chain**, which occurs on the inner mitochondrial membrane. In this phase, the NADH releases the hydrogen ions and high-energy electrons it picked up during glycolysis and the citric acid cycle. The energy from these electrons is used to convert large quantities of ADP into ATP. The electrons transfer through a series of carrier proteins. At the end of the electron transport chain the free electrons and H^+ ions bond with oxygen. The oxygen and H^+ ions form water, which is released from the cell as a waste product. Each electron transfer releases energy.

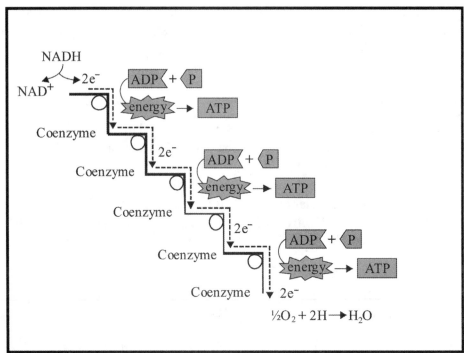

Figure 3.16 Electron Transport Chain

ANAEROBIC RESPIRATION

Anaerobic respiration, or **fermentation,** is the process by which sugars break down in the absence of oxygen. Our muscle cells, fungi, and some bacteria are capable of carrying out anaerobic respiration. These cells convert the products of glycolysis into either alcohol or **lactic acid**. Glycolysis releases energy, while the production of alcohol or lactic acid provides NAD^+, the electron carrier needed for glycolysis.

Yeast and some bacteria can carry out alcoholic fermentation. Yeast produces **ethanol** (C_2H_5OH) through a process called **alcoholic fermentation**. The chemical equation representing this process is shown in Equation 3.3. Carbon dioxide gas is released during alcohol formation. This carbon dioxide gas is responsible for the holes in bread. Yeast is commonly put in bread to make it rise. The fermentation of the yeast produces carbon dioxide, which becomes trapped in the dough, forming small bubbles and causing the bread to rise. Carbon dioxide produced by yeast in beer gives the beer its bubbles. Other uses of alcoholic fermentation are the making of breads, beer, wine and liquor.

$$C_6H_{12}O_6 \rightarrow 2C_2H_5OH + 2CO_2 + \text{energy} \qquad \text{Equation 3.3}$$

Animal cells cannot perform alcoholic fermentation. Instead, they produce lactic acid from the products of glycolysis, through the process of **lactic acid fermentation**. Human muscle cells produce lactic acid during strenuous exercise. During strenuous exercise, a person cannot take in enough oxygen through breathing to supply all the muscles with the necessary oxygen. As a result, lactic acid fermentation occurs to supply the muscles with the needed energy. The day after intense physical activity, muscles are sore due to the presence of lactic acid. Some bacteria use lactic acid fermentation to obtain food energy.

CHEMOSYNTHESIS

Chemosynthesis is the process by which inorganic chemicals are broken down to release energy. The only known organisms that are able to carry out chemosynthesis are **bacteria**. These organisms form the base of the food chain around thermal vents found on the ocean floor. They may also be found around other aquatic volcanic vents like those around Yellowstone National Park.

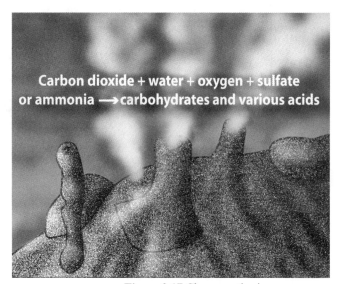

Figure 3.17 Chemosynthesis

Chemosynthetic bacteria can oxidize sulfates or ammonia to produce two free electrons. The two free electrons are used to fix carbon dioxide into carbohydrates. This process is similar to the way that green plants utilize light energy and carbon dioxide to produce carbohydrates. These bacteria are an important part of the nitrogen cycle. Some of these bacteria have adapted to conditions that could have existed on the early earth, leading some scientists to hypothesize that these are actually living representatives of the earliest life on earth.

COMPARING PHOTOSYNTHESIS, CELLULAR RESPIRATION, AND CHEMO-SYNTHESIS

All organisms must be able to obtain and convert energy to carry out life functions, such as growth and reproduction. **Photosynthesis** and **chemosynthesis** are ways that organisms can trap energy from the environment and convert it into a biologically useful energy source. **Cellular respiration** is a way that organisms can break down energy sources to carry out life's processes. Photosynthesis takes place in plants, algae and some bacteria. Cellular respiration takes place in all eukaryotic (have a true nucleus) cells and some prokaryotic (no true nucleus) cells. Chemosynthesis takes place only in prokaryotic cells.

Table 3.2 Comparison of Photosynthesis, Cellular Respiration and Chemosynthesis

	Photosynthesis	**Cellular Respiration**	**Chemosynthesis**
Function	energy storage	energy release	energy storage
Location	chloroplasts	mitochondria	prokaryotic cells
Reactants	CO_2 and H_2O	$C_6H_{12}O_6$ and O_2	$CO_2 + H_2O + O_2$ + sulfate or ammonia
Products	$C_6H_{12}O_6$ and O_2	CO_2 and H_2O	carbohydrates and varied acids
Chemical Equation	$6CO_2 + 6H_2O + \text{light} \rightarrow C_6H_{12}O_6 + 6O_2$	$6O_2 + C_6H_{12}O_6 \rightarrow 6CO_2 + 6H_2O + \text{energy}$	varies

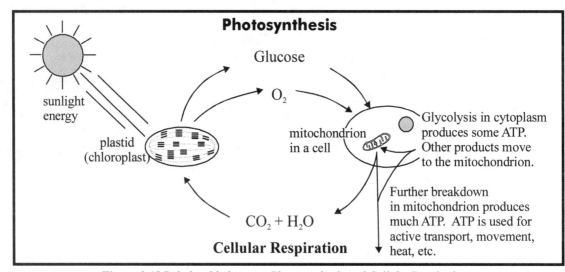

Figure 3.18 Relationship between Photosynthesis and Cellular Respiration

Section Review 3: Obtaining Cellular Energy

A. Terms

photosynthesis	light-dependent phase	glycolysis
Calvin cycle	light-independent phase	Krebs cycle
chloroplast	carbon fixation	electron transport chain
thylakoid	cellular respiration	alcoholic fermentation
chlorophyll	aerobic respiration	lactic acid fermentation
pigment	anaerobic respiration	chemosynthesis
		plastid

B. Multiple Choice

1. What form of energy is used by cells?

    A. enzymes   B. cofactors   C. ATP   D. DNA

2. The process of releasing energy from the chemical breakdown of compounds in a cell is

    A. hesitation.   B. expiration.   C. elimination.   D. respiration.

3. In photosynthesis, plants use carbon dioxide, water and light to produce

    A. carbon monoxide.   C. glucose and oxygen.

    B. energy.   D. chlorophyll.

4. What is released when ATP is broken down into ADP and one phosphate?

    A. oxygen   B. water   C. energy   D. hydrogen

5. The Krebs Cycle and the electron transport chain phases of cellular respiration take place in which organelle?

    A. nucleus   C. ribosome

    B. cytoplasm   D. mitochondrion

6. The process by which the energy from the Sun is used to create glucose molecules is known as

    A. cellular respiration.   C. chemosynthesis.

    B. photosynthesis.   D. fermentation.

7. Photosynthesis takes place inside

    A. mitochondria.   C. animal cells.

    B. chloroplasts.   D. none of the above.

C. Short Answer

1. Compare and contrast aerobic and anaerobic respiration.

2. Compare and contrast alcoholic and lactic acid fermentation.

3. What is the chemical equation for photosynthesis and cellular respiration?

D. Complete the following exercise.

For each of the following statements, decide which process it relates to: photosynthesis (P), respiration (R), or both (B). Mark each statement accordingly.

1. ___ Carbon dioxide is a reactant in the reaction.

2. ___ End product is ATP

3. ___ Converts energy from one form to another

4. ___ Takes place in mitochondria

5. ___ Produces carbon dioxide

6. ___ Takes place in chloroplasts

7. ___ Glucose changed into energy for cells

8. ___ Produces oxygen

9. ___ Uses cofactors

10. ___ Oxygen is a reactant in the reaction

11. ___ Produces glucose

12. ___ Uses chlorophyll

13. ___ Has an electron transport chain

14. ___ Light, water, and chlorophyll create glucose

Activity

Fill in the concept map below using the following terms: *cell respiration*; H_2O; CO_2; O_2; $C_6H_{12}O_6$; *energy*.

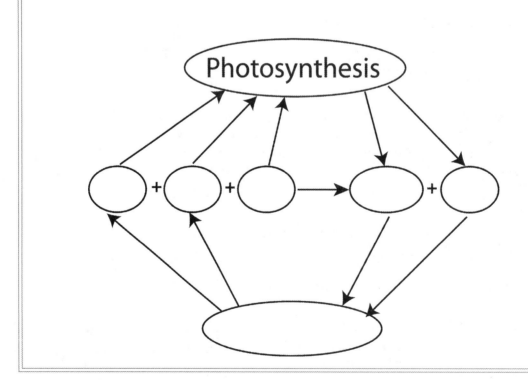

CHAPTER 3 REVIEW

A. Choose the best answer.

1. What do complex carbohydrates break down into?

   A. enzymes

   B. amino acids

   C. simple sugars

   D. ATP

2. Which of the following biomolecules are fat molecules that store energy?

   A. proteins   B. nucleic acids   C. carbohydrates   D. lipids

3. Which of the following elements can be found in all living and previously living organisms?

   A. helium   B. sulfur   C. carbon   D. nitrogen

4. Which biomolecule is a polymer assembled from some combination of the 20 amino acids?

   A. lipids   B. DNA   C. protein   D. nucleotide

5. Which proteins in the cell speed up chemical reactions?

   A. lipids   B. DNA   C. enzymes   D. glucose

6. Where does cellular respiration takes place?

   A. an animal cell only

   B. a plant cell only

   C. both plant and animal cells

   D. neither plant or animal cells

7. The chemical energy supply for all living cells is contained in a molecule that, when broken down, releases the energy so that it may be used for activities such as muscle contractions, photosynthesis and locomotion. This molecule that is a storehouse of energy is

   A. ATP.   B. DNA.   C. RNA.   D. ADP.

8. To obtain and use cellular energy plant cells use

   A. photosynthesis only.

   B. photosynthesis and cellular respiration.

   C. cellular respiration only.

   D. chemosynthesis.

9. How is cellular energy stored?

   A. chemical bonds

   B. enzymes

   C. membrane potential

   D. protein shapes

10. Pepsin, a digestive enzyme in the human stomach has an optimum pH that can be described as

    A. basic.   B. neutral.   C. acidic.   D. very acidic.

11. _____ are the main product of the cell.

    A. Lipids   B. Amino acids   C. Proteins   D. Carbohydrates

12. A coenzyme is a non–protein molecule that activates the enzyme. What is the difference in the molecular structure of the protein and the co–enzyme?

    A. A coenzyme contains amino acids, but a protein does not.

    B. A protein contains amino acids, but a coenzyme does not.

    C. A coenzyme contains high energy ionic bonds, but a protein does not.

    D. A protein contain high energy ionic bonds, but a coenzyme does not.

13. Which of the following foods represents the largest source of protein?

    A. potato chips   B. oranges   C. chicken   D. cauliflower

14. What are the largest carbohydrates called?

    A. monosaccharides   C. oligosaccharides

    B. disaccharides   D. polysaccharides

15. What chemical reagent is used to test for carbohydrates?

    A. Benedict's solution   C. phenylpthalein

    B. iodine   D. sodium hydroxide

16. What does the equation below represent?

$$C_6H_{12}O_6 + 6O_2 \rightarrow 6CO_2 + 6H_2O$$

    A. photosynthesis   C. simple diffusion

    B. cellular respiration   D. kinetic energy of motion

17. What is the primary purpose for photosynthesis?

    A. to trap and store solar energy in chemical form

    B. to release chemical energy from glucose into usable cellular energy

    C. to move molecules from one side of the membrane to the other

    D. to use chemical energy from water and oxygen

18. What biologically important molecule is a product of photosynthesis?

    A. O_2 B. CO_2 C. H_2O D. $C_6H_{12}O_6$

Chapter 4
Nucleic Acids and Cell Division

ALABAMA HSGT IN SCIENCE STANDARDS COVERED IN THIS CHAPTER INCLUDE:

5a	Recognizing that cells differentiate to perform specific functions.
6	Describe the roles of mitotic and meiotic divisions during reproduction, growth and repair of cells.
6a	Comparing sperm and egg formation in terms of ploidy.
6b	Comparing sexual and asexual reproduction.
8	Identify the structure and function of DNA, RNA and protein.
8c	Relating normal patterns of genetic inheritance to genetic variation.

THE ROLE OF DNA

The genetic basis of life is a molecule called **DNA** or **deoxyribonucleic acid**. DNA is carried in the nucleus of all cells and performs two primary functions. First, it carries the code for all the genes of an organism, which in turn create the proteins that perform all the work of living. Second, the code of the DNA itself is the template for future generations. First, we will look at the role of DNA in protein synthesis and then its role in heredity.

DNA, RNA AND PROTEIN SYNTHESIS

DNA

DNA is a complex molecule with a double helix shape like a twisted ladder. Each side of the helix is composed of a strand of **nucleotides** that are the building blocks of nucleic acids. Each nucleotide contains a phosphate group, the sugar **deoxyribose** and a **nitrogenous base**. There are four bases in DNA, and they form pairs. The bases are **adenine** (A), **thymine** (T), **guanine** (G) and **cytosine** (C). A and T always pair, and G and C always pair. The A-T and G-C pairings are called **complementary pairs**. Each pair forms one of the rungs of the ladder as shown in Figure 4.1.

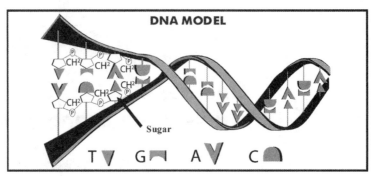

Figure 4.1 Model of DNA

The DNA molecule carries the code for all the genes of the organism. **Genes** are pieces of the DNA molecule that code for specific proteins. The process of making genes into proteins is called **protein synthesis**.

DNA is located in the nucleus of the cell. The assembly of proteins occurs outside of the nucleus, on the ribosome. The manufacture of proteins involves three steps:

1. The DNA code of the gene segment must be copied in the nucleus of the cell.

2. The code must then be carried from the nucleus into the cytoplasm and finally to a ribosome.

3. The protein is then assembled from the code and released from the ribosome.

These steps are carried out by RNA or ribonucleic acid.

RNA

RNA (ribonucleic acid) is a molecule used to translate the code from the DNA molecule into protein. It is similar to DNA except it is single stranded. Its sugar is **ribose**. RNA, like DNA, has four nitrogenous bases. It shares adenine, guanine and cytosine but replaces thymine with **uracil** (U). Hence, the bases A and U pair up instead of A and T. There are several types of RNA. Messenger, ribosomal and transfer RNA are <u>all</u> involved in protein synthesis.

Activity	
Determine the corresponding mRNA molecules from the given DNA strand.	
DNA Strand	**mRNA molecule**
1. ATTGCTCCAAAC	
2. TTACGCGGTAAA	
3. CTCACTCGGGAT	
4. CATACTGGCTAT	
5. GCTTTCGGAATT	

PROTEIN SYNTHESIS

TRANSCRIPTION

The first step of protein synthesis is the manufacture of a specific kind of RNA called **messenger RNA (mRNA)**. This copying process is called **transcription**. Transcription begins when a region of the DNA double helix unwinds and separates, as shown in Figure 4.2. The separated segment is a gene, and it serves as a template for the soon-to-be-formed mRNA strand.

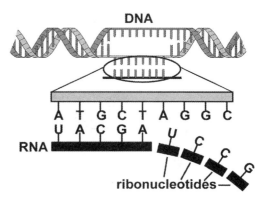

Figure 4.2 Transcription

The mRNA strand is assembled from individual RNA nucleotides that are present in the nucleus. An enzyme called **RNA polymerase** picks up these unattached nucleotide bases and matches them to their complementary bases on the DNA template strand. This continues until the entire gene segment has been paired, and a complete mRNA strand has been formed. This mRNA strand has a sequence that is complementary to the original gene segment. At that point, the mRNA separates and leaves the nucleus, moving out into the cytoplasm to settle on the **ribosome**, an organelle composed of another kind of RNA called **ribosomal RNA (rRNA)**. Here on the surface of the ribosome, the process of translation begins.

TRANSLATION

Translation is the step in protein synthesis where mRNA is decoded (translated) and a corresponding polypeptide is formed. (Remember that a polypeptide is made up of **amino acids**.) Let's look at the "language" of mRNA.

One way to think of a strand of mRNA is as a chain of nucleotides, as in:

AUGACAGAUUAG

While this is correct, a more accurate way of thinking of the chain is that it is divided into segments consisting of three nucleotides each, as in:

AUG ACA GAU UAG

The mRNA strand is not *actually* divided, but writing its code in this way emphasizes an important concept: the **codon**. The three-nucleotide codon has the specific function of corresponding to a particular amino acid. Here is how it works: The molecule of mRNA is bound to the surface of the ribosome at the first three-nucleotide segment, called the **start codon**. The cytoplasm in which they float contains, among other things, amino acids and a third kind of RNA — **transfer RNA (tRNA)**. Transfer RNA is a molecule of RNA that contains a three-part nucleotide segment called an **anticodon**, which is the exact complement of one mRNA codon. The anticodon corresponds exactly to one of the 20 kinds of amino acids. Once the tRNA binds the amino acid, it travels to the ribosome surface. There, the three tRNA nucleotide bases (the anticodon) pair with their three complementary mRNA bases (the codon). The amino acid that is bound to the tRNA is then added to the growing polypeptide chain at the surface of the ribosome, as shown in Figure 4.3.

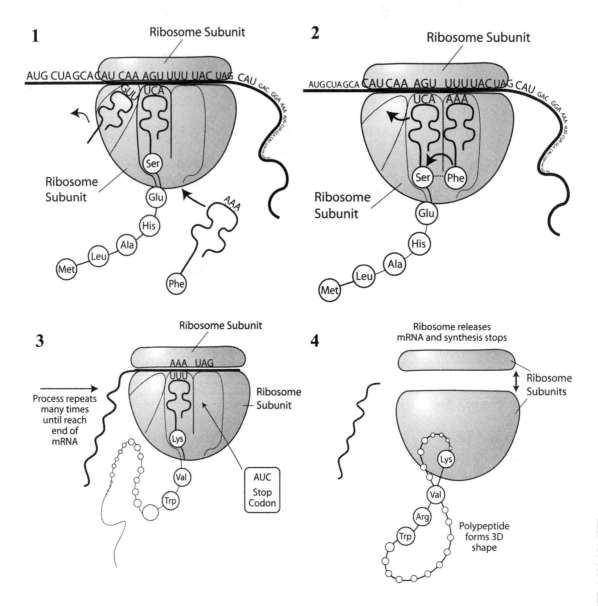

Figure 4.3 Translation Process

The ribosome facilitates this process by moving along the mRNA chain until it reaches a **stop codon**, a three-nucleotide segment that tells the ribosome that the translation process is complete. The ribosome then releases the newly-formed polypeptide chain, which moves out into the cell as a fully functioning protein.

There are many proteins within every cell. Proteins make up **enzymes** that help to carry out reactions within the cell. Proteins also compose **hormones**, which are chemical messengers that regulate some body functions. Proteins provide structure and act as energy sources. They transport other molecules and are part of our bodies' defenses against disease. In short, proteins are essential for survival because almost everything that happens in the cell involves proteins.

Section Review 1:   DNA, RNA and Protein Synthesis

A. Terms

DNA	deoxyribose	transcription	amino acid
gene	base	messenger RNA (mRNA)	translation
RNA	ribosome		transfer RNA (tRNA)
anticodon	adenine	ribosomal RNA (rRNA)	enzyme
polymerase	cytosine	codon	hormone
guanine	uracil	protein synthesis	thymine
nucleotide	ribose	complementary pairs	start codon
		stop codon	

B. Multiple Choice

1. Protein synthesis begins with the manufacture of a molecule of

    A. mRNA.   B. rRNA.   C. tRNA.   D. nucleotide.

2. Ribosomes are made of

    A. mRNA.   B. rRNA.   C. tRNA.   D. protein.

3. Proteins are made up of polypeptide chains. Polypeptide chains are composed of

    A. mRNA.   B. rRNA.   C. tRNA.   D. amino acids.

4. Transfer RNA (tRNA) carries

    A. the mRNA to the ribosome.   C. an amino acid to the ribosome.

    B. the nucleotide bases to the mRNA.   D. an amino acid to the cytoplasm.

5. Which of the following is the first step in protein synthesis?

    A. tRNA bonds to an amino acid in the cytoplasm.

    B. DNA unravels to expose an mRNA segment.

    C. DNA unravels to expose a gene segment.

    D. mRNA bonds to tRNA.

C. Short Answer

1. Describe the process of translation.

2. Which sugars are found in DNA and RNA?

3. What are proteins made of?

4. List the DNA bases that pair and the RNA bases that pair.

5. What role does DNA play in protein synthesis?

DNA REPLICATION

In the last section, we examined the role that DNA plays in protein synthesis. In this section, we will examine the pivotal role that DNA plays in **cell division**.

Cells must be able to divide in order for the organism to grow, reproduce and repair itself. Multicellular organisms are made up of two kinds of cells: reproductive cells and somatic (or body) cells. Both kinds of cells contain DNA, which is stored in the nucleus in the form of chromatin. **Chromatin** consists of long strands of DNA, jumbled up with proteins, that together form a kind of disorganized mass of genetic material in the nucleus. When the cell is ready to divide, the chromatin coils and condenses to form chromosomes. **Reproductive cells** (sex cells) have a single set, or **haploid** number (n), of chromosomes. **Somatic cells** (body cells) have two sets, or a **diploid** number (2n), of chromosomes.

When the cell divides, the chromosomes must be distributed between the newly produced cells. This means that the DNA must be able to copy itself, which it does through the process of **replication**.

During replication, the double strands of the DNA helix break apart, unzipping like a zipper, to become two individual strands. In a process very similar to that of mRNA formation, new DNA strands are assembled from the free-floating nucleotides in the cell's nucleus. An enzyme called **DNA polymerase** collects the nucleotide bases and matches them to their complementary pair along the single-strand DNA. When the entire process is complete, two new DNA double helices identical to the original helix have been formed. The replication process is just one part of the cell cycle.

THE CELL CYCLE

The **cell cycle** is the sequence of stages through which a cell passes between one cell division and the next. The length of time it takes a cell to complete the cell cycle varies from one cell to another. Some cells complete the entire cycle in a few minutes, and other cells spend their entire life frozen in a particular phase.

Most of the cell cycle is spent in **interphase** as shown in Figure 4.4. Interphase consists of three major parts: G_1, S and G_2. During the G_1 phase of interphase, the cell grows in size. In the S phase, replication of the DNA

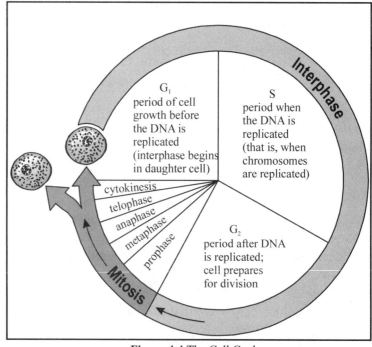

Figure 4.4 The Cell Cycle

containing the genetic material occurs, which gives the cell a double amount of DNA. In the G_2 phase, the cell prepares for mitosis by replicating organelles and increasing the amount of cytoplasm.

MITOSIS

All of the cells in the body, with the exception of reproductive cells, are called **somatic cells**. Some examples are heart cells, liver cells and skin cells. Somatic cells undergo a process called mitosis. **Mitosis** is a type of cell division that generates two daughter cells with the identical components of the mother cell.

The daughter cells that result from mitotic cell division are identical to each other as well as to the parent cell. The daughter cells have the same (diploid) number of chromosomes as the parent cell. Mitosis is the mechanism for **asexual reproduction**, which only requires one parent. Mitosis also allows multicellular organisms to grow and replace cells. The stages of mitosis are:

Prophase: The nucleus of the cell organizes the chromatin material into thread-like structures called chromosomes. The centriole, in animal cells only, divides and moves to each end of the cell. Spindles form between the centrioles.

Metaphase: The chromosomes attached at the center, or centromeres, line up on the spindle at the center of the cell.

Anaphase: Chromosomes separate at the center, and the spindles pull them toward either end of the cell. A nuclear membrane forms around the chromosomes as they disorganize.

Telophase: Chromatin again forms from the chromosomes, and a cell membrane begins to grow across the center between the two new nuclei.

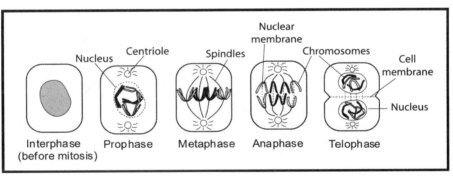

Figure 4.5 Stages of Mitosis

CYTOKINESIS

Cytokinesis, the division of the cell cytoplasm, usually follows mitosis. Cytokinesis generally begins during the telophase of mitosis. It finalizes the production of two new daughter cells, each with approximately half of the cytoplasm and organelles as well as one of the two nuclei formed during mitosis. The processes of mitosis and cytokinesis are together called **cell division**.

MEIOSIS

Meiosis is a type of cell division necessary for **sexual reproduction**. It is limited to the reproductive cells in the testes, namely the sperm cells, and the reproductive cells in the ovaries, namely the eggs. Meiosis produces four reproductive cells or **gametes**. These four cells contain half the number (haploid) of chromosomes of the mother cell, and the

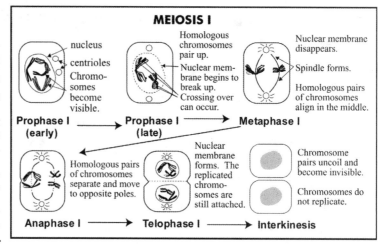

Figure 4.6 Meiosis I

chromosomes are not identical. There are two phases of cell division: **meiosis I** and **meiosis II**. Before meiosis begins, each pair of chromosomes replicates while the cell is in its resting phase (interphase).

During meiosis I, each set of replicated chromosomes lines up with its homologous pair. **Homologous chromosomes** are matched pairs of chromosomes. Homologous chromosomes are similar in size and shape and carry the same kinds of genes. However, they are not identical because each set usually comes from a different parent. The homologous pairs of chromosomes can break and exchange segments during the **crossing over** process, a source of genetic variation. The homologous pairs of chromosomes then separate. The cell splits into two daughter cells, each containing one pair of the homologous chromosomes. **Interkinesis** is the resting period before meiosis II begins.

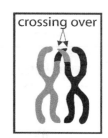

Figure 4.7 Crossing Over of Chromosomes

During meiosis II, the two daughter cells divide again without replication of the chromosomes. The result is four gametes, each having half the number of chromosomes of the mother cell.

In males, all 4 gametes produce a long whip-like tail. In females, 1 gamete forms an egg cell with a large supply of stored nutrients. The other 3 gametes, called **polar bodies**, disintegrate.

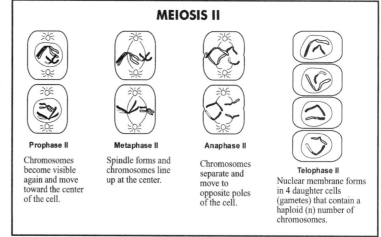

Figure 4.8 Meiosis II

In humans, the body cells have 23 different pairs or a diploid (2n) number of 46 chromosomes total. Each egg and each sperm have 23 single or haploid (n) number of chromosomes.

Section Review 2: Reproduction of Cells

A. Terms

reproductive cells	chromatin	replication	meiosis
haploid	cell cycle	metaphase	sexual reproduction
somatic cells	interphase	anaphase	gamete
diploid	asexual reproduction	telophase	crossing over
homologous chromosomes	prophase	cytokinesis	interkinesis
	mitosis	cell division	polar bodies

B. Multiple Choice

1. All body cells, except the sperm and the ova, are _____ cells.
   A. germ   B. reproductive   C. somatic   D. spindle

2. The type of nuclear division that produces gametes is
   A. meiosis.   B. cytokinesis.   C. interphase.   D. mitosis.

3. When DNA is in long strands prior to coiling, it is in the form of
   A. chromosomes.   B. centromeres.   C. chromatin.   D. chromatids.

4. A type of nuclear division that takes place in somatic cells is
   A. meiosis.   B. cytokinesis.   C. interphase.   D. mitosis.

5. During interphase, the cell
   A. splits its homologous pairs.
   B. grows, replicates DNA and prepares for cell division.
   C. divides the number of chromosomes in half.
   D. becomes separated by a cellular membrane.

6. The length of time it takes for a cell to complete the cell cycle is
   A. around two hours.   C. the same for each kind of cell.
   B. different for each cell.   D. around two minutes.

7. Interkinesis follows
   A. fertilization.   B. mitosis.   C. meiosis II.   D. meiosis I.

C. Short Answer

1. Why is sexual reproduction dependent on meiosis?

2. The normal number of chromosomes in a yellow pine tree is 24. With pictures taken from a high-powered microscope, you determine that the pollen from the yellow pine only has 12 chromosomes. How can this be explained?

3. Which type of cell division results in a diploid number of chromosomes in the new cells? Which type of cell division results in a haploid number of chromosomes in the new cells?

4. Anaphase in both mitosis and meiosis is the phase in which chromosomes get separated and pulled to opposite ends of the poles. Explain how anaphase in mitosis is different from anaphase I in meiosis. Draw a diagram of these two phases to help explain the difference.

ASEXUAL VS. SEXUAL REPRODUCTION

Asexual reproduction by mitosis is a careful copying mechanism. Some unicellular organisms, like amoeba produce asexually. Many plants also produce asexually. There are several mechanisms by which this occurs. However, the offspring produced are always genetically identical to the parent.

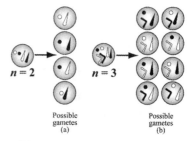

Figure 4.9 Possible Gametes of Offspring

In contrast, **sexual reproduction** by meiosis brings with it the enormous potential for genetic variability. The number of possible chromosome combinations in the gametes is 2^n, where n is the haploid chromosome number and 2 is the number of chromosomes in a homologous pair. Look at Figure 4.9, which shows the possible distribution of chromosomes into homologous pairs at meiosis in organisms with small numbers of chromosomes (in this case 2 and 3).

When n=2, four distinct distributions are possible. When n=3, eight distinct distributions are possible. If humans have a haploid number of n=23, then 2^{23}, or 8,388,608 distinct distributions are possible. Remember, this is only the genetic variation that occurs *before* fertilization.

FERTILIZATION AND CELL DIFFERENTIATION

The haploid gametes produced during meiosis are spermatozoa in males and ova in females. During **fertilization**, these gametes fuse to form a new diploid parent cell called the **zygote**. The zygote is one cell with a set of 2n chromosomes. Each parent contributes one homolog to each homologous pair of chromosomes. To grow in size, it then begins the process of mitosis becoming an **embryo**.

The group of cells produced in the very early stages of the embryo's growth are similar to the original zygote. They are called embryonic **stem cells**. Eventually, when the embryo reaches 20 –150 cells in size, this group begins to produce cells that are different from themselves. This process is called **cell differentiation**. The cells become specialized and later become tissues. As each cell differentiates, it produces proteins characteristic to its specific function.

Stem cells have the capability to become any type of cell. This is possible because genes within the cell can be "turned on" or "turned off" at specific times. Every cell of the organism has the same genetic information that was present in the initial zygote. Thus, cell differentiation occurs by the selective activation or inactivation of only some of these genes. For example, some cells could become liver cells while other cells become skin cells, but both of these cell types contain genes for every other cell type within the organism.

In the next chapter, we will discuss genes and the role they play in heredity.

Section Review 3: Reproduction, Fertilization & Cell Differentiation

A. Terms

fertilization   zygote   asexual reproduction   cell differentiation
embryo   stem cells   sexual reproduction   stem cells

B. Multiple Choice

1. In fertilization, gametes fuse to form a(n)

    A. embryo.   B. soatic cell.   C. zygote.   D. reproductive cell.

2. Stem cells are

    A. cells that can produce any type of offspring cell.

    B. cells that contain stem structures used in reproduction.

    C. haploid cells that can produce any type of offspring cell.

    D. found only in plant cells.

3. A dove has a diploid number of 16 chromosomes. How many possible distributions of chromosomes can occur in the homologous pairs of a dove's gametes?

    A. 16   B. 32   C. 256   D. 65,536

4. A zygote becomes an embryo through the process of

    A. mitosis.   B. meiosis.   C. cell differentiation.   D. fertilization.

5. What process of reproduction brings with it the greatest potential for genetic variability?

    A. mitosis.   B. meiosis.   C. cell differentiation.   D. interkinesis.

6. Mitosis is to _____ as Meiosis is to _____.

    A. asexual reproduction; sexual reproduction   C. cellular respiration; photosynthesis

    B. sexual reproduction; asexual reproduction   D. embryo; zygote

7. What process causes stem cells to become unique?

    A. embryo   B. cell differentiation   C. cell respiration   D. meiosis

8. What type of organisms usually reproduces asexually?

    A. multicellular   B. unicellular   C. bi-cellular   D. differentiation

9. What gives stem cells the ability to become any type of cell?

    A. the activation or inactivation of specific genes during developmental stages

    B. the presence or absence of specific genes within the zygote

    C. the formation or dissipation of a nuclear envelop

    D. growth of an embryo

10. Mitosis is a small part of what larger cellular process?

    A. cell differentiation   B. meiosis   C. cell cycle   D. gametes

CHAPTER 4 REVIEW

A. Choose the best answer.

CHAPTER
REVIEW

1. Chromosomes line up on spindles in the center of a cell
   during +

   A. anaphase.   B. telophase.   C. metaphase.   D. prophase.

2. In the DNA molecule, guanine pairs with another base called

   A. quinine.   B. riboflavin.   C. cytosine.   D. thymine.

3. The long strands of DNA are made up of

   A. elastic rubber bases.   C. sugar and phosphates.

   B. sugar nucleotides and potassium.   D. oxygen and nucleotides.

4. The sections of DNA that resemble rungs on a ladder are called

   A. genetic codes.   C. base pairs.

   B. reprocessors.   D. lipid pairs.

5. Mitosis generates

   A. daughter cells identical to the mother cell.
   B. many reproductive cells.
   C. diseased cells.
   D. gametes.

6. Meiosis is a type of cell division that

   A. leads to genetic mutation.   C. is necessary for sexual reproduction.

   B. causes deformity.   D. causes alleles to deform.

7. DNA can make exact copies of itself. This process is called

   A. translation.   B. duplication.   C. replication.   D. transcription.

8. A type of cellular reproduction when the nuclear division of somatic cells takes place
   is

   A. meiosis.   B. cytokinesis.   C. interphase.   D. mitosis.

9. When preparing for cell division, the chromatin condenses and becomes a

   A. gene.   B. chromosome.   C. protein.   D. codon.

10. The molecule that transports the code of information from DNA to the ribosome is
    A. tRNA.   B. rRNA.   C. mRNA.   D. an amino acid.

11. The process in which paired twin chromosomes exchange pieces of DNA during meiosis is called
    A. crossing over.   B. fertilization.   C. self pollination.   D. replication.

12. Somatic cells have two sets of chromosomes, one from the mother and one from the father. These matched pairs of chromosomes are called
    A. clones.   C. homologous chromosomes.
    B. gametes.   D. mutations.

13. During translation, adenine on mRNA will pair with which base on tRNA?
    A. uracil   B. guanine   C. thymine   D. cytosine

14. Amino acids that are not yet part of a polypeptide are found in which part of the cell?
    A. mitochondria   C. Golgi apparatus
    B. cytoplasm   D. nucleus

15. The number of chromosomes in gametes is referred to as
    A. chromatin.   C. heterozygous.
    B. haploid.   D. controlled.

16. Prior to cell differentiation, all the cells in an embryo are
    A. the same.   B. stem cells.   C. gametes.   D. A and B.

17. A fruit fly has a haploid number of 4 chromosomes. How many possible distributions of chromosomes can occur in its homologous pairs?
    A. 4   B. 8   C. 16   D. 256

18. What is the function of a stop codon?
    A. to instruct tRNA to stop delivering amino acids to mRNA
    B. to instruct the ribosome to stop delivering amino acids to mRNA
    C. to instruct the ribosome to stop the translation process and release the protein
    D. to instruct the ribosome to stop the transcription process and release the protein

19. A diploid cell has a chromosome number of 32. It produces a new cell with a chromosome number of 16. What process led to the formation of the new cell?
    A. mitosis   B. meiosis   C. diffusion   D. homeostasis

20. Which example below requires mitosis?

    A. female fish making eggs

    B. new embryo growing inside an egg

    C. male kangaroo producing sperm

    D. male pine cone producing pollen grains

21. If an organism has an haploid number of 16, how many possible chromosome distributions are there?

    A. 32

    B. 65,536

    C. 655,365

    D. 1.8×10^{19}

22. What type of cell division do skin cells use?

    A. asexual

    B. sexual

    C. repetitive

    D. duplicate

23. Approximately how much time do cells spend in G_1, S and G_2?

    A. 25% of their time

    B. 50% of their time

    C. 75% of their time

    D. 100% of their time

24. What does DNA ultimately produce?

    A. carbohydrates

    B. sugars

    C. fats

    D. proteins

25. How does crossing over aid organisms?

    A. It increases genetic variations.

    B. It decreases genetic variations.

    C. It maintains zero genetic variations.

    D. Crossing over does not aid organisms.

26. What type of reproduction do multicellular vertebrates use?

    A. asexual

    B. sexual

    C. zygote

    D. haploid

27. At the end of Meiosis II, how many egg cells are produced by the human female?

    A. 4

    B. 3

    C. 2

    D. 1

28. What ultimately causes the genetic variability during cell division?

    A. the physical configuration of homologous chromosomes during metaphase

    B. the development of the cell membrane during telophase

    C. the separation of chromosomes during prophase

    D. the division of cytoplasm during cytokinesis

29. What is the first step in the formation of a protein?

    A. transcription

    B. translation

    C. hormones

    D. prophase

30. What is a triplet set of nucleotides more commonly called?

    A. anti-codon

    B. codon

    C. zygote

    D. rRNA

Chapter 5
Genetics, Heredity and Biotechnology

ALABAMA HSGT IN SCIENCE STANDARDS COVERED IN THIS CHAPTER INCLUDE:

7	Apply Mendel's law to determine phenotypic and genotypic probabilities of offspring.
7a	Defining important genetic terms, including dihybrid cross, monohybrid cross, phenotype, genotype, homozygous, heterozygous, dominant trait, recessive trait, incomplete dominance, codominance and allele.
7b	Interpreting inheritance patterns shown in graphs and charts.
7c	Calculating genotypic and phenotypic percentages and ratios using a Punnett square.
8a	Explaining relationships among DNA, genes and chromosomes.
8b	Listing significant contributions of biotechnology to society, including agricultural and medical practices.
8c	Relating normal patterns of genetic inheritance to genetic variation.
8d	Relating ways chance, mutagen and genetic engineering increase diversity.
8e	Relating genetic disorders and disease to patterns of genetic inheritance.

GENETIC EXPRESSION

Genes, which are specific portions of DNA, determine hereditary characteristics. Genes carry traits that can pass from one generation to the next. **Alleles** are different molecular forms of a gene. Each parent passes on one allele for each trait to the offspring. Each offspring has two alleles for each trait. The expression of physical characteristics depends on the genes that both parents contribute for that particular characteristic. **Genotype** is the term for the combination of alleles inherited from the parents.

Genes are either dominant or recessive. The **dominant gene** is the trait that will most likely express itself. If both alleles are dominant, or one is dominant and one is recessive, the trait expressed will be the dominant one. In order for expression of the **recessive gene** to occur, both alleles must be the recessive ones. For example, a mother might pass on a gene for having dimples, and the father might pass on a gene for not having dimples. Having dimples is dominant over not having dimples, so the offspring will have dimples even though it inherits one allele of each trait. For the offspring not to have dimples, both the mother and father must pass along the allele for not having dimples. The **phenotype** is the physical expression of the traits. The phenotype does not necessarily reveal the combination of alleles.

When studying the expression of the traits, geneticists use letters as symbols for the different traits. Capital letters are used for dominant alleles and lowercase letters for recessive alleles. For dimples, the symbol could be D. For no dimples, the symbol could be d. The genotype of the offspring having one gene for dimples and one gene for no dimples is Dd. The phenotype for this example is having dimples.

If an individual inherits two of the same alleles (either dominant or recessive) for a particular characteristic, the individual is **homozygous**. If the offspring inherits one dominant allele and one recessive allele, such as in the example in the above paragraph, the individual is **heterozygous**.

A **Punnett square** is used to express the possible combinations for a certain trait an offspring may inherit from the parents. The Punnett square shows possible genotypes and phenotypes of one offspring. Figure 5.1 below shows an example of a **monohybrid cross**, which involves one trait, done on a Punnett square.

The Punnett Square

The Punnett square is a tool geneticists use to determine the possible genotype of one offspring. The possible alleles donated by one parent are written across the top and the possible alleles donated by the other parent are written along the left side. In the example, the cross between two heterozygous parents is examined.

D = allele for dimples

d = allele for no dimples

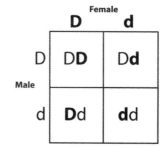

Each time this male and female produce an offspring, there is a 3/4 (or 75%) chance the offspring will have dimples and a 1/4 (or 25%) chance the offspring will have no dimples.

Figure 5.1 Punnett Square for Dimples/No Dimples

When looking at a Punnett square, it is possible to determine the probability or percent chance of having offspring with a particular characteristic. In the example shown above, the possibility the offspring produced will have no dimples is ¼ or 25 percent chance. The one comes from the box dd and the four comes from the total number of boxes. Each time these parents produce an offspring there is a ¼ or 25 percent chance the offspring will not have dimples. Conversely, there is a ¾ or 75 percent chance the offspring will have dimples.

The phenotype depends not only on which genes are present, but also on the environment. Environmental differences have an effect on the expression of traits in an organism. For example, a plant seed may have the genetic ability to have green tissues, to flower and to bear fruit, but it must be in the correct environmental conditions. If the required amount of light, water and nutrients are not present, those genes may not be expressed.

Temperature also affects the expression of genes. Primrose plants will bloom red flowers at room temperature and white at higher temperatures. At low temperatures, Himalayan rabbits and Siamese cats have dark extremities like ears, nose and feet. Warmer areas of the animals' bodies are lighter colored.

MENDEL'S CONTRIBUTION TO GENETICS

Around 1850, **Gregor Mendel** (1822 – 1884) began his work at an Austrian monastery. Many biologists call Mendel "the father of genetics" for his studies on plant inheritance. Mendel and his assistants grew, bred, counted and observed over 28,000 pea plants.

Pea plants are very useful when conducting genetic studies because the pea plant has a very simple genetic make up. It has only seven chromosomes, its traits can be easily observed, and it can **cross-pollinate** (have two different parents) or **self-pollinate** (have only one parent). Table 5.1 lists some of the pea plant traits along with their attributes. To begin his experiments, Mendel used plants that were true breeders for one trait. **True breeders** have a known genetic history and will self-pollinate to produce offspring identical to itself.

Table 5.1 Possible Traits of Pea Plants

Seed Shape	Round* Wrinkled		Pod Color	Green* Yellow	
Seed Color	Yellow* Green		Flower Position	Axial* Terminal	
Seed Coat Color	Gray* White		Plant Height	Tall* Short	
Pod Shape	Smooth* Constricted				

*Dominant

Activity

Use the given genotypes to determine the probable genotypes of offspring from each mating.

1. GG (male), Gg (female)

2. Jj (male), jj (female)

3. pp (male), PP (female)

PRINCIPLE OF DOMINANCE

Through his experiments, Mendel discovered a basic principle of genetics, the principle of dominance. Mendel's **principle of dominance** states that some forms of a gene or trait are dominant over other traits, which are called recessive. A dominant trait will mask or hide the presence of a recessive trait. When Mendel crossed a true breeding tall pea plant with a true breeding short pea plant, he saw that all the offspring plants were tall. The tallness trait *masks* the recessive shortness trait. The crossing of the true breeders is the **parental generation**, or the **P** generation. The offspring produced are the first filial generation or F_1 generation. The offspring of the F_1 generation are called the second filial or F_2 generation.

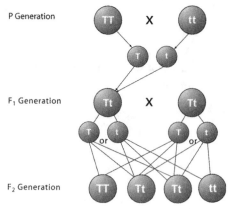

Figure 5.2 Possible Gametes of Offspring

PRINCIPLE OF SEGREGATION

Crossing plants from the F_1 generation creates the F_2 generation. Mendel soon discovered that a predictable ratio of phenotypes appeared. For every one recessive plant, there were three dominant plants present. Mendel realized that this ratio could only occur if the alleles separate sometime during gamete formation.

As a result, Mendel developed his **principle of segregation**. This principle states that when forming sex cells, the paired alleles separate so that each egg or sperm only carries one form of the allele. The two forms of the allele come together again during fertilization.

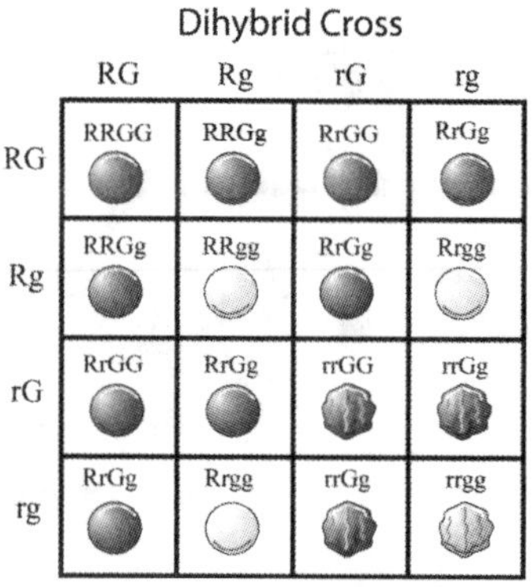

Figure 5.3 Dihybrid Cross of F1 Heterozygous Offspring

PRINCIPLE OF INDEPENDENT ASSORTMENT

When Mendel began to study **dihybrid crosses**, which involve two traits, he noticed another interesting irregularity. Mendel crossed plants that were homozygous for two traits: seed color and seed texture. Round seed texture and green color are both dominant traits. Mendel assigned the dominant homozygous P generation the genotype (RRGG). Wrinkled seed texture and yellow color are both recessive traits. The recessive homozygous P generation seeds were assigned the genotype (rrgg). When (RRGG) was crossed with (rrgg), the resulting F_1 generation was entirely heterozygous (RrGg). The F_1 generation was then allowed to self-pollinate, resulting in an F_1 dihybrid cross of (RrGg) with (RrGg). The result was an F_2 generation with a distinct distribution of traits, as depicted in Figure 5.3. Counting up the genotypes of the F_2 generation should give you the result that 9/16 of them will have the round, green phenotype, 3/16 will have the round, yellow phenotype, 3/16 will have the wrinkled, green phenotype and 1/16 will have the wrinkled, yellow phenotype.

The consistent observation of this trend led to the development of **the principle of independent assortment**. This principle states that each pair of alleles segregates independently during the formation of the egg or sperm. For example, the allele for green seed color may be accompanied by the allele for round texture in some gametes and by wrinkled texture in others. The alleles for seed color segregate independently of those for seed texture.

Section Review 1: Genetics

A. Terms

gene	phenotype	Gregory Mendel
allele	homozygous	true breeder
genotype	heterozygous	principle of dominance
dominant gene	Punnett square	principle of segregation
recessive gene	monohybrid cross	dihybrid cross
self-pollinate	cross-pollinate	principle of independent assortment

B. Multiple Choice

1. The combination of alleles inherited is called the

    A. heterozygote.   B. phenotype.   C. genotype.   D. Punnett square.

2. The expression of traits is called the

    A. phenotype.   B. genotype.   C. mutation.   D. allele.

3. If an individual inherits one dominant allele and one recessive allele, the genotype is

    A. homozygous.   B. recessive.   C. heterozygous.   D. phenotype.

4. If an individual inherits two of the same allele, either both dominant or both recessive for a particular characteristic, the individual's genotype is

    A. heterozygous.   B. phenotypic.   C. homozygous.   D. mutated.

5. Use a Punnett square to predict the cross of a homozygous green parent with a homozygous yellow parent if yellow is dominant over green. The phenotype of the offspring will be

    A. all yellow.   C. neither yellow nor green.

    B. all green.   D. some yellow and some green.

C. Short Answer

1. The gene for cystic fibrosis is a recessive trait. This disorder causes the body cells to secrete large amounts of mucus that can damage the lungs, liver, and pancreas. If one out of 20 people is a carrier of this disorder, why is only one out of 1,600 babies born with cystic fibrosis?

2. What is the relationship between phenotype and genotype?

3. Compare homozygous alleles to heterozygous alleles.

4. What specifically determines hereditary characteristics in an individual?

MODES OF INHERITANCE

SEX-LINKED TRAITS

Sex chromosomes are the chromosomes responsible for determining the sex of an organism. These chromosomes carry the genes responsible for sex determination as well as other traits. They are the 23rd pair of chromosomes and are sometimes called X or Y chromosomes. Males have the genotype XY and females have the genotype XX. In females, one X comes from their mother and one X comes from their father. In males, the X chromosome comes from their mother and the Y chromosome comes from their father.

Punnett Square for Color Blindness

	X^B	X^b
X^B	X^{B}X^B	X^{B}X^b
Y	X^{B}Y	X^{b}Y

B = Normal
b = Color Blind

Figure 5.4 Punnett Square for Color Blindness

If a recessive trait, like color blindness, is located on the X chromosome, it is not very likely that females will have the phenotype for this condition. It is more likely that males will have the condition since they only have one X chromosome. Males do not have another X chromosome or a duplicate copy of the gene. A female that has a recessive gene on one X chromosome is a **carrier** for that trait.

Examine the Punnett square in Figure 5.4, which shows the cross of a female who is heterozygous for color blindness with a normal male. This Punnett square shows how a mother contributes to the color blindness of her sons.

INCOMPLETE DOMINANCE

Incomplete dominance is the situation when one trait is not completely dominant over the other. Think of it as blending of the two traits. All of the offspring in the F$_1$ generation will show a phenotype that is a blending of both the parents. If the F$_1$ generation is self-pollinated, the ratio of the offspring will appear in a predictable pattern. One offspring will look like one parent, two offspring will look like both parents, and one offspring will look like the other parent.

A cross between a red and a white four o'clock flower demonstrates this point. One flower in the parental generation is red with genotype R^{1}R^1. The other flower is white with genotype R^{2}R^2. The offspring of this cross appear pink and have a genotype of R^{1}R^2. See Figure 5.5 to the right for the genotypes and the phenotypes of the P, F$_1$ and F$_2$ generations.

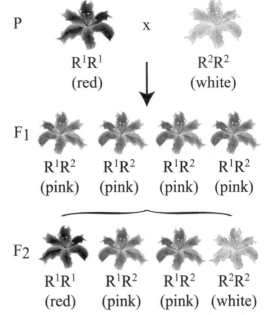

Figure 5.5 Genotypes and Phenotypes of P, F$_1$ and F$_2$ Generations of 4 o 'clock Flower

CO-DOMINANCE

When both traits appear in the F_1 generation and contribute to the phenotype of the offspring, the trait is **co-dominant**. One example occurs in horses, in which the trait for red hair is co-dominant with the trait for white hair. A roan is a horse that has both traits. The horse appears to look pinkish-brown from far away. However, if you look closely at the coat of this animal, you will notice that both solid red and solid white hairs found on the coat give the animal its unique color.

Though they sound similar, there are two main differences between the situations of co-dominance and incomplete dominance. When one allele is incompletely dominant over another, the blended result occurs because *neither allele is fully expressed*. That is why the F_1 generation four o'clock flower is a *totally different color* (pink). In contrast, when two alleles are co-dominant, *both alleles are completely expressed*. The result is a combination of the two, rather than a blending. The roan horse's hair may look pink from afar, but it is actually a combination of distinct red hair and white hair.

MULTIPLE ALLELES AND POLYGENIC TRAITS

Certain traits like blood type, hair color and eye color, are determined by two genes from each parent for every trait. Whenever there are different molecular forms of the same gene, each form is called an **allele**. Although each individual only has two alleles, there can be many different combinations of alleles in that same population. For instance, hamster hair color is controlled by one gene with alleles for black, brown, agouti (multi-colored), gray, albino and others. Each allele can result in a different coloration.

Polygenic traits are the result of the interaction of multiple genes. It is commonly known, for instance, that high blood pressure has a strong hereditary linkage. The phenotype for hypertension is not, however, controlled by a single gene that lends itself to elevating or lowering blood pressure. Rather, it is the result of the interaction between one's weight (partially controlled by one or more genes), their ability to process fats in general and cholesterol in particular (several metabolic genes), their ability to process and move various salts through the bloodstream (transport genes) and their lifestyle habits, such as smoking and drinking (which may or may not be the result of the expression of several genes that express themselves as addictive behavior). Of course, each of the genes involved may also have multiple alleles, which vastly expands the complexity of the interaction.

Activity		
Pretend the color crosses shown are inherited in one animal species co-dominantly, while the same coloration is inherited by another animal species in an incompletely dominant way. Determine the phenotype of each cross.		

	Red × Blue	**Yellow × Blue**	**Red × White**
Species 1	co-dominant _____	co-dominant _____	co-dominant _____
Species 2	incomplete _____	incomplete _____	incomplete _____
	Green × Red	**Brown × White**	**Violet × Black**
Species 1	co-dominant _____	co-dominant _____	co-dominant _____
Species 2	incomplete _____	incomplete _____	incomplete _____

GENETIC PEDIGREES

A pedigree is a graphical chart used to identify the lineage of individuals. Pedigrees are useful when the genotype of individuals is unknown. Pedigrees are used when breeding animals like dogs or race horses. Pedigrees help show the inheritance of genetic disorders within families. Often pedigrees represent males with a square and females with a circle. People born or diagnosed with a disorder are often shaded or colored. Each pedigree has a key to help you determine the best way to understand the information displayed.

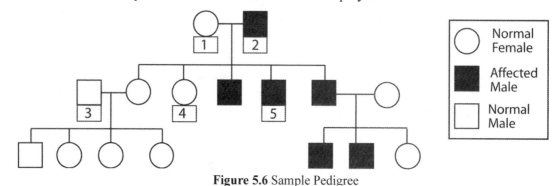

Figure 5.6 Sample Pedigree

Section Review 2: Modes of Inheritance

A. Terms

sex chromosomes   carrier   incomplete dominance

co–dominance   multiple alleles   polygenic traits

B. Multiple Choice

1. A male has the genotype XY. Which parent is responsible for giving the son the Y chromosome?

   A. mother

   B. father

   C. both the father and the mother

   D. neither the father nor the mother

2. What is the difference between co-dominance and incomplete dominance?

   A. Co-dominant traits are blended and incompletely dominant traits appear together.

   B. Co-dominant traits are recessive and incompletely dominant traits appear together.

   C. Co-dominant traits appear together and incompletely dominant traits are blended.

   D. Co-dominant traits are recessive and incompletely dominant traits are blended.

3. A cross between a black guinea pig and a white guinea pig produces a grayish guinea pig. What information do you need to determine if the production of a grayish offspring is a result of co-dominance or multiple alleles?

   A. the phenotype of the guinea pig's litter mates

   B. the number of alleles per gene

   C. the genotype of both parents

   D. either A or B

4. Roan horse and cattle fur is a common example of

    A. incomplete dominance.   C. multiple alleles.

    B. co-dominance.   D. polygenic traits.

C. Short Answer

1. The phenotype for blood type is an example of a multiple allele trait. The three alleles are A, B and O. A and B are co-dominant to O. Determine the phenotypes of the offspring in each of the situations below.

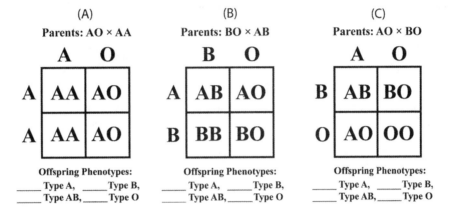

2. Given the information that the offspring phenotypes for blood type are 2/4 AB and 2/4 AO, draw a corresponding Punnett square

MUTATIONS

Mutations are mistakes or misconnections in the duplication of the chromatin material. Mutations usually occur in the nucleus of the cell during the replication process of cell division. Some mutations are harmful to an organism, and some are beneficial. Mutations are believed to play a significant role in creating the diversity of life on Earth today. Geneticists classify mutations into two groups: **gene mutations** and **chromosomal mutations**.

Gene mutations are mistakes that affect individual genes on a chromosome. For instance, one base on the DNA strand substitutes for another base. A substitution of bases will change the codon and, therefore, the amino acid. Consequently, the protein being synthesized may be different from what the DNA originally coded for, thus affecting one or more functions within the organism. Gene mutations also occur by the insertion or deletion of nucleotides from a gene.

Chromosomal mutations are mistakes that affect the whole chromosome. Recall that during meiosis, homologous chromosomes pair and may exchange segments through a process called crossing over. If errors occur during crossing over, chromosomal mutations result. There are four major categories of chromosomal mutations:

- **Duplication mutations** occur when a chromosome segment attaches to a homologous chromosome that has not lost the complementary segment. One chromosome will then carry two copies of one gene or a set of genes.

- **Deletion mutations** occur when a chromosome segment breaks off and does not reattach itself. When cell division is complete, the new cell will lack the genes carried by the segment that broke off.
- **Inversion mutations** occur when a segment of chromosome breaks off and then reattaches itself to the original chromosome, but backwards.
- **Translocation mutations** occur when a chromosome segment attaches itself to a nonhomologous chromosome.

Mutations in the somatic cells affect only the tissues of the organism. Mutations occurring in the reproductive cells may be transmitted to the gametes formed in meiosis and thus pass on to future descendants. These mutations can cause abnormal development and a variety of genetic diseases.

Although mutations do occur spontaneously, environmental factors increase the likelihood of mutations. These environmental factors are called **mutagens.** Radiation exposure can alter sex cells in humans, which directly affects the offspring by increasing the number of mutations. Natural mutation-causing chemicals in food and man-made chemicals and pollutants can cause mutations. Extremely high temperatures and some kinds of viruses can also cause mutations.

GENETIC DISORDERS AND DISEASES

Damage to human DNA happens at a rate of approximately 10,000 occurrences per cell per day. Fortunately, cells have repair mechanisms for correcting most of the errors. Additionally, many mutations that are not corrected have little to no effect on the organism. Some mutations though, including those that affect the reproductive cells, have negative effects on the organism and/or the organism's offspring.

Sickle-cell anemia, the result of two recessive genes, is a genetic disease that causes the red blood cells to take on a sickle, or crescent, shape. The distorted red blood cells cannot get through tiny blood vessels, preventing oxygen and nutrients from getting to organs. Sickle cell anemia leads to frequent and severe infections, damage to major organs and episodes of intense pain in the back, chest, abdomen and extremities.

Hemophilia is a sex-linked, recessive condition involving failure of blood to clot properly. The X chromosome carries the trait. The heterozygous mother carries the recessive trait and passes it on to approximately half of her sons, who will exhibit the disease since they have only the one X chromosome. Her daughters have a 1 in 2 chance of being carriers of the disease, and 1 in 2 sons will have the disease.

Queen Victoria of England was a hemophilia carrier. Her children married into other royal families of Europe. Thus, the condition quickly spread through these royal families.

A person with **Down's syndrome** has inherited an extra copy of chromosome 21, and therefore, has 47 total chromosomes instead of the usual 46 found in humans. The extra chromosome is the result of **nondisjunction**, the failure of one pair of homologous chromosomes to separate during meiosis. The extra genetic material interferes with normal growth and development and results in mild to severe learning disabilities, a small skull, extra folds of skin under the eyes, a flattened nose bridge and low muscle tone throughout the body.

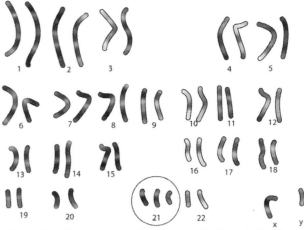

Figure 5.7 Chromosomes of a Person with Down's Syndrome

Down's syndrome may also lead to medical conditions that include heart abnormalities and thyroid problems.

Phenylketonuria (PKU) is an inherited disease resulting from a missing enzyme needed to change the amino acid phenylalanine to tyrosine. Since the chemical change cannot take place, phenylalanine builds up in the blood and urine and causes brain damage. Doctors test infants for this defect at birth. If the infant has the defect, the doctor gives the baby a special protein that prevents the disease from developing during the first 5 years while the child's brain is growing.

Cystic Fibrosis (CF) is a genetic disorder passed to children from their parents. CF is caused by a mutation of the CFTR gene. To develop CF an individual must have both recessive forms of the CFTR gene. CF causes many problems in affected individuals including: increased mucus in the lungs, lung infection, lung disease, poor growth rate, clubbing of fingers, decreased life span and infertility. Individuals with CF are usually discovered in childhood with a sweat test or a genetic test. There is no treatment for CF; however, the symptoms can be lessened with antibiotics, breathing treatments and exercise.

Tay-Sachs is another genetic disorder inherited by children from their parents. Tay-Sachs is a recessive genetic disease. It is caused by any mutations to the HEXA gene found on chromosome 15. This disease results in the build up of fatty acids in the nerve tissues. Symptoms of this disease include blindness, deafness, difficulty swallowing and eventual death. Infants born with this disease usually do not live past the age of 3. Two rare forms of the disease include juvenile TSD and adult/late onset TSD. Individuals with juvenile TSD have a life expectancy of 5 – 15 yrs. Individuals with adult TSD can manage the disease with drugs.

Section Review 3:   Mutations

A. Terms

mutation	chromosomal mutation	inversion mutation
gene mutation	deletion mutation	translocation mutation

B. Multiple Choice

1. A change in the chromosome structure caused by radiation, chemicals, pollutants or during replication is a/an

    A. mutation.   B. allele.   C. gene.   D. replicator.

2. A change in the nitrogen bases on the DNA strand is what kind of mutation?

    A. chromosome mutation   C. gene mutation

    B. segregated mutation   D. nondisjunction mutation

3. Which of the four types of mutations cause a change in the arrangement, rather than the number, of genes on a chromosome?

    A. deletion   C. translocation

    B. deletion and translocation   D. translocation and inversion

BIOTECHNOLOGY

Biotechnology is the commercial application of biological products and has been in existence for thousands of years. It includes the production of wine, beer, cheese and antibiotics, but today it more commonly refers to processes that manipulate DNA. Such processes include recombinant DNA technology, genetic engineering of agricultural crops, gene therapy, cloning and DNA fingerprinting.

RECOMBINANT DNA TECHNOLOGY

The ideas behind **recombinant DNA technology** revolve around the concept of protein synthesis. Since DNA codes for the placement of amino acids to form proteins, changing the DNA can produce a different protein. To create a recombinant DNA molecule, the DNA of one organism is cut into pieces. Then, a piece that produces a desired protein is inserted into another organism's DNA. The organism with the new piece of DNA will then produce the desired protein.

DNA molecules can be cut by substances called restriction enzymes. **Restriction enzymes** are enzymes that cut DNA at particular sites. They also leave "sticky ends" of DNA that link the new pieces of DNA. Another enzyme is used to bind the new piece of DNA to the carrier DNA. DNA changed in this way is referred to as **transformed**. Recombinant DNA is often created using the widely-studied bacteria *Escherichia coli* (*E. coli*). *E. coli* bacteria contain **plasmids**, which are small loops of DNA. The carrier can also be a virus, since some viruses incorporate themselves into their DNA hosts.

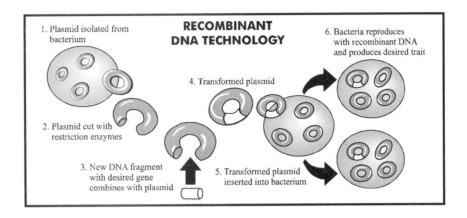

Figure 5.8 Recombinant DNA Technology

GENETIC ENGINEERING OF AGRICULTURAL CROPS

Figure 5.9 Rice Farm

Many scientists and researchers believe that recombinant technology holds great potential for improvements in agricultural products. There have already been many successes with the technology. These modified crops and animals allow farms to produce higher quality and more bountiful products, which in turn give the farmers a greater earning potential. For centuries, traditional methods of plant hybridization and selective animal breeding have been widely used to improve the genetic characteristics of various agricultural products. **Recombinant technology** takes this to an improved level by allowing scientists to transfer specific genetic material in a very precise and controlled manner and in a shorter period of time than traditional methods. For example, in plant crops the characteristics of pest resistance and improved product quality are highly desirable.

Recombinant technology has already resulted in improved strains of corn, soybeans and cotton. Insect-resistant crops and herbicide-tolerant crops have been created using recombinant technology. These improvements also enable farmers to reduce the use of chemicals, which reduces costs for the farmers, as well as helping to reduce environmental damage and run-off pollution. Rot-resistant tomatoes have been made possible by agricultural biotechnology. This improved variety allows grocery stores to offer naturally vine-ripened tomatoes instead of tomatoes that were picked green and artificially ripened on their way to the store.

Some improved products show promise for a global impact on the problem of malnutrition. Researchers working in cooperation with the International Rice Research Institute have used genetic engineering to develop an improved variety of rice. This hybrid "golden rice" has been designed to overcome Vitamin A deficiency and to combat iron-deficiency anemia. A diet containing this improved rice could prevent blindness in millions of children in Third World countries. Another product in development is a variety of rice that will grow in the 33 million acres of land in China that have salty soil.

There are many questions about the possible long term effects of this new technology. One concern is that **genetically modified foods** may be detrimental to human health. Genetically engineered foods may cause unexpected allergic reactions in people, since proteins not naturally found in the product have been inserted. Without labeling, a person with allergies may find it difficult to avoid a known food allergen if part of the food causing the allergy is genetically added into another food product. In many European and Asian countries, modified foods must be labeled as such, but in the United States, the FDA has not yet required consumer information labeling.

Genetically modified crops could pose some threat to the environment. Since herbicide-tolerant crop plants do not die when exposed to the weed-killing chemicals, some crops might be sprayed more heavily to ensure greater weed control. Some studies have indicated that the destruction of plant life naturally surrounding the crops reduces the habitats and food supplies of birds and beneficial insects.

Genetic pollution can occur through the cross-pollination of genetically modified and non-genetically modified plants by wind, birds and insects. Also, farmers who want to grow non-genetically modified crops may have a hard time avoiding genetic pollution if their farms are located near fields with genetically modified plants.

Genetically modified plants may also have some negative impact on the agricultural economy. Much of the research funding for genetically modified crops comes from companies that produce herbicides, pesticides and genetically modified seeds. Usually, genetically-modified seeds must be used with the same chemicals utilized in their development, which makes the farmers dependent on the company producing the herbicides and pesticides. In addition, genetically modified seed is more expensive than traditional seed, but reduced costs in other areas, such as chemicals, may offset that increase.

BIOTECHNOLOGY IN MEDICINE

Figure 5.10
Biotech Analyst

The medical industry is a strong proponent of biotechnology. The vaccine for Hepatitis B is a recombinant product. Human insulin and growth hormone as well as a clot-dissolving medication have been created using recombinant DNA technology. **Interferon** is a recombinant product used to fight cancer and a broad array of other diseases. **Monoclonal antibodies** are exact copies of an antibody that bind to a specific antigen, such as a cancer cell. These antibodies have been created and are used as therapy for breast cancer and non-Hodgkin's lymphoma. The antibodies are created from genetically altered mice that produce human antibodies. Research is ongoing to produce antibodies to target cells responsible for causing other diseases. As with all medications, side effects are evaluated, and each drug must prove to be more beneficial than harmful before it is approved for use.

In addition to medications, **gene therapy** is used to help cure diseases. The idea is that if a defective protein is replaced with a good one, then the disease caused by the defective protein can be eliminated. Gene therapy has the greatest potential for success in treating diseases with only one defective gene. Diseases that could be helped by gene therapy include *cystic fibrosis*, *gout*, *rickets*, *sickle-cell anemia* and *inherited high cholesterol*. Research into the use of gene therapy on people with these diseases is highly regulated.

Gene therapy is currently used in people who have **SCID, severe combined immunodeficiency**. People with this disease are also called "bubble babies" because they must be kept in sterile, bubble-like environments to prevent even minor infections, which can kill them. Using gene therapy, cells with the gene to make a certain protein are introduced into the body via the white blood cells. The new cells can then multiply and produce the protein necessary to have a functional immune system.

STEM CELL RESEARCH

Stem cells are cells found in the human body that have yet to become a specialized type of cell. They are a "pre-cell." Stem cells have the amazing ability to become any type of cell or tissue. For example, a stem cell could develop into a nerve cell or a liver cell. The potential for using stem cells to help cure many chronic human diseases is great. Stem cells could help people with *nerve damage*, *Alzheimer's*, *Parkinson's* or *arthritis*. There are three main sources of stem cells available. Stem cells can be harvested from adult bone marrow, umbilical cord blood after delivery or from human embryos. The harvesting of stem cells from human embryos usually results in the death of that embryo. Many people oppose using embryonic stem cells in medicine. There are other avenues of harvesting stem cells, however. Sources such as bone marrow and umbilical cord blood are being researched as possible alternatives to the use of embryonic stem cells. More research is needed to determine the full range of therapeutic possibilities of stem cells.

CLONING

Cloning is the creation of genetically identical organisms. The cloning of Dolly the sheep from an adult sheep cell in 1997 created great debate about the possibility of cloning humans. In the United States, federal research funds are not given to scientists who research human cloning, but the research is not banned.

Figure 5.11 Dolly and Her Offspring Bonnie

The possible benefits of human cloning include allowing a childless couple to have a child, creating tissues for transplantation that would not be rejected by their host and using genetically altered cells to treat people with Alzheimer's or Parkinson's, both diseases caused by the death of specific cells within the brain. Another application is to create therapeutic proteins, like antibodies, through the modification of the cells and then cloning the cells to have several copies.

Although creating a human clone is theoretically possible, it would be very difficult. Dolly was the 277th attempt in cloning a mammal and her death sparked a huge array of new research questions. Both scientific and moral questions must be debated, researched and solved if cloning technology is ever to become mainstream science.

DNA FINGERPRINTING

With the exception of identical twins, every person's DNA is different. **DNA fingerprinting** is the identification of a person using his or her DNA. Laboratory tests are performed by forensic scientists to determine if the suspect of a crime, for example, was present at the scene of the crime. It is also used to determine paternity, that is, the father of a child. This process has a high degree of accuracy at greater than 99%. A DNA fingerprint is not the same as an actual fingerprint taken by inking your finger. Neither is it a blueprint of your entire DNA sequence. Rather, it is the analysis of a small number of sequences of DNA that are known to vary among individuals a great deal. These sequences are analyzed to get a probability of a match. That means that DNA fingerprinting can be used to compare sample DNA from, say, a crime scene to sample DNA taken from a suspect. It cannot be used to tell who you are, independent of a comparative sample.

DNA fingerprinting is performed by cutting DNA with enzymes and separating the fragments using electrophoresis. **Electrophoresis** uses electrical charges to separate pieces of molecules based on both size and charge. The nucleic acids of DNA have a consistent negative charge imparted by their phosphate backbone, and thus migrate toward the positive terminal. The speed at which they migrate depends on both the size and molecular structure of the fragments. The result is a column of bands, each representing a specific fragment of DNA. Since two identical samples of DNA will both fragment and migrate in the same fashion, matching bands indicate that the DNA of those samples is the same, and thus the person from which those samples came is one and the same person.

In years past, there have been errors in the results of DNA fingerprinting. Today, however, there is only a tiny possibility of error, a fraction of a percent, since such advances have been made in the precision and accuracy of electrophoretic techniques that DNA differing by a single base pair can now be easily resolved.

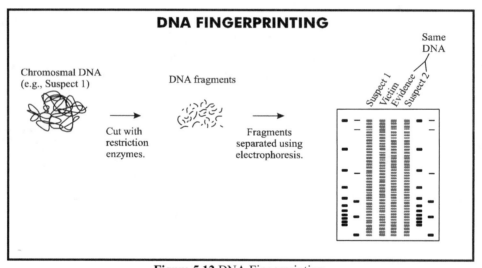

Figure 5.12 DNA Fingerprinting

Human Genome Project

The **genome** is an organism's complete set of DNA, which carries the information needed for the production of proteins. These proteins are responsible for determining how an organism looks and for performing most life functions, including metabolizing foods, fighting infections and maintaining homeostatic controls. Humans have 46 chromosomes that contain 30,000 genes made up of approximately 3 billion base pairs.

Launched in 1990, the **Human Genome Project** (HGP) sought to identify all human genes and determine all of the base pair sequences in all human chromosomes. The goal of the project was to chart variations in the sequence of base pairs in humans and to begin labeling the functions of genes. In addition to sequencing the human genome, the project also planned to sequence other organisms of vital interest to the biological field. Some of these organisms are the bacterium, *E. coli*; the yeast, *S. cerevisiae*; plus the roundworm, fruitfly and mouse. Chromosome 22 was the first chromosome sequenced and was completed in December 1999. This chromosome was chosen as the first one to sequence, because at over 33 million base pairs, it is relatively small. The Human Genome Project was completed in 2003, thanks to the contributions of biologists throughout the world.

A beneficial consequence of the HGP is the technologies that were developed in order to conduct the project. In fact, the development of faster sequencing technology resulted in the completion of the first set of goals far ahead of schedule. Scientists are hopeful that by knowing the human genome, drugs can be designed based on individual genetic profiles, diagnoses of diseases will be improved and cures may be found for many genetic diseases.

The Human Genome Project has many accompanying ethical, legal and social issues, some more obvious than others. The importance of these issues is so great that the organizers of the HGP set aside a percentage of the project budget specifically to study them. Some of the concerns addressed are the use of genetic information, the confidentiality of personal genetic information, the possibility of discrimination based on genetic information and reproductive issues.

Section Review 4:   Biotechnology

A. Terms

biotechnology	plasmid	stem cell
recombinant DNA	genetic pollution	cloning
restriction enzyme	monoclonal antibody	DNA fingerprinting
transformed	gene therapy	electrophoresis

B. Multiple Choice

1. The commercial application of biological products is

    A. illegal.   B. biotechnology.   C. unethical.   D. agricultural.

2. A small loop of DNA in a bacterium is called a

    A. plasmid.   C. polypeptide.

    B. protein.   D. transformed loop.

3. Strawberries have been created to resist the harmful effects of frost. This is an application of what?

    A. genetic engineering   C. DNA fingerprinting

    B. gene therapy   D. cloning

4. A person with a defect in a gene that codes for a specific protein could be a candidate for which of the following?

    A. cloning

    B. DNA fingerprinting

    C. gene therapy

    D. protein injections

5. Which of the following is a potential carrier of DNA to create recombinant products?

    A. clone   B. virus   C. enzyme   D. electrophoresis

C. Short Answer

1. What are some positive and negative aspects of cloning humans?

2. How is genetically modified food beneficial to farmers? How can it be harmful?

3. Give an example of an advance in biotechnology that you have heard about in the news or read about in this chapter. Explain the benefits of the application of biotechnology as well as possible negative effects.

Activity

Recently, black bear populations in Dundelbur, Alabama have been declining. As a result, the Department of Natural Resources (DNR) closely monitors hunters in the area. Persons caught harvesting bear in this area face stiff fines and possible jail time. Clarence Obvious was reported to your DNR office as a possible bear poacher. As the local DNR representative, you must find him and discover if he is innocent or guilty. You get a warrant to search his freezer and discover three questionable meat samples. Clarence claims that these samples are from a deer, a boar (male hog) and a sow (female hog) he shot earlier this year. You send these samples to your DNA lab. At the lab, known samples of bear, sow, boar and deer are compared with Clarence's meat.

Examine the PCR results for yourself.

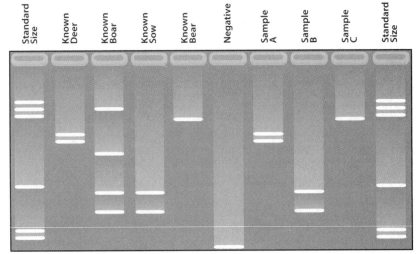

Was there bear meat in his freezer?

Is Clarence innocent? How do you know?

CHAPTER 5 REVIEW

A. Choose the best answer.

1. Down's syndrome is caused by

    A. hemophilia.

    B. thyroid disease.

    C. chromosome mutation.

    D. injury during pregnancy.

2. Use a Punnett square to predict the cross of a homozygous tall parent with a homozygous short parent if tall is dominant over short. The phenotypes of the offspring will be

    A. all tall.

    B. all short.

    C. neither short nor tall.

    D. some tall and some short.

3. The medical industry is helped by biotechnology

    A. through the development of better treatments and drugs.

    B. through the more effective disposal of wastes.

    C. by better helping people deal with loss of a loved one.

    D. through better care for the ill members of society.

4. Stem cells

    A. only come from human embryos.

    B. can definitely help many people with diseases.

    C. are found on the ends of neurons.

    D. are undifferentiated cells capable of becoming any tissue.

5. A police officer is at a crime scene and is collecting samples of blood, hair and skin. What is the officer probably going to do with the samples?

    A. The officer is cleaning the crime scene based on protocol.

    B. The officer is keeping samples to be filed with the police report.

    C. The officer is going to have the samples analyzed for a DNA fingerprint.

    D. The officer will show them to the victim's family, the judge and the prosecutor.

6. Phenylketonuria (PKU) is a genetic disease in which the enzyme needed to convert the amino acid phenylalanine into tyrosine is missing. Phenylalanine builds up in the blood and urine resulting in brain damage. How might this disease be treated successfully?

   A. Babies with PKU should be fed a diet high in phenylalanine.

   B. Babies with PKU should be tested for brain damage after eating foods that contain phenylalanine.

   C. Babies with PKU should be fed a diet which contains an equal mix of the amino acids phenylalanine and tyrosine.

   D. Babies with PKU should be fed a special diet with low amounts of the amino acid phenylalanine.

7. Genetically altered DNA is referred to as

   A. restricted.   B. fingerprinted.   C. transformed.   D. monoclonal.

B. Short Answer

A variety of pea plant may be either purple (A) or white (a); two purple pea plants are crossed, and it is known that the genotypes of the parent plants are both heterozygous dominant. **Use this information and the information given in the Punnett square to answer questions 8 – 10.**

	A	a
A	AA	Aa
a	Aa	aa

8. Which trait is dominant? Which trait is recessive?

9. What percentage of the flowers will be purple? How many will be white?

10. What are the genotypes and phenotypes of the parents?

11. Name at least two products created through recombinant DNA technology.

12. How can genetically modified plants be harmful to the environment? Give at least two reasons.

13. Which of the following biomolecules will move the fastest toward the positive terminal? Circle the correct molecule.

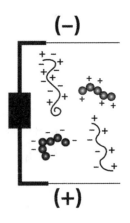

(−)

(+)

Chapter 6
Taxonomy

ALABAMA HSGT IN SCIENCE STANDARDS COVERED IN THIS CHAPTER INCLUDE:

9	Differentiate between the previous five- kingdom and current six-kingdom classification systems.
9a	Sequencing taxa from most inclusive to least inclusive in the classification of living things.
9b	Identifying organisms using a dichotomous key.
9c	Identifying ways in which organism from the Monera, Protista and fungi kingdoms are beneficial and harmful.
9d	Justifying the grouping of viruses in a category separate from living things.
9e	Writing scientific names accurately by using binomial nomenclature.
10	Distinguish between monocots and dicots, angiosperms and gymnosperms, and vascular and non-vascular plants.
10a	Describing the histology of roots, stems, leaves and flowers.
11	Classify animals according to type of skeletal structure, method of fertilization and reproduction, body symmetry, body coverings and locomotion.

BIOLOGICAL CLASSIFICATION

Biologists classify living things according to the traits they share. **Taxonomy** is the classification of an organism based on several features, such as structure, behavior, development, genetic makeup (DNA), nutritional needs and methods of obtaining food. Evolutionary theory is the basis for this classification system. Taxonomy divides organisms into several categories that start out broadly and become more specific. These categories are **kingdom**, **phylum**, **class**, **order**, **family**, **genus** and **species**.

Occasionally, subphylum, subclasses and suborders are used to further delineate characteristics among the primary classifications.

The previously accepted five kingdom classification system included the kingdoms monera, protista, fungi, plantae and animalia. The discovery of exceptional bacteria called archaebacteria caused a shift in the classification system. Archaebacteria were found to thrive in conditions previously thought uninhabitable, like hot springs or volcanic vents. Further study revealed that these bacteria had structurally unique cell walls and advanced DNA and RNA characteristics. The current classification system now has six kingdoms including archaebacteria, monera, protista, fungi, plantae and animalia.

Figure 6.1 Classification System for Organisms

Table 6.1 lists the six **kingdoms** based on general characteristics. Each kingdom further divides into **phylum**, to name organisms in the kingdoms of Eubacteria. Phylum further break down into **classes**, and classes break down into **orders**. The categories become progressively more detailed and include fewer organisms as they are further broken down into **family**, **genus** and **species**. The species is the most specific category. Organisms of the same species are grouped based on the ability to breed and produce fertile offspring.

To remember the order of the subdivisions, memorize the silly sentence, "King Phillip Came Over From Greece Sneezing." The first letter of each of the words in this sentence is also the first letter of each of the classification categories for organisms.

Table 6.1 The Six Kingdoms

Super Kingdom	Kingdom	Basic Characteristic	Example
Prokaryotes	Eubacteria	found everywhere	cyanobacteria
	Archaebacteria	live without oxygen, get their energy from inorganic matter or light, found in extreme habitats	halophiles
Eukaryotes	Protista	one-celled or multicellular, true nucleus	amoeba
	Fungi	multicellular, food from dead organisms, cannot move	mushroom
	Plantae	multicellular, cannot move, make their own food, cell walls	tree
	Animalia	multicellular, moves about, depends on others for food	horse

Figure 6.2 Carl Linnaeus

Carl Linnaeus (1707 – 1778), a Swedish botanist, devised the current system for classifying organisms. Linnaeus used **binomial nomenclature**, a system of naming organisms using a two-part name to label the species. The binomial name is written in Latin and is considered the scientific name. It consists of the generic name (genus) and the specific epithet (species). The entire scientific name is italicized or underlined, and the genus name is capitalized as in *Homo sapiens* for humans. Table 6.2 is a complete classification of three members of the kingdom Animalia, which we will examine later in the chapter.

A classification system is necessary to distinguish among the great number of organisms and to avoid confusion created by the use of common names. Common names are used for many organisms, but not all organisms have common names and some have multiple common names.

Table 6.2 Examples of Classifications

Example:	Human	Grasshopper	Wolf
Kingdom	Animalia	Animalia	Animalia
Phylum	Chordata	Arthropoda	Chordata
Class	Mammalia	Insecta	Mammalia
Order	Primate	Orthoptera	Carnivora
Family	Homindae	Locuslidea	Canidae
Genus	*Homo*	*Schistocerca*	*Canis*
Species	*sapiens*	*americana*	*lupus*

The hierarchical classification devised by Linnaeus has been, and still is, quite useful in organizing organisms. However, there are limitations. For instance, even though classification is based on evolutionary theory, it does not reflect the idea that evolutionary processes are continual, and species are not fixed. Changes will occur over time and, therefore, classification will also have to change. Also, classification does not take into account the variation that exists among individuals within a species. All domestic dogs have the scientific name *Canis lupus familiaris*, but a great deal of variation exists among different breeds of dogs and even among individual dogs of the same breed.

Finally, the most definitive test to determine if organisms are of the same species is to confirm their ability to breed successfully, producing fertile offspring. However, controlled breeding of wild organisms for the purpose of observation and study can sometimes be impractical, if not impossible. Also, sometimes closely related species can interbreed, such as in the mating of a horse and donkey to produce a mule. Classification has been instrumental in bringing about an understanding of similarities and possible evolutionary relationships of organisms. However, it is not static and may need to change with the discovery of new organisms and as more evidence of evolutionary patterns surface.

VIRUSES ARE DIFFERENT FROM LIVING THINGS

A **virus** is a small particle that contains proteins and hereditary material (DNA or RNA), but it is not alive. The virus is surrounded by a protein coat or **capsid**. Recall that a cell can do all of the things that other organisms can do, such as eat and reproduce. However, a virus particle cannot eat, and it can only reproduce inside a cell. Outside the cell, a virus particle does nothing and remains inactive. Viruses are cell-specific, meaning they can only infect a cell if the capsid of the virus can fit into a receptor site in the host cell membrane.

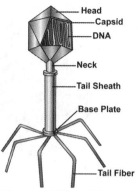

Figure 6.3 Virus Schematic

KINGDOMS ARCHAEBACTERIA AND EUBACTERIA

BACTERIA

Members of the kingdoms Archaebacteria and Eubacteria are collectively called **monerans**. These prokaryotic organisms are found in nearly every ecological niche on the planet, including soil, water, surfaces of animals and plants, animal intestines, and in many of the more extreme environments. Archaeabacteria and Eubacteria differ in their habitats and the ways in which they obtain energy.

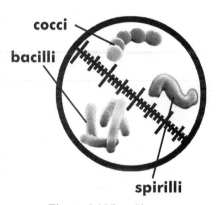

Figure 6.4 Virus Shapes

Archaeabacteria are **anaerobic**, meaning they cannot tolerate oxygen. These organisms are found in the most extreme habitats. **Methanogens** produce methane, a gas, and live in places such as the intestines of cows and other ruminants and in the soil. **Halophiles** live in highly concentrated bodies of salt water, such as the Dead Sea and the Great Salt Lake. **Thermoacidophiles** convert sulfur to sulfuric acid, creating hot acid springs. These amazing species can handle temperatures near 80° Celsius and pH levels as low as 2. They are found in places such as the acidic sulfur springs in Yellowstone National Park and in undersea vents called **smokers**.

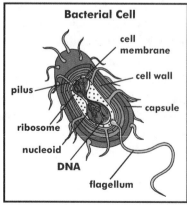

Figure 6.5 Idealized Bacterial Cell

Organisms in the kingdom Eubacteria are the "true bacteria" and are thought to have evolved separately from the Archaebacteria. Eubacteria are classified as heterotrophic, autotrophic or chematrophic. **Heterotrophs,** found nearly everywhere, need organic molecules as an energy source and feed on living organisms, dead organisms or organic wastes. **Autotrophs** are photosynthetic and are found in ponds, lakes, streams and most areas of land. **Chematrophs** obtain energy from the breakdown of inorganic, or non-living, substances such as nitrogen and sulfur compounds. Some chematrophs are important in converting atmospheric nitrogen into forms that can be used by plants.

All bacteria are microscopic and, as shown in Figure 6.4, on page 124, occur in three main shapes: cocci (spheres), bacilli (rods) or spirilli (spirals). Some are mobile and use a **flagellum** (plural form: flagella), a long extension that spins like a propeller, to move. Others have **pili** (singular form: pilus) which are small hair-like extensions all over the surface of the bacteria.

Pili allow the bacteria to attach to and grow on a surface. Pili are also used for gathering food and to aid in reproduction. Bacteria have a cell membrane and a specialized cell wall. The cell wall, however, is made of different material than the cell wall of a plant. Being prokaryotes, bacteria do not have membrane-bound organelles or a nucleus.

Bacteria reproduce through **binary fission**, where a cell divides in half. It is a process similar to mitosis (see Figure 6.6). They can also reproduce by **conjugation**, a process through which genetic material is exchanged between two cells with the aid of a special pilus that is hollow. Bacteria reproduce very rapidly and double the number of organisms at each division, with some bacteria producing a new generation approximately every twenty minutes. This rate of reproduction continues until nutrients are used up.

Bacteria are found everywhere, and most are harmless. They live on our skin and in our digestive tract and prevent harmful bacteria from colonizing and causing infection. Bacteria living in our digestive tract help digest fats and produce vitamin K. In the environment, they are important **decomposers**, feeding on dead matter. Some bacteria process raw sewage, removing harmful bacteria. Beneficial bacteria are used in the food industry to make cheese, vinegar, soy sauce and yogurt. They are also used in biotechnology to make recombinant products and are able to convert nitrogen into a form that is usable by plants and animals.

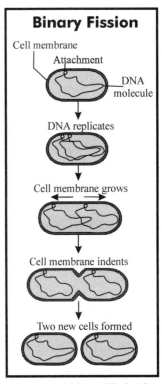

Figure 6.6 Binary Fission in Bacteria

Some bacteria cause disease by reproducing and damaging tissue or releasing toxins that interfere with cellular functions. Examples of bacterial illnesses include tuberculosis, typhus, diptheria, cholera, tetanus, tooth decay, gum disease, strep throat and other streptococcal infections. In many cases, bacterial infections can be prevented by maintaining cleanliness. Washing hands is an important way to prevent the spread of infections. Many disinfectants are available to kill bacteria on surfaces, and antibiotics can get rid of infections in humans and animals when used properly. Antibiotics are drugs, derived from living organisms or manufactured synthetically, that kill bacteria without harming the host. Frequent or improper use of antibiotics eliminates those bacteria that are susceptible to the antibiotics, but allows the resistant strains to reproduce and pass their resistance on to offspring. Bacterial resistance is becoming more common, creating new challenges in maintaining health.

Section Review 1: Biological Classification

A. Terms

anaerobic	autotroph	conjugation	order
methanogen	chematroph	decomposer	family
halophile	flagella	taxonomy	genus
thermoacidophile	pili	kingdom	species
heterotroph	binary fission	phylum/division	binomial nomenclature
		class	

B. Multiple Choice

1. Which of the following groups of categories is listed from broadest to most specific?

   A. family, order, class

   B. phylum, class, kingdom

   C. order, family, genus

   D. genus, family, species

2. The two-part system used to name organisms is called

   A. dual identification.

   B. binomial nomenclature.

   C. double nomenclature.

   D. Linnaean nomenclature.

3. What is the proper way to write a scientific name in Latin?

   A. all caps and italicized

   B. kingdom capitalized and species lowercase, all in italics

   C. listing all categories in italics

   D. genus capitalized and species lowercase, all in italics or underlined

4. Humans belong in which order?

   A. Mammalia   B. Homo   C. Primate   D. Chordata

5. Bacteria reproduce through

   A. binary fission or conjugation.

   B. spirilli or cocci.

   C. autotrophs or heterotrophs.

   D. mitosis and meiosis.

6. Bacteria capable of movement do so by using their

   A. pili.   B. binary fission.   C. flagella.   D. bacilli.

7. The capsid coating on a virus serves to

   A. identify the capsid of another virus to breed.

   B. identify a receptor site on a prospective host cell.

   C. identify necessary food items in the host cell.

   D. assist in locomotion of the virus in the host cell.

C. Short Answer

1. Name several features used to classify organisms.

2. Discuss three limitations of the current classification system.

3. Discuss positive and negative effects of bacteria.

KINGDOM PROTISTA

Kingdom Protista contains a diverse group of unicellular and multicellular organisms. All protist cells are eukaryotic with a membrane-bound nucleus. Protists can be *plant-like*, *animal-like* or *fungus-like.*

PLANT-LIKE PROTISTS

Plant-like protists are known as **algae** and may be unicellular or multicellular. Although algae come in different colors, all algae have chlorophyll-containing chloroplasts and can make their own food. Algae are divided into six phyla according to their pigments and how they store food.

Euglenas have characteristics of both plants and animals. They are both autotrophic and heterotrophic. Euglena live in fresh water, move around with a flagellum and have no cell wall. They have an eyespot that responds to light.

Golden algae or **diatoms** are single-celled algae that have chloroplasts filled with chlorophyll and store their own food in the form of oil. They have a cell wall and a golden brown pigment that covers the green color of the chlorophyll. These algae are found in salt water and are an important source of food for marine animals. When they die, they form the diatomaceous earth used in products such as detergents, paint removers, and scouring powders as well as chalk and limestone. Diatom shells contain silica, the main element in glass; it is used in road paint to make the yellow lines visible at night.

Dinoflagellates are found in both fresh and salt water. They have red pigment and move around using two flagella. They also glow in the dark and are a source of food to marine animals. When these algae have occasional "blooms" and over-populate in the water, they produce a "red tide" which creates massive fish kills.

The other three phyla of algae are distinguished by their color. **Green algae** store food in the form of starch. They can be either one-celled or multicellular, and can live in water or out of water (such as in tree trunks). **Red algae** are multicellular and produce a type of starch on which they live. Irish moss is a type of red algae that is used to give toothpaste and pudding its smoothness. **Brown algae** are multicellular and vary in size. **Kelp** is a type of brown algae and is an important food source for many people around the world. Algae carry on photosynthesis and play an important role as producers in the environment, producing about $\frac{1}{2}$ of the Earth's organic material and about $\frac{3}{4}$ of its oxygen.

ANIMAL-LIKE PROTISTS

Animal-like protists are one-celled organisms known as **protozoa**. Many protozoa are parasites living in water, on soil, and on living and dead organisms. There are four phyla of protozoa, traditionally, divided according to their method of movement.

Ciliates have hair-like structures called cilia that help them move freely. A paramecium is a typical ciliate. They can live in fresh and salt water. They have oral grooves to take in food, making them heterotrophic. Ciliates reproduce by fission and conjugation.

Flagellates live in fresh and salt water and, as their name implies, move by one or more flagella. Some flagellates are parasites, and many cause disease. Trypanosome is a flagellate that causes African sleeping sickness in humans and other animals when it is transmitted by the bite of the tsetse fly.

Amoeboids (sometimes called sarcodines) move by pseudopods, which means false feet. An amoeba is a typical species of the sarcodina phylum. They change shape as they surround their food. Some amoebas have hard shells.

Sporozoa is a phylum containing only parasites that feed on the blood of humans and other animals. Malaria is a disease that attacks humans when sporozoa are transmitted to the human bloodstream in the bite of a mosquito. Sporozoa have no way of moving on their own.

PLANKTON

Plankton is the name of a combined organism made up of protozoa and algae. Plankton are essential to life on earth. They produce much of the oxygen other organisms in the world need to survive. They are the "grass" of the sea from which all marine animals get their nourishment.

Fungus-like protists include several phyla that have features of both protists and fungi. They include slime molds and water molds. They obtain energy from decomposing organic material. Slime mold is a phylum of organisms found in damp soil and on rotting wood.

Slime molds are decomposers. They have two life stages. One stage is a flat, sideways mass that moves like an amoeba. A second reproductive state is an upright stage which is similar to fungus. The reproductive stage produces using spores that develop into zygotes.

Water molds, downy mildews and white rusts are all included in another phylum. Most feed on dead organisms, and some are parasitic to plants or animals. It was one of the water molds that attacked the potato crop in Ireland in the 1840s causing a famine that resulted in the death of over a million people.

Section Review 2: Protists

A. Terms

plant-like protists	protozoa	flagellates	sporozoans
algae	ciliates	amoeboids	plankton
animal-like protists	cilia	pseudopod	fungus-like protists

B. Multiple Choice

1. All algae are

    A. autotrophs.   B. heterotrophs.   C. decomposers.   D. ciliates.

2. Which member of the protist kingdom causes "red tides"?

   A. algae   B. Euglena   C. dinoflagellates   D. protozoa

3. How are animal-like protists grouped?

   A. size   C. method of movement

   B. habitat   D. number of diseases they cause

4. Why are algae important?

   A. They create color on Earth.   C. They are decomposers.

   B. They produce the most nitrogen on Earth.   D. They produce most of the oxygen on Earth.

5. Fungus-like protists are

   A. decomposers.   B. autotrophs.   C. consumers.   D. producers.

C. Complete the following two exercises.

1. Identify the animal-like and plant-like characteristics of the Euglena.

2. Describe the primary difference between algae and protozoa.

KINGDOM FUNGI

Figure 6.7 Fungi

Fungi are heterotrophic organisms that secrete enzymes, allowing them to digest their food. They are also **saprophytes**, which are organisms that live in or on matter that they decompose as they use it for food. Some fungi are edible while other species are poisonous. Fungi live in aquatic environments, soil, mud and decaying plants. They include black bread mold, yeast, mushrooms and truffles. The fungus *Penicillium* is responsible for the flavors of Roquefort and Camembert cheeses. The widely-used antibiotic penicillin is also derived from a species of this group.

A **lichen** is a type of fungus that grows together with algae or cyanobacteria, creating a symbiotic relationship. Rocks and dead trees are broken down into soil by lichens. The algae or cyanobacteria provide food through photosynthesis, and the fungi provide protection and structure. Some lichens cannot grow in areas with high pollution, so they are often used as an indicator of the level of pollution in an area.

Another symbiotic relationship exists between fungi and vascular plants, called **mycorrhizae** ("fungus roots"). The fungi penetrate the root of the plant and then extend into the soil. It is not known exactly how the fungi help the plants thrive, but it is thought that minerals in the soil are converted by the fungi into a more usable form for the plants and that the presence of the fungi increases water uptake. The fungi obtain sugars, amino acids and other organic substances from the plants.

Fungi reproduce sexually and asexually with reproductive cells called **spores**. Spores are produced sexually by the fruiting body, the visible portion of a reproductive structure like a mushroom. The spore is released into the air, and if conditions are right, it grows into an individual on its own. The fruiting body forms gametes that reproduce sexually. Fungi reproduce asexually through mitosis or budding. **Budding** occurs when a piece of the organism becomes detached and continues to live and grow on its own as a complete structure.

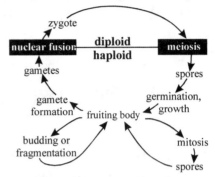

Figure 6.8 Fungus Lifecycle

Some fungal species cause disease by growing on and causing irritation to the skin, hair, nails or mucus membranes of animals. Many are not harmful, but they are irritating and difficult to eliminate. Fungal spores can also be inhaled and cause infections in the lungs and other organs. These types of infections are not very common but can cause permanent damage.

Fungi, along with bacteria, are the great recyclers. Together, they keep the earth from becoming buried under mountains of waste.

Section Review 3: Fungi

A. Terms

saprophytes	mycorrhizae	Euglenas	budding
lichen	spores	fruiting body	fungi

B. Multiple Choice

1. Examples of fungi include

    A. dinoflagellates and algae.

    B. cyanobacteria and monera.

    C. mushrooms and yeast.

    D. sporozoa and sarcodines.

2. A saprophyte is an organism that

    A. feeds off of plants.

    B. feeds off of dead matter.

    C. feeds off of spores.

    D. feeds off of photosynthesizers.

3. Fungi secrete enzymes to

    A. break down materials so they can absorb them.

    B. catalyze chemical reactions in the air.

    C. help photosynthesis take place by activating plastids.

    D. none of the above.

C. Complete the following two exercises.

1. Name ways in which fungi cause disease.

2. Discuss the symbiotic relationship between fungi and other organisms.

THE KINGDOM PLANTAE

The plant kingdom consists of multicellular organisms that have eukaryotic cells. Almost all use photosynthesis to obtain food. The life cycle of a plant consists of two distinct generations. This type of life cycle is called **alternation of generations**. Alternation of generations includes a sexual phase, called **gametophyte**, alternating with an asexual phase, called **sporophyte**. Gametophytes produce egg and sperm that join to produce a sporophyte generation. Sporophytes contain **spores**, or reproductive cells, that undergo meiosis and give rise to the gametophyte generation. The life cycle then begins again. Some plants spend most of their life cycles as sporophytes, while other plants spend most of their lives as gametophytes.

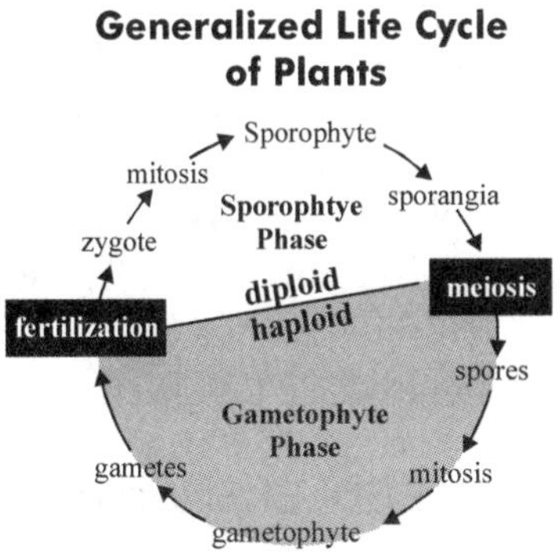

Generalized Life Cycle of Plants

Sporophyte

mitosis · Sporophtye Phase · sporangia

zygote

diploid · meiosis

fertilization · haploid

spores

Gametophyte Phase

gametes · mitosis

gametophyte

Figure 6.9 Plant Lifecycle

There are many different types of plants, with a variety of structure types. Plants can be non-vascular, vascular and seedless, or vascular and seed bearing. **Non-vascular plants** lack tissues used to transport substances like water and sugars. Instead, they absorb nutrients through their cells. **Vascular plants** contain specialized structures for conducting substances. Some vascular plants develop from seeds. Others develop from spores.

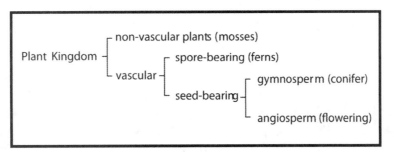

Plant Kingdom ┬ non-vascular plants (mosses)
             └ vascular ┬ spore-bearing (ferns)
                        └ seed-bearing ┬ gymnosperm (conifer)
                                       └ angiosperm (flowering)

Figure 6.10 Divisions Within the Plant Kingdom

NON-VASCULAR PLANTS

Bryophytes are non-vascular, seedless plants that live in moist habitats. They include the mosses, liverworts and hornworts. Mosses are the most common. The bryophytes have leaf-like, root-like and stem-like parts. They do not have a true root structure. Their cells are elongated to better absorb moisture, and their leaves have a **cuticle**, a waxy covering to help retain moisture. They tend to be small plants due to the lack of roots and tissues that would support more extensive growth.

VASCULAR PLANTS

Vascular plants have tube-like structures throughout the plant that allow them to transport materials. Unlike the bryophytes which must take water and minerals directly into their cells, vascular plants use roots to absorb water and minerals and then use their vascular system to transport nutrients to the cells and organs of the plant. **Xylem** are vessels that conduct water and minerals from the roots to the rest of the plant. **Phloem** are vessels that conduct starch and sugar from the leaves, the site of photosynthesis, to the other parts of the plant. Collectively, the xylem and phloem are called **vascular tissue**. Vascular

Figure 6.11 Types of Vascular Plants

plants are not limited in size like the non-vascular bryophytes, and they can live in drier climates.

SEEDLESS VASCULAR PLANTS

The **seedless vascular plants** produce spores and include the ferns, whiskbrooms, lycophytes and horseferns. Seedless vascular plants must live in moist environments because they are aquatic organisms for part of their lives. Only the ferns are abundant today. The stems of ferns are usually **rhizomes** which grow underground. Roots grow from the rhizome down into the soil. The leaves of the fern, called **fronds**, grow up from the rhizome and have a cuticle to help retain moisture. Ferns

Figure 6.12 Fern

reproduce using spores located in a cluster called **sori**. Sori are often found on the back of fertile fronds. Since ferns are vascular, they are not as limited in size as the bryophytes. However, because they reproduce using spores, ferns still require water to complete their lifecycle.

VASCULAR SEED-BEARING GYMNOSPERMS

Figure 6.13 Gymnosperm

Gymnosperms are non-flowering, vascular plants, many of which produce cones. The most abundant group of gymnosperms is the **conifers**. Gymnosperm seeds are located on the outside of the plant, usually on a scale of a cone. They are not enclosed in fruit. The conifers have both male and female cones. The male cones are small, and they produce

Figure 6.14 Cones

pollen. The female cones contain the ovule and are much larger. Pollen is transported by the wind to the female cones where fertilization takes place. The sporophyte stage is dominant. Conifers have needle-like leaves and are evergreen, which means they do not shed all of their leaves in the winter. Conifers include *pine trees*, *fir trees* and *redwoods*. The wood and other parts of conifers are used for lumber, paper and synthetic products such as rayon, paint thinner, varnish and plastic glues.

VASCULAR SEED-BEARING ANGIOSPERMS

Angiosperms are flowering plants, comprising the most abundant group of plants. They have roots, stems, leaves, flowers and seeds and have adapted to live almost anywhere. Their seeds are enclosed within a fruit. Many angiosperms are **deciduous**, which means they lose their leaves once a year. Most of our food comes from angiosperms, and products from flowering plants include cotton, dyes, pigments, medicines, tea and spices. Maple trees, tomato plants and rose bushes are examples of flowering plants.

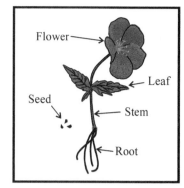

Figure 6.15 Angiosperm Structures

Roots anchor the plant, absorb water and minerals and store food. Attached to them are small projections called **root hairs,** which increase the absorbing surface of the root. At the tip of the root is a **root cap**, which consists of thick-walled dead cells that protect the growing tip as it pushes its way through the soil.

Stems are support for leaves and reproductive parts as well as protection for the transport system of the plant. In **herbaceous** plants, which are most of the annuals, the stems are flexible. In the **woody** plants which live from season to season, stems are rigid and hard. The **cambium** layer located near the vascular tissue is responsible for increasing the diameter of the stem. A protective covering of **epidermis** covers the entire plant, much like our skin. Just inside the epidermis is the **cortex**, which also helps to protect the plant.

Leaves are the factories of the plant. They use the energy from the Sun and make sugar. Their cells contain chlorophyll, which carries on the work of photosynthesis. Leaves are covered with a waxy substance called **cuticle**, which helps protect them. Tiny openings called **stomata**, usually located on the underside of the leaf, allow carbon dioxide to enter the plant and oxygen and water to escape from the plant. Transpiration is the process where plants exchange gases with the atmosphere.

Angiosperms are further divided into **monocots** and **dicots**. This grouping is based on the number of cotyledons the seed possesses, along with other characteristics. A **cotyledon** is a seed leaf that provides nutrition to the developing seed. You can think of it as the first leaf of the plant able to perform photosynthesis. **Monocots** have one cotyledon. Other monocot characteristics include parallel veins in their leaves, a fibrous root system and floral parts arranged in threes or fives. Examples of monocots are grasses, palms, lilies and orchids.

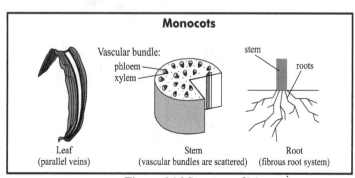

Figure 6.16 Structure of Monocots

The **dicots** have two cotyledons, net-veined leaves, a taproot system and floral parts arranged in fours or fives. A **taproot** is a large central root. Also, their vascular tissue is arranged in a circle around the outside of the stem. Most fruit trees are dicots as are roses, melons and beans.

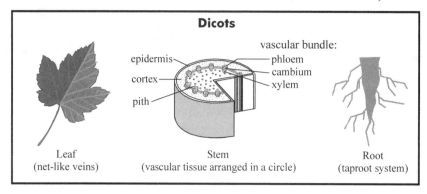

Dicots

vascular bundle:
epidermis — phloem
cortex — cambium
— xylem
pith

Leaf
(net-like veins)

Stem
(vascular tissue arranged in a circle)

Root
(taproot system)

Figure 6.17 Structure of Dicots

SEXUAL REPRODUCTION IN PLANTS

The **flower** is the reproductive organ that produces **seeds** and **pollen**. The **stamen** is the *male* structure of the flower. The **pistil** is the *female* organ of the flower. At the top of the stamen is the **anther** which produces pollen through the process of meiosis. At the bottom of the pistil is the **ovary** which undergoes meiosis to produce the **ovule**. During pollination, pollen grains stick to the top of the pistil called the **stigma**. From there, the pollen grain grows a **pollen tube** down through the **style** to the ovary where it fertilizes an ovule. The ovule develops into a seed.

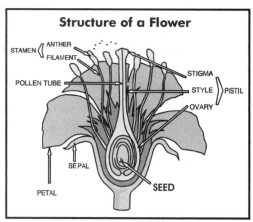

Structure of a Flower

STAMEN — ANTHER
FILAMENT
POLLEN TUBE
STIGMA
STYLE — PISTIL
OVARY
SEPAL
PETAL
SEED

Figure 6.18 Structure of a Flower

Self pollination occurs when the pollen of a flower is transferred to the stigma of the same flower. In **cross pollination**, the pollen from one flower sticks to insects which in turn deposit the pollen on other flowers. Look at the scanning electron microscope image of pollen grains shown in Figure 6.19. Pollen grains from several different types of flowers are shown.

Figure 6.19 Seven Different Types of Pollen

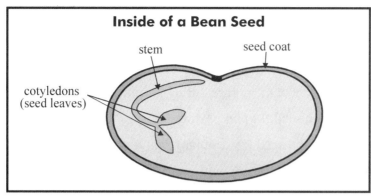

Inside of a Bean Seed

stem

seed coat

cotyledons
(seed leaves)

Figure 6.20 Germination of Seed

Germination is the process of a seed coat splitting and a young plant beginning to grow. Conditions such as moisture, oxygen and appropriate temperature must be right for germination to occur. Since water is required, it often coincides with spring rains. Moisture softens the seed coat and causes it to swell. The seedling needs oxygen to carry on respiration. Lower temperatures and darkness are needed to stimulate growth in dormant seeds.

Section Review 4: The Plant Kingdom

A. Terms

alternation of generations	root hairs	ovary	flower
gametophyte	rootcap	ovule	seeds
sporophyte	stems	stigma	pollen
spores	herbaceous	pollen tube	stamen
non-vascular plants	woody	style	pistil
cuticle	cambium	self pollination	anther
xylem	epidermis	cross pollination	taproot
phloem	cortex	germination	angiosperms
vascular tissue	leaves	dicots	roots
rhizomes	stomata	cotyledon	gymnosperms
	monocots	fronds	bryophytes

B. Multiple Choice

1. Mosses are

    A. vascular plants.   C. non-vascular plants.

    B. gymnosperms.   D. angiosperms.

2. The cuticle helps leaves

    A. have brighter color.   C. grow faster.

    B. retain moisture.   D. capture sunlight.

3. Instead of seeds, ferns produce

    A. flowers.   B. water.   C. cones.   D. spores.

4. Gymnosperm seeds are often found
   A. in a flower.
   C. on the cone.
   B. in the bark of the tree.
   D. on the root.

5. Why is it important for the seed coat to rupture during germination?
   A. It allows light to get to the seed for photosynthesis.
   B. It allows oxygen to get to the seed for cellular respiration.
   C. It enables fungi to create a relationship with the new seed.
   D. It helps animals to find the seeds and use them as a food source.

6. In cross pollination, the flower is
   A. fertilized artificially.
   C. fertilized by insects carrying pollen.
   B. sterile.
   D. fertilized by itself.

7. What flower part produces pollen?
   A. anther   B. style   C. pistil   D. stigma

8. What is the largest group of plants?
   A. bryophytes   B. ferns   C. flowering plants   D. gymnosperms

9. What plant group has net-like veins on its leaves?
   A. monocot   B. dicot   C. bryophyte   D. conifer

10. How do non-vascular plants differ from vascular plants?
    A. non-vascular plants lack xylem and phloem
    B. vascular plants lack xylem and phloem
    C. vascular plants produce spores only
    D. non-vascular plants are not limited to size.

C. Short Answer

1. Describe the difference between deciduous and evergreen trees.

2. Describe the functions of the roots, stems, leaves and flowers of plants.

3. Compare the seeds of gymnosperms to the seeds of angiosperms.

4. What is the purpose of vascular tissue in plants?

5. Why does germination usually happen in the spring?

6. If a plant were to lose its leaves in early summer, what effect might this have on the survival of the plant?

7. Without looking at the roots or leaves of a flowering plant, could you tell if it was a monocot or dicot?

INVERTEBRATES

PHYLUM PORIFERA: SPONGES

Characteristics: The sponge is the most primitive and the simplest member of the animal kingdom. It is multicellular but has a hollow body. A sponge passively absorbs food and oxygen from the water passing through its pores. Sponges reproduce both asexually and sexually. Adult sponges are **sessile**, meaning they cannot move. They attach themselves to a hard surface. All sponges live in water. Most live in ocean salt water, but some sponges have adapted to a freshwater environment.

Figure 6.21 Sponge

External Features:	
Ostia	Pores which allow water, food and oxygen to enter the hollow body.
Spicules	Hard spike-like structures that provide a framework for the sponge's body. Spicules are composed of calcium carbonate or silicon dioxide.
Epidermis	The outer cell covering of the body.
Internal Features:	
Collar cells	Specialized cells for digestion.
Amoebocytes	Internal cells that circulate nutrients and produce gametes for sexual reproduction.
Asexual Reproduction:	
Budding	The growth of a new organism on the body of the parent. This "bud" breaks off to form a new sponge.
Fragmentation	When parts of a sponge are broken off and form new sponges.
Regeneration	The ability to grow back a broken or injured part.
Gemmules	Groups of amoebocytes enclosed in a hard, protective covering that become dormant when conditions become unfavorable for growth in winter. Warmer temperatures cause the outer wall to dissolve and the amoebocyte cells develop into an immature sponge.
Sexual Reproduction:	
Hermaphrodites	Possess gonads of both sexes and as a result can produce both sperm and eggs.
Gametes	Sex cells, a generic term for either ovum or sperm.
Larva	Once an egg is fertilized in sexual reproduction, a sponge larva develops. The larva is an immature sponge not resembling the adult.

PHYLUM CNIDARIA (OR COELENTERATA): HYDRA AND JELLY FISH

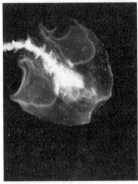

Characteristics: Cnidaria are primitive animals, but are a step above sponges. They possess a single digestive cavity, with arm-like projections around their mouths. Cnidaria have two body types: polyps, which are sessile, and medusas, which are free-swimming. They have an offensive system in the form of stinging cells, and some have a defensive system in the form of movement. Cnidaria have radial symmetry. These creatures react to their environment according to the information received through their "nerve net." They are sensitive to light variations, gravity, touch and chemicals. Cnidaria reproduce by budding, regeneration, or gametes. They can live in fresh or salt water, and live as individuals or in colonies.

Figure 6.22 Cnidarian

External Features:	
Tentacles	Projections of cells which capture food and aid locomotion.
Nematocyst	A stinging cell that contains a coiled thread which will shoot out and inject toxins into the prey. Figure 6.23 is a scanning electron microscope image of a discharged nematocyst.
Polyps	Tube-like sessile bodies
Medusas	Bell or cup-shaped free-swimming bodies.
Ectoderm	Outer layer of body covering.
Internal Features:	
Coelenteron	A cup-shaped single digestive cavity.
Radial symmetry	Regular circular arrangement of body parts around a central area.
Reproduction:	
Dioecious	Contains either male or female gonads, not both.
Regeneration	Asexual reproduction in which missing or broken parts are able to grow back.

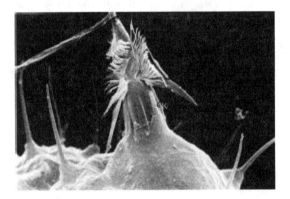

Figure 6.23 Nematocyst of Cnidarian

Figure 6.24 Flatworm

PHYLUM PLATYHELMINTHES: Flatworms (Planaria, Tapeworms, Liver flukes)

Characteristics: *Flatworm* is the common, descriptive name for three classes of primitive worms: planaria, tapeworm and liver fluke. All platyhelminthes have ribbon-like bodies with dorsal and ventral surfaces, made up of three layers of tissue. The free-living planaria have a digestive system. All can live in fresh and salt water, while only the two parasitic forms live in hosts, including humans, at some stage of development.

External Features:	
Dorsal surface	The upper surface of the body of the animal (the "back")
Ventral surface	The under surface of the body of the animal (the "belly")
Head	All flatworms have a head. On the planaria, the head is a triangular shaped front end with eyespots.
Mouth	Planaria have a mouth through which food and water enters.
Pharynx	Planaria have a pharynx, a tube-like structure in the middle of the dorsal surface.
Internal Features:	
Digestive system	**Gastrovascular cavity** – an internal organ that breaks down food into usable substances. This cavity has a single opening that serves as mouth and anus.
Excretory system	**Flame bulbs** – cells that secrete excess water and waste through pores.
Nervous system	**Eyespots** – darkened spots on the head of the dorsal surface; sensitive to touch and light. **Nerve mass** – two nerve cords and a nerve net extending throughout the length of the body.
Reproductive system	• Flatworms can reproduce asexually by **fission**. Fission is the spontaneous division of body parts which develop into new organisms identical to the parent. • Flatworms also reproduce sexually. They are **hermaphrodites**, animals that have both male and female gonads. However, they usually exchange sperm with another individual for fertilization. • Flatworms can regenerate when injured.

Harmful Features: Tapeworms and liver flukes are parasites, meaning they obtain food from other living organisms. Tapeworms live in the intestines of other animals. They absorb food from their host and reproduce rapidly.

PHYLUM NEMATODA: ROUNDWORMS (ASCARIS, TRICHINELLA, AND HOOKWORMS)

Figure 6.25 Roundworm

Characteristics: All nematodes have a digestive tract that allows food to enter through the mouth, travel down a tube-like structure and exit through the anus. All nematodes have a body cavity and muscle system around their digestive tract, giving them a cylindrical (round) shape that tapers at both ends. They reproduce sexually, being either male or female (dioecious). Nematodes can be decomposers, that consume organic matter in the soil, predators that eat other worms and each other, or parasites that inhabit both animals and humans with sickening and sometimes fatal results. They can live anywhere.

External Features:	
Anterior	Front or head end of an organism.
Posterior	Tail or back end of an organism.
Anus	Posterior opening through which wastes are removed.
Internal Features:	
Digestive System	**Digestive tube**–continuous cellular path through which food is taken in at the mouth, digested and waste is discarded out of the body through the anus.
Muscular System	Continuous group of cells which stretch and contract and provide locomotion for the organism.
Reproductive System	**Dioecious**–have male or female gonads, but not both.

Harmful Features: The ascaris worms are free-living decomposers in the soil. Some are also parasites and can be harmful to humans, animals and plants. The trichina worm is found in undercooked pork. It causes trichinosis in humans. Trichinosis is accompanied by severe pain, fever and weakness. Hookworms burrow through the skin of their host and move through the bloodstream to the intestines causing infection, blood loss and tissue damage. They can cause physical and mental retardation in children.

PHYLUM ANNELIDA: SEGMENTED WORMS (EARTHWORMS, POLYCHAETES AND LEECHES)

Characteristics: There are three classes of Annelida. The two most familiar are the earthworm and the leech. The third class of annelids is the polychaete worms. These segmented worms live exclusively in marine environments. Mostly, they live buried in sediment at the bottom of the ocean. All the annelida have segmented bodies, allowing for improved movement; and a coelum, allowing space for more

Figure 6.26 Annelid

complex body systems. Leeches and earthworms are hermaphrodites, though they usually do not fertilize their own eggs. Polychaete worms are sexually dioecious, with separate male and female. They have a complete digestive system with specialized organs, a closed circulatory system, tube-like hearts that pump blood, an incomplete excretory system, a two layered muscular system and a nervous system that responds to the environment: light, touch, chemicals and temperature.

External Features:	
Segmented	Body is divided into ring-like sections.
Prostomium	Small lip on the anterior end covering the mouth.
Skin	Epidermal covering of the body.
Setae	Pair of bristles located on body segments enabling worms to move.
Clitellum	Swollen area near the anterior which produces a cocoon to collect eggs and sperm as they are released from the body
Bilateral symmetry	Right and left sides are a mirror image of each other
Internal Features:	The annelids have a coelom–a fluid-filled body cavity.
Digestive System	**Pharynx** – muscular cavity at the rear of the mouth **Esophagus** – tube connecting the mouth to internal digestive organs **Crop** – thin-walled storage structure **Gizzard** – thick-walled structure where food is ground up by muscle action **Intestines** – area where food diffuses into the blood
Circulatory System	**Aortic Arch** – five tube-like hearts that pump blood into two main tubes, which extend through the body **Blood** – fluid that transports food through body and removes waste
Excretory System	**Nephridia** – organs located in the segments of the earthworm. Nephridia collect waste materials and excrete the waste through pores on the surface of the body
Nervous System	**Ganglia** – bulb-like enlargements of nerve tissue, making up the "brain" of small animals **Nerve cords** – a series of cells which extend the length of the body and carry nerve impulses between the body and the ganglia
Muscular System	Two layers of cells: one layer runs lengthwise throughout the body, and the other layer is circular around the body to aid locomotion
Reproductive System	The **clitellum** is part of the reproductive structure that secretes fluid and forms a cocoon where the eggs are deposited

Helpful Features: Earthworms play an important role in the environment. They loosen and aerate soil as they feed on decaying matter. They are a source of food for birds and other animals. Leeches are used both in alternative medicine practice and in the development of synthetic medicines, using the substances that they secrete. One substance is a powerful anticoagulant, and another is considered to be a defense against the spread of some cancers. Contrary to popular belief, cutting an earthworm in half does NOT result in two earthworms; it merely kills the earthworm. Segmented worms, including earthworms, can regrow some lost segments, but usually no more than 4 – 10 segments of the tail.

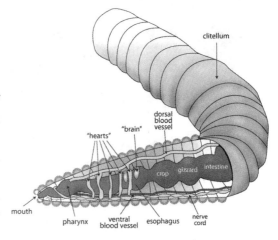

Figure 6.27 The Digestive System of a Worm

PHYLUM MOLLUSCA: MUSSELS, CLAMS, OYSTERS, SQUID, OCTOPUS, SNAILS

Characteristics: All mollusks have soft bodies arranged in three distinct parts: the head-foot, which encases movement and sensory organs; the visceral mass, containing organs of digestion, excretion (together known as "guts") and reproduction; and a mantle, specialized tissue forms a shell. The shells, themselves, are specialized. Bivalves are hinged with a bendable ligament: clams, mussels, etc.; univalves are one solid piece: snails, slugs, etc. The class of Cephalopoda typically have thin internal shells (the octopus and squid). All mollusks have bilateral symmetry, coelom, reproduce by gametes and are found in fresh water, in salt water or on land.

External Features:	
Mantle	Membrane covering the visceral mass (Some secrete a hard covering or shell.)
Foot	Muscular extension used for locomotion and burrowing
Univalve	Having a one-part shell
Bivalve	Having a two-part shell
Internal Features:	
The main part of the mollusk containing the gonads, digestive system, excretory organs, and heart are found in the visceral mass.	
Digestive System	Mollusks have a **radula** which is a tongue-like structure used for scraping food from an object.
Circulatory System	Features similar to a heart-like organ, vessels and open space in the coelom
Nervous System	Mollusks have small organs sensitive to light called **eyespots**

Mollusks, in general, are known for their muscular "foot" that propels them through ocean sand or garden dirt. However, cephalopods (squid and octopus) propel themselves by water expulsion through their mantle cavities. They are active predatory animals, displaying complex intelligence.

PHYLUM ECHINODERMATA: STARFISH, SEA URCHINS, SEA CUCUMBERS

Figure 6.28
Echinoderm

Characteristics: These creatures, named for their "spiny" skin, are adapted to life in salt water. They reproduce by regeneration and gametes. They lack a well-defined head region and are formed with radial symmetry (though they develop from bilaterally symmetrical larvae). While they lack blood vessels and an excretory system, all echinoderms have tube feet and a unique water-vascular system. In *Echinodermata*, the water-vascular system acts as a circulatory, excretory and respiratory system. This system is used in locomotion, transport of food and waste and in respiration (much like gills in fish). The water-vascular system uses muscle contractions to force water into specified canals within the Echinoderm's body. This system is very potent, but very slow. The unique combination of water canals and muscular contractions allow some members of the phylum, particularly the starfish, to pry open mollusk shells for food. In order to consume the mollusk, the starfish extends its stomach inside out, into the mollusk shell and then digest the animal while it is still alive.

External Features:	**Endoskeleton** – small calcium plates covered with the epidermis
	Tube feet – small suction organs on their underside used for holding and locomotion
Internal Features:	**Water-vascular system** – (described in the characteristics) made up of a series of ring and radial canals through which water passes

PHYLUM ARTHROPODA

Characteristics: Arthropods are invertebrate animals with **exoskeletons**. An exoskeleton is like an outside skeleton that gives the animal support and protection. Because the exoskeleton is on the outside and does not grow, arthropods must periodically **molt**, shedding their exoskeletons. All arthropods have jointed appendages. They have complex digestive systems and an open circulatory system, meaning blood is not contained in vessels. Classes of arthropods include crustaceans, arachnids, diplopods, chilopods and insects.

Figure 6.29
An Arachnid

Class: Crustacean (Crayfish, Lobster, Shrimp, Crab)

Figure 6.30 A Crustacean

Characteristics: Crustaceans have a hard covering, jointed legs, bilateral symmetry, ventral nervous system, dorsal heart and three part body cavity made of head, thorax and abdomen. The head and thorax are fused together and called the cephalothorax. The sensory organs include the antennae and antennules. Crustaceans have well-developed jaws, called mandibles, that move laterally (from side to side). Aquatic crustaceans have a tail to aid in locomotion through water. Crustaceans can live in fresh water, salt water and on land. They reproduce by gametes and most develop from larvae.

External Features:	
Jointed legs	Appendages attached to the abdomen adapted for gathering food, chewing, sensing the environment and aiding in reproduction
Carapace	A hard protective outer shell which covers the head and thorax
Cephalothorax	A fused head and middle section
Antennae	An organ which extends from the head, used for touch
Antennules	Short appendages used for touch, taste, and balance
Mandibles	True jaws for crushing food
Maxillae	Two mouth parts used for holding food
Internal Systems:	
Respiratory System	All, even the ones that live on land, have **gills** for breathing.
Circulatory System	**Arteries** carry blood from the heart to the other organs in the body. The blood then leaves the arteries and flows in the spaces between the body organs and then to the gills to exchange carbon dioxide for oxygen. It then returns to the heart.
Excretory System	Crustaceans have excretory organs called **green glands** which remove excess water and wastes from the blood.
Nervous System	Crustaceans have a fused **ganglia** that branches into nerves to the compound eyes, antennae and antennules. Compound eyes have many lenses which detect light and motion. Two nerves run around the esophagus and join the ventral nerve cord which extends down the length of the body.

Class: Insecta (Beetles, Flies, Crickets, Grasshoppers, etc.)

Figure 6.31 Insects

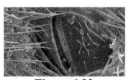

Figure 6.32
Spiracle on Cricket

Characteristics: This class of arthropods has hard bodies, three body sections and three pairs of jointed legs. Insects are classified according to the type of mouth parts they have. They have only one pair of antennae and a trachea. Insects undergo complete or incomplete metamorphosis in their development. Most insects have wings, biting mouth parts and legs. The image to the right is a scanning electron microscope image of the spiracle of a cricket.

External Features:	
Head	Contains one pair of antennae, compound eyes and mouth parts
Thorax	Midsection has three parts: first, a pair of legs; second, a pair of legs and forewings; and a pair of legs and hind wings
Abdomen	Back part of the body used for egg laying in females
Legs	Appendages used to move insect.
Internal Systems:	
Digestive System	**Labrum** – upper lip **Labium** – lower lip **Gastric caeca** – Glands in the stomach that secrete enzymes **Rectum** – an enlargement at the end of the intestine
Respiratory System	**Air sacs** – structures that pump air into the trachea **Trachea** – main air tube from the pharynx to the lungs **Tracheoles** – fine branches of the trachea, which carry oxygen and carbon dioxide to and from the body cells **Spiracles** – openings in the abdomen through which air is exchanged
Circulatory System	Vessel called the **aorta** which carries blood from the heart to the head
Excretory System	**Malpighian tubules** remove wastes from the blood
Nervous System	Includes a brain and a ventral cord made of a chain of ganglia that extends to all parts of the body. In addition to compound eyes, insects have a hearing organ called the **tympanum**. The tympanum is a membrane that is vibrated by sound waves.
Reproductive System	Insects reproduce sexually **Testes** – male reproductive organs which produce sperm **Ovaries** – female reproductive organs which produce egg **Seminal receptacles** – a sack-like structure that stores sperm **Ovipositor** – structure at the rear of a female that is used to lay eggs

Special Features:	
Metamorphosis	Process in which an insect goes through stages of development as it matures into an adult. In complete metamorphosis, an insect goes through four phases: egg, larva, pupa and adult. In incomplete metamorphosis, an insect goes through three stages: egg, nymph and adult.
Nymph	Stage of development in incomplete metamorphosis between egg and adult. Nymphs look like adults, but do not have wings or reproductive organs.
Larva	Stage of development in complete metamorphosis when the insect hatches from the egg. Larvae are worm-like and do not resemble adults.
Pupa	Stage of development in complete metamorphosis between the larva stage and the adult stage. During the pupa stage, the insect usually forms a cocoon in which its body is transformed into the adult.
Cocoon	Silky structure around the pupa of an insect
Chrysalis	Another name for the pupa of an insect

Helpful Features: Some insects are beneficial to humans. Bees pollinate plants and produce honey. Figure 6.33 is a bee pollinating a flower. Here you can clearly see the pollen basket loaded with pollen being transported from one flower to another. Some insects are used to control the population of other insects.

Harmful Features: Some insects are harmful to humans. They bite, sting, spread disease and destroy crops.

Adaptive Characteristics: Bees and ants have highly organized societies like the bees and ants. Each member has a special job that is necessary for the survival of the colony. This arrangement

Figure 6.33 Bee with Pollen Basket

is called **division of labor**. Some insects have defense mechanisms, such as mimicry, or producing chemical scent or having a bad taste.

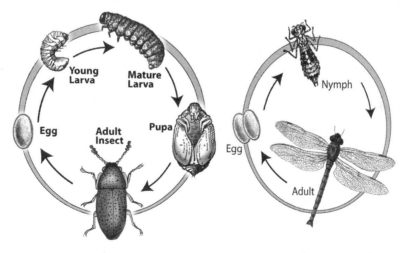

Complete Metamorphosis   Incomplete Metamorphosis
Figure 6.34 Metamorphosis

Section Review 5: Invertebrate

A. Terms

ostia	ventral surface	univalve	antennae
spicules	posterior	bivalve	mandibles
hermaphrodites	setae	radula	tympanum
nematocyst	bilateral symmetry	eyespot	ovipositor
polyps	crop	tube feet	metamorphosis
medusas	gizzard	water vascular	nymph
ectoderm	nephridia	system	pupa
radial symmetry	ganglia	exoskeletons	cocoon/chrysalis
dioecious	mantle	molting	division of labor
dorsal surface	foot	carapace	cephalothorax

B. Multiple Choice

1. The simplest animal is a/an

   A. earthworm   B. sponge   C. eel   D. canary

2. Flukes are parasitic and have a complex life cycle with at least two hosts, often humans and water snails. How do they cause infection in humans?

   A. They travel through the digestive tract creating tumors along the way.

   B. They wrap around hair and pull it out.

   C. They cause blindness by laying eggs on eyes.

   D. They lay eggs in the bladder and cause tissue damage.

3. Starfish have special structures that help them climb and obtain food. These structures are called

   A. bivalves.   B. segments.   C. tube feet.   D. exoskeletons.

4. Which class has the most members?

   A. Arthropoda   B. Insecta   C. Arachnida   D. Crustacean

5. The only invertebrates with the ability to fly are

   A. arachnids.   B. crustaceans.   C. insects.   D. mollusks.

C. Short Answer

1. Why do garden plants thrive in soil that has many earthworms?

2. Name a roundworm that causes illness in humans. How does a person contract the illness? How could the illness be prevented?

3. What are the stages of complete metamorphosis and incomplete metamorphosis? Describe the similarities and differences between a larva and a nymph.

Vertebrates

PHYLUM CHORDATA

All fish, amphibians, reptiles, birds and mammals belong to this phylum. Fish, amphibians and reptiles are **ectothermic** animals. Their body temperature fluctuates with their surroundings. Birds and mammals are **endothermic**. These animals maintain their body temperature through metabolism and the use of fur or feathers.

Characteristics: Members of this phylum have a **notochord**, a firm but flexible rod that provides stability for the body. This notochord often transforms into a vertebral column in later stages of life. A hollow nerve tube is positioned on the dorsal side above the notochord. At some point in development, all chordates also have **gill slit** structures, sometimes called pharyngeal pouches. All chordates also have a postanal **tail**. In some chordates, the tail disappears during the embryonic stage. Different classes of chordates have adapted to live in salt water, fresh water, land and air. All have highly developed body systems: an **endoskeleton** (internal skeleton) made of bones, cartilage or both; a **closed circulatory system;** and a well developed **nervous system** containing brain, spinal cord and nerves which help them to respond to their environment.

Class: Osteichthyes (Bony Fish)

Figure 6.35 Bony Fish

Characteristics: This class is well-adapted to life in the water. They have streamlined bodies for ease of locomotion in water; scales for protection and flexibility; fins for balance and movement; a swim bladder for maneuverability in depths and an oxygen source; **a lateral line** system that senses changes in water pressure and detects external obstacles; and bones, plus the notochord, for stability and body structure. With a few exceptions, fish are ectothermic. Fertilization is largely an external process; however, some fish have internal structures that allow for fertilization within the body of the fish and allow the fish to bear live offspring.

External Features:	
Scales	small, flattened bony plates forming a body covering
Fins	wing-like structures that aid locomotion and balance
Internal Systems:	
Digestive System	complete digestive system
Respiratory System	**gills** absorb dissolved oxygen from water
Circulatory System	two-chambered heart
Excretory System	**kidney** which is an organ that filters the blood and removes nitrogenous waste and excess water
Nervous System	two-part brain
	Cerebellum – part of the brain that controls muscles and balance
	Medulla oblongata – part of the brain that controls involuntary actions
Skeletal System	flexible cartilage of the notochord, present as an embryo is replaced by bone. A bony skeleton give support and protection to internal organs.

Special Features: Fish have a **swim bladder**, which is a sac-like organ that fills with air enabling the fish to float.

Class: Amphibia (Frogs, Toads, Salamanders, etc.)

Characteristics: Amphibians have adapted to life on land and in water. Amphibians are also ectothermic like fish. Their smooth skin absorbs essential moisture and gases. This thin skin must be kept moist by mucus glands, preventing the amphibian from drying out. The moist skin also helps in respiration and has pigment cells. An amphibian life cycle begins by external fertilization (the release of sperm and eggs into water). The fertilized eggs hatch into larvae. In the case of frogs and toads, the larvae are called tadpoles. Tadpoles have gills and a tail in the

Figure 6.36 Amphibian

early stages of development. During metamorphosis, which occurs in the aquatic atmosphere, tadpoles develop legs and lungs and move onto land as adult frogs or toads.

External Features:	
Pigment	coloring matter in the cells
Mucus	thick liquid produced by cells for moistening skin
Internal Systems:	
Digestive System	complete digestive system **Tongue** – a muscular organ attached to the front of the mouth used for obtaining food **Cloaca** – a chamber where the digestive, excretory and reproductive organs empty their contents to be expelled from the body
Respiratory System	Amphibians breath through the skin, the lining of the mouth when inactive, and through the lungs when active. **Nares** – external openings to the olfactory nerves for smelling **Glottis** – an opening in the pharynx leading to the larynx **Larynx** – a structure for making noise at the entrance of the trachea
Circulatory System	three-chambered heart pumps blood between heart and body and between heart and lungs. Vessels carry blood to and from cells of the body.
Excretory System	**Kidney** – an organ which filters the blood and removes nitrogenous wastes and excess water. **Bladder** – a sack-like structure which holds liquid wastes from the kidney
Nervous System	Brain is more developed than in the fish. The nervous system is composed of a brain and a spinal cord. Sense organs are incompletely developed for hearing, smelling, tasting, and seeing. **Eustachian tube** – a canal connecting the middle ear to the mouth cavity. **Tympanic membrane** – a membrane that functions as an eardrum which picks up vibrations from the air
Muscular System	highly developed in all amphibians in the case of the frog, powerful muscles in the back legs adapted for jumping.
Reproductive System	a complete reproductive system exists with dioecious individuals
Skeletal System	skull and nine vertebrae enclose the brain and spine, respectively **Pectoral girdle** – bony structure that supports the front legs **Pelvic girdle** – bony structure that supports the hind legs

Class: Reptilia (Snakes, Lizards, Turtles, etc.)

Characteristics: Reptiles are adapted to a life spent, for the most part, on land. Their body system adaptations include the following. They have a completely internal fertilization system, a respiratory system dependent upon bringing air through lungs, the body support system of a bony endoskeleton and dry, scaly skin covering the body which resists drying out. Most reptiles lay **amniotic eggs** also called "land eggs" which have tough, leathery shells that resist drying out. Amniotic eggs are filled with a developing embryo and fluids to feed it. Reptiles are ectothermic and have developed responses to protect themselves from the effects of extreme

Figure 6.37 Reptile

temperatures. Many of these animals have claws and well developed jaws and teeth for defense.

Class: Aves (Birds)

Figure 6.38 Bird of Paradise

Characteristics: All birds have feathers, which distinguishes them from any other animal. Feathers are an obvious adaptation that give birds the ability to fly; however, there are other important features which contribute to this ability, like hollow bones, internal air sacs, and streamlined bodies. They have a variety of beak, wing and claw structures, depending on their environment. Water birds are adapted to swim or wade. Birds of prey have hooked claws, powerful beaks and keen sight. Flightless birds live all over the world. They have strong legs and feet. The beak of a bird is a physical adaptation that fits its diet and habitat. Birds have complex and highly developed systems: a respiratory system with lungs, a circulatory system with a four-chambered heart and a nervous system, giving birds excellent eyesight, and in some birds, the ability to migrate. Birds are one of only two classes of animals that are endothermic, (warm blooded) the other being mammals. They are internally fertilized and produce amniotic eggs. A bird's chief feature, it's feathers, are not only structures for movement and warmth, but function as camouflage and for attracting mates.

Class: Mammalia (Mammals)

Characteristics: Mammals are the other class of endothermic animals. All mammals produce milk for their young and have fur, in varying amounts, covering their bodies. Mammals have complete and highly specialized systems. They have a four-chambered heart, a complex brain that reacts not only through instinct but also learns through interaction with the environment, a reproductive system structured for internal fertilization and most often give birth to live young. The young usually have an extended time of parental care. Almost all mammals have two pairs of limbs. Mammals also have teeth of different shapes, adapted to their diets.

Figure 6.39 Tibetan Fox

External Features:	
Differs according to their Order, Family, Genus and species.	
Internal Systems:	
Digestive System	complete digestive system
Respiratory System	This system consists of lungs, trachea, bronchi, bronchioles, air sacs and alveoli
Circulatory System	Blood circulates through the body in a series of arteries, capillaries and veins
	Arteries – tube-like vessels that carry blood away from the heart
	Aorta – the major artery that carries blood away from the heart
	Capillaries – blood vessels that connect arteries and veins
	Veins – blood vessels that carry oxygen-depleted blood to the heart
Excretory System	complete excretory system
Nervous System	highly specialized
	Cerebral hemisphere – the division of the brain into right or left side which controls a part of the body
	Cerebrum – part of the brain that controls the senses, thought and conscious activities of the body
Reproductive System	Highly developed to provide protection and nourishment for the developing young within the body of the female
Skeletal System	complete skeletal system

Adaptive Characteristics of Mammals: Monotremes are mammals that lay eggs. Marsupials are mammals that carry their young in pouches. Placentals are mammals with a placenta that enables the young to develop while protected inside the mother's body. The young mammal, an embryo, is implanted in the uterus and has a certain gestation period, depending on the size and number of offspring. Most mammals provide parental care for their young. Other adaptations include the following: limbs of different kinds of mammals are adapted to moving in different environments; teeth of different mammals are adapted to eating different foods; and migration and hibernation are two ways that mammals adapt to changes in weather.

SEXUAL REPRODUCTION IN ANIMALS

1. Animals producing gametes that are fertilized externally do so in large masses. Female frogs and fish lay eggs in water. Males deposit their sperm onto the eggs. **Fertilization** takes place in the water and depends on the chance meeting of the egg and sperm. Therefore, the more gametes produced by each parent, the more likely that fertilization will occur.

2. Animals producing **gametes** that are fertilized internally are much more certain of offspring being produced. Since the **zygotes** of these animals are usually carried internally, space for growth is limited. The females of these animals produce only a small number of gametes at a time.

3. The release of gametes is controlled by the hormone level in the animal. The **pheromones** (chemical Messengers) released by some animals can attract mates. **Photoperiod** is the environmental factor of light that triggers hormonal surges in females and causes **estrus,** or the period known as "heat."

4. Several hormones in humans are responsible for the release of gametes and the receptivity of the male to promote fertilization. Both sexes release **luteinizing hormones (LH)** and **follicle-stimulating hormones (FSH).** In **males, testosterone** and **gonadotropin** are needed for gamete production. In **females, progesterone** and **estrogen** are needed in preparation for the implantation of the embryo.

ASEXUAL REPRODUCTION IN ANIMALS

Asexual reproduction is the ability of an organism to reproduce itself without producing sperm and egg. Asexual reproduction occurs in lower forms of animals. Organisms in the phyla Porifera, Cnidaria and Platyhelminthes can reproduce asexually by cell division, budding, regeneration or fission.

Section Review 6: Vertebrate

A. Terms

notochord	sweat glands	endoskeleton	amniotic egg
gill slits	lateral line	keel	sebaceous glands
ectothermic	swim bladder	endothermic	uterus
mammary glands	external fertilization	internal fertilization	placenta

B. Multiple Choice

1. Fish have a unique sense organ that runs the length of the body, is sensitive to pressure changes, and gives them the ability to detect movement. This organ is called the

    A. notochord. B. vertebrae. C. lateral line. D. scales.

2. If an animal does not maintain a constant body temperature and has a body temperature similar to its environment's, the animal is

    A. ectothermic. B. endothermic. C. a scavenger. D. a parasite.

3. Frogs, salamanders and toads are

    A. reptiles. B. amphibians. C. arthropods. D. mammals.

4. Birds and mammals are able to maintain a constant internal temperature because they are

    A. ectothermic. B. endothermic. C. carnivorous. D. cold-blooded.

5. An example of an egg-laying mammal is

    A. a kangaroo. B. a platypus. C. an elephant. D. a bat.

6. The group of mammals whose offspring are delivered very early in development, and complete development in a pouch, are

    A. monotremes. B. marsupials. C. placentals. D. reptiles.

USING A DICHOTOMOUS KEY

The identification of biological organisms can be performed using tools such as the **dichotomous key**. A dichotomous key is an organized set of questions, each with yes or no answers. The paired answers indicate mutually exclusive characteristics of biological organisms. You simply compare the characteristics of an unknown organism against an appropriate dichotomous key. The key begins with general characteristics and leads to questions which indicate progressively more specific characteristics. By following the key and making the correct choices, you should be able to identify your specimen to the indicated taxonomic level.

An example using known organisms follows: Pick an organism and follow the key to determine its taxonomic classification.

PICK AN ORGANISM

1. Does the organism have an exoskeleton?

    Yes... Go to question 2.
    No... Go to question 4.

2. Does the organism have 8 legs?

    Yes... It is of Class Arachnida, Order Araneae.
    No... Go to question 3.

3. Does the organism dwell exclusively on land?

    Yes... It is of Phylum Arthropoda, Subphylum Crustacean, Class Malacostraca, Order Isapoda, Suborder Dniscidea.
    No... Go to question 4.

4. Does the organism have an endoskeleton?

    Yes... Go to question 5.
    No... Go to question 6.

5. Does the organism dwell exclusively in the water?

    Yes...Go to question 6
    No... Go to question 7

6. Does the organism have stinging tentacles?

    Yes... It is of Phylum Cnidaria, Class Scyphozoa
    No... Go to question 7.

7. Does the organism have 5 legs?

    a. Yes... It is of Phylum Echinodermata, Class Asteroidea
    b. No... Go to question 8.

8. Does the organism carry live young in a pouch?

    a. Yes... Go to question 9.
    b. No... Go to question 10.

9. Does it climb trees?

    a. Yes... It is of Class Mammalia, Subclass Marsupialia, Order Diprodonia, Suborder Vombatiformes.
    b. No... It is of Class Mammalia, Subclass Marsupialia, Order Diprodonia, Suborder Phalangerida, Genua Macropus

10. Is the organism a mammal?

    a. Yes.... Go to 11.
    b. No... It is of Phylum Chordata, Class Actinoptergii, Order Perciformes, Family Scrombridae, Genus Thunnus

11. Does the adult organism have teeth?

    a. Yes... It is of Phylum Chordata, Class Mammalia, Order Cetacea, Suborder Odontoceti.
    b. No... It is of Phylum Chordata, Class Mammalia, Order Cetacea, Suborder Mysticeti.

Were you able to identify all the animals? If not, one glitch might be that some of these sub-categories go beyond the knowledge that has been outlined in our text. These are easily investigated by going online and searching simply for the animal name. You will be surprised at how much you learn.

Practice Exercise:

Try this as a practice exercise: Use Wikipedia®, the free encyclopedia (online at http://en.wikipedia.org/) to search the term Vombatiformes. If you answered the questions in the dichotomous key correctly, you know that one member of this sub-order is the koala. There is only one other member of this sub-order; all the others are extinct. Find out what other animal belongs to the sub-order Vombatiformes.

CHAPTER 6 REVIEW

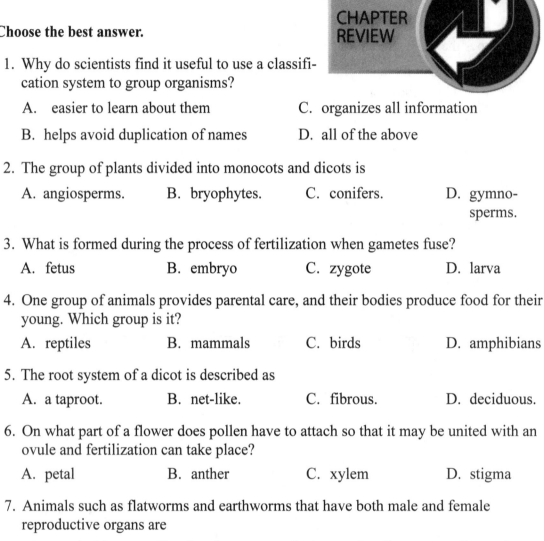

CHAPTER
REVIEW

Choose the best answer.

1. Why do scientists find it useful to use a classification system to group organisms?

    A. easier to learn about them

    B. helps avoid duplication of names

    C. organizes all information

    D. all of the above

2. The group of plants divided into monocots and dicots is

    A. angiosperms.   B. bryophytes.   C. conifers.   D. gymnosperms.

3. What is formed during the process of fertilization when gametes fuse?

    A. fetus   B. embryo   C. zygote   D. larva

4. One group of animals provides parental care, and their bodies produce food for their young. Which group is it?

    A. reptiles   B. mammals   C. birds   D. amphibians

5. The root system of a dicot is described as

    A. a taproot.   B. net-like.   C. fibrous.   D. deciduous.

6. On what part of a flower does pollen have to attach so that it may be united with an ovule and fertilization can take place?

    A. petal   B. anther   C. xylem   D. stigma

7. Animals such as flatworms and earthworms that have both male and female reproductive organs are

    A. arachnids.   B. dioecious.   C. hermaphrodites.   D. angiosperms.

8. Beetles, bees and flies have a larval stage in their development in which the young organisms look very different than their adult counterparts. These insects then enter a pupal stage where marked changes in body form take place after which an adult emerges. This type of development is

    A. incomplete metamorphosis.

    B. complete metamorphosis.

    C. placental.

    D. differentiation.

9. The organ that some fish have that has better adapted them to life in water by making them virtually weightless and, therefore, decreasing the amount of energy needed for movement is the

    A. lateral line.   B. notochord.   C. air bladder.   D. keel.

10. Water escapes from plants through tiny openings called

    A. stomata. B. root hairs. C. root cap. D. cotyledon.

11. Roots anchor plants, take in water and minerals, and

    A. make leaves. B. make water. C. store food. D. use ozone.

12. Which is the sexual phase of the alternation of generations?

    A. gametophyte B. placenta C. sporophyte D. cotyledon

13. All echinoderms live

    A. in the ocean. B. on land. C. in fresh water. D. as parasites.

14. What characteristics do all vertebrates share in common at some time in their lives?

    A. gill slits and exoskeleton C. notochord and exoskeleton

    B. spinal cord and endoskeleton D. gill slits and endoskeleton

15. Which plant group is evergreen, has seeds in a cone, and has xylem and phloem?

    A. gymnosperms B. angiosperms C. bryophytes D. gametophyte

16. Earthworms have both male and female sex organs. What are they called?

    A. nematocysts B. organisms C. hermaphrodites D. mucus

17. Since their moist, mucus-covered skin offers little protection, identify the group of animals whose health is often used by humans as an indicator of pollution.

    A. amphibians B. reptiles C. mammals D. arachnids

18. In seed-bearing plants, what is the structure that provides nutrition to the developing seed and is sometimes the first photosynthetic leaf?

    A. seed coat B. root C. cotyledon D. ovule

19. Mammals have glands that

    A. secrete oils. C. produce milk.

    B. secrete sweat. D. do all of the above.

20. The two major divisions of the kingdom Plantae are

    A. gymnosperms and angiosperms. C. mosses and ferns.

    B. vascular and non-vascular. D. monocots and dicots.

21. Viruses

    A. can eat and metabolize food.
    B. can reproduce only when inside a host cell.
    C. can reproduce on their own at anytime.
    D. eat and metabolize food only when inside a host cell.

22. The special tissue that produces a shell in mollusks is the

    A. hermaphrodite.　　B. cephalothorax.　　C. mantle.　　　D. chitin.

23. The tongue of the frog is attached to the front of its mouth. This adaptation may be beneficial to the frog for

    A. making sounds.　　　　　　C. breathing.

    B. snatching insects.　　　　　D. smelling.

24. The pectoral and pelvic girdles of the frog give it greater efficiency of movement. They serve as attachments for the

    A. neck.　　　　B. typanum.　　　　C. legs.　　　　D. cloaca.

25. Which vertebrate is MOST adapted to living on land?

    A. salmon　　　　　　　　　C. poison dart frog

    B. hammerhead shark　　　　D. iguana

26. Which phylum has a unique water-vascular system used for locomotion?

    A. annelids　　　B. arthropods　　　C. mammals　　　D. echinoderms

27. What phylum contains the simplest animal form?

    A. nematoda　　　B. annelida　　　C. cnidaria　　　D. porifera

28. What group of animals has segmented bodies?

    A. nematoda　　　B. annelida　　　C. cnidaria　　　D. porifera

29. What group of animals is classified according to the type of mouth parts it has?

    A. insects　　　B. echinodermata　　C. cnidaria　　　D. reptile

30. What is the term for the tissue that plants use to transport food?

    A. xylem　　　B. phloem　　　C. sori　　　D. pollen

31. What is the term for an egg laying mammal?

    A. placental　　　B. marsupial　　　C. monotreme　　　D. cold blooded

32. How are birds and mammals similar?

    A. They are both endothermic.　　C. They both have scales.

    B. They are both ectothermic.　　D. They both make their own food.

33. How are reptile eggs similar to bird eggs?

    A. They both have a thick shell to retain moisture.

    B. They both have a thin shell to exchange water with their environment.

    C. They both have a thin permeable shell.

    D. They both are hard.

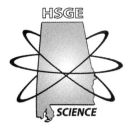

Chapter 7
Evolution

10b	Recognizing chemical and physical adaptions of plants.
12	Describe protective adaptions of animals, including mimicry, camouflage, bead type, migration and hibernation.
12a	Identifying ways in which the theory of evolution explains the nature and diversity of organisms.
12b	Describing natural selection, survival of the fittest, geographic isolation and fossil record.

BIOLOGICAL CLASSIFICATION

Scientists estimate that there may be up to 14 million different species inhabiting the planet. Approximately 1.75 million species have been scientifically named and described, including 250,000 plant species and 792,000 animal species. The variation among organisms is called **biodiversity**. Biodiversity includes ecosystem diversity, species diversity and genetic diversity.

Ecosystem diversity is the variety of ecosystems available. An ecosystem is a community of organisms and their environment. Forests, prairies, coral reefs and lakes are examples of ecosystems.

Species diversity is the number of different species of organisms. Within an ecosystem, the activities of all organisms are interwoven and interrelated. Each ecosystem is bound by a dependence between organisms within the ecosystem. The organisms that cannot adapt or no longer have a function in an ecosystem are soon gone. On the other hand, if an organism vital to an ecosystem is removed, its absence will eventually affect the entire ecosystem in some way.

Genetic diversity distinguishes among individuals within a species. Mixing of the gene pools promotes diversity and creates physical and genetic changes in the offspring. According to the theory of **evolution**, new species evolve from preexisting species over long periods of time. This evolution of new species promotes diversity. However, evolution does not always affect the entire species. Organisms within the same species may evolve differently over time, or remain unchanged, depending on their needs and environment.

Adaptation is a change in structure or function that allows an organism to be more successful. Adaptation is another way species can diversify. **Extinction** is the condition where there are no living representatives of an organism. Extinction impacts biodiversity by reducing the number of species.

CLASSIFICATION AND EVOLUTIONARY RELATIONSHIPS

We learned about taxonomy, or how organisms are classified, in Chapter 6. The question remains, what features separate organisms into differnt groups? Evolutionary relationships are the main factor when classifying living things. Most biologists assume that organisms with common traits come from a common ancestor. Scientists also use similarities in physical structures, embryo development, genetic information, reproductive strategies, nutritional strategies and biochemical similarities to classify organisms.

Anatomical similarities are evident in the study of homologous structures and vestigial organs. **Homologous structures** develop from a common ancestor and are similar in shape, but have different functions. The human arm, the wing of a bird and the flipper of a whale are all homologous structures. They contain the same bones. In fact, we see a similar pattern of limb arrangement in all land dwelling (or previously land dwelling) organisms. The limb pattern is one bone, two bones and then many bones. Biologists believe these structures come from a common ancestor. Their different functions correspond to their use in different environments. A whale uses a flipper for swimming, a bird uses a wing for flying. A human uses his arm for a variety of tasks including swimming, locomotion, and food gathering. A whale, a bird and a human all belong in the same phylum, Chordata.

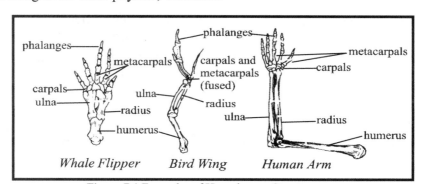

Figure 7.1 Examples of Homologous Structures

Vestigial organs, structures that are no longer used or have greatly decreased in importance, are another anatomical similarity. Whales and some snakes have a pelvis and femur, structures necessary for walking, but whales and snakes no longer have any use for these structures. These structures may have become smaller, since they are unused. Their presence also suggests a common ancestor.

Scientists agree that studying the embryonic development of an organism often leads to a greater understanding of the evolutionary history of that organism. The early development of an embryo is the most important time during its life cycle. Like laying a foundation for a house, the structures and tissues formed at the beginning of development lay the basis for many other tissues later in life. Vertebrates (organisms with a backbone or spine) pass through some stages that are similar to each other. The more closely related an organism is, the more similar its stages of development will be. The stages of embryonic development for several different organisms are shown in Figure 7.2.

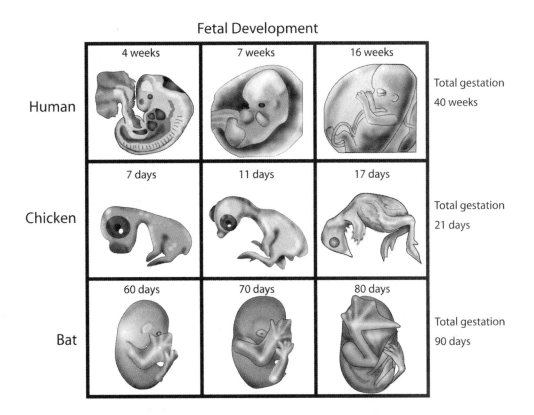

Figure 7.2 Examples of Embryonic Development

Some organisms, such as fungi and animals, are grouped partially based on their method of reproduction. Examples of distinguishing characteristics in animals include whether or not reproduction is sexual or asexual and whether or not fertilization occurs internally or externally.

Organisms are also grouped based on their nutritional strategies, or the way they acquire their food. The exception to this general rule is the kingdom Plantae, as almost all plants produce their food through photosynthesis. Most organisms in the other kingdoms are heterotrophs, meaning they feed off other forms of life. The prokaryotes and fungi both feed on dead organic matter. Animals get their food by ingestion. Nutritional strategies may also subdivide a kingdom. For example, the protists are grouped in different division based on how they store their reserve food supply.

Biochemical similarities demonstrate relationships among various organisms. DNA sequences are studied and compared. The closer the sequences, the more closely related the organisms. Humans and chimpanzees show a great deal of overlap in their DNA sequences. Humans and reptiles show some similarities, but there is less overlap than between the human and chimpanzee sequences. When the DNA from humans and yeast are compared, there is very little overlap. This suggests that humans and chimpanzees are much more closely related than humans and yeast. Another example is the horseshoe crab. The horseshoe crab was once grouped with other crabs, but is now grouped with the spiders based on genetic data.

Section Review 1: Biological Classification

A. Terms

biodiversity	adaptation	virus	homologous structure
ecosystem diversity	extinction	capsid	vestigial organ
species diversity	genetic diversity		evolution

B. Multiple Choice

1. The dodo bird was a flightless bird that became extinct in the last century. Although its disappearance had no significant recorded impact on other members of the ecosystem, it did affect one aspect of the ecosystem. What is it?

   A. the ability for other species to adapt

   B. the genetic diversity of other species

   C. the biodiversity of the ecosystem as a whole

   D. the process of evolution within the ecosystem

Use the following scenario to answer questions 2 – 3.

   Lake Lanier is a man-made lake in Georgia. The floor of the lake is filled with dead trees and construction debris remaining from the time of its construction. Over time, these items have become the natural habitat of the organisms living in the lake.

2. If a new species of fish were transferred from a natural lake to Lake Lanier, which of the following would be altered?

   A. the fish's ability to adapt   C. the ecosystem of the lake

   B. the ecosystem of the fish   D. the ability of other fish to adapt

3. The newly-transferred fish turns out to hungrily consume two other species of fish in the lake, eventually causing their extinction. What is a correct description of this circumstance?

   A. The species diversity of the ecosystem initially increased, then decreased.

   B. The genetic diversity of the ecosystem initially increased, then decreased.

   C. The genetic diversity of the ecosystem immediately decreased.

   D. The species diversity of the ecosystem immediately decreased.

4. Wisdom teeth are the common name for the third molar in humans. They generally appear much later than all other adult teeth, and usually not until the age of 18. The teeth have no noticeable purpose to the modern human and are often pulled to make room for the other teeth in the mouth. The continued presence of wisdom teeth is a good example of

A. homologous structures in humans.

C. genetic diversity in humans.

B. vestigial structures in humans.

D. adaptation to better dental care.

5. A homologous structure is not always obvious. For instance, the wings of an insect are not homologous to those of a bird, because they did not evolve from the same ancestor. However the wings of a bird are homologous to the flippers of a whale. Pick the pair that is most likely to be homologs.

A. the forelimbs of a salamander and a turtle

B. the dorsal fins of a dolphin and a shark

C. the spines of a porcupine and a sea anemone

D. the long necks of an ostrich and a giraffe

C. Short Answer

1. Name at least two types of diversity.

2. What factors influence genetic diversity?

3. Compare and contrast cells and viruses.

THE FOSSIL RECORD: MORE EVIDENCE OF EVOLUTION

The evolutionary relationships used to classify organisms give several types of evidence for evolution, such as the existence of homologous structures, vestigial organs and biochemical similarities. Fossils also provide evidence for the change in organisms over time. A **fossil** is the recognizable remains or body impressions of an organism that lived in the past. The **fossil record** refers to all fossils that have been found since the study of fossils began. Fossils are useful in determining the age of rocks. Fossils recognized as unique to certain time periods are called **index fossils**. Most fossils come from organisms that have hard body parts. Things like bone or shells will fossilize more readily than soft-bodied organisms. Generally speaking, the older the layer, the greater the difference of the organism from today's species. Thus, fossils can be used to show how organisms have changed or evolved over time.

There are many processes on the earth's surface that break down and destroy living tissue. Trees and animals rot and become food for other living creatures. Fossils are more likely to form when animals are buried very quickly. Occasionally, the conditions are right for fossil formation. Catastrophic events, like floods, mud slides, ash deposition from volcanes, and earthquakes usually lead to the formation of fossils. The rarity of fossils makes each one valuable to scientific thought. In fact, estimates indicate that the fossil record only represents about 0.1% of all the organisms that have lived on the planet. It is important to note that no one knows exactly how many organisms have lived or do currently live on Earth.

GAPS IN THE FOSSIL RECORD

Figure 7.3 Trilobite Fossil

The fossil record is an important tool scientists use when attempting to better understand the history of the Earth. However, it is important to note the record itself is not complete. There are many gaps present in the record that cause much speculation in the academic community. Most scientists agree that there are gaps in the fossil record. However, scientists are not in agreement on the explanation of these gaps. The gaps have been explained in three ways: **not all fossils have been discovered, not enough animals were fossilized** or **the theory of evolution is "not evolved enough."**

As more evidence becomes available **all** theories and ideas undergo a refinement process. Darwin was unaware of how traits were passed from the parent to the offspring. The discovery of genes helped refine the theory of evolution, showing the mechanism by which animals evolve. Recent work with DNA has helped clarify relationships among living species. As technology advances, so too will our understanding of the natural world.

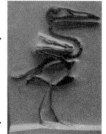

Figure 7.4 Fossil

Carbon dating is a type of **absolute dating**, which uses the rate of **radioactive decay** of isotopes to determine the age of rocks and fossils. Isotopes are elements that have the same number of protons in the nucleus but differ in number of neutrons. In some isotopes, the nuclei are unstable because the forces binding protons and neutrons together are not very strong. These nuclei break apart or decay in a process known as **radioactivity**. Unstable isotopes, called **radioactive parents**, decay and form other more stable elements called **daughter products**. This decay happens at a measurable rate. The calculation of the ratio of parent to daughter products is known as **radiometric dating**. **Half-life** is the time required for one-half of the parent isotope in a rock to decay into a daughter product. **Carbon-14** has a half-life of 5,730 years. Carbon-14 decays into its daughter product, nitrogen-14. By comparing the number of parent and daughter isotopes, a scientist can determine the age of a fossil using the known half-life of carbon-14. For example, if a fossil contains one-quarter carbon-14 isotopes, and three-quarters nitrogen-14 isotopes, then a scientist can estimate that the fossil has existed for two half lives, or 11,460 years. Other radioactive isotopes such as uranium-238, thorium-232, rubidium-87, and potassium-40 are frequently used in radiometric dating; however, their half-life is too long to determine the age of living organisms on Earth.

Based on radiometric dating of rock layers, scientists agree that Earth is around 4.55 billion years old. The oldest rocks found on Earth are 3.8 billion years old. During much of that time, only bacteria inhabited the earth. Eukaryotic cells have only developed in the past 1.8 billion years. The early atmosphere of Earth was a **reducing atmosphere** and contained no free oxygen. It consisted of gases released from volcanic activity occurring underneath the surface of Earth. As plant life developed, the process of photosynthesis resulted in the creation of atmospheric oxygen. Most of the oxygen build up in the atmosphere was a result of photosynthetic plants in the ocean, such as algae. Today's **oxidizing atmosphere** contains nitrogen, oxygen, carbon dioxide and water vapor. The idea of an ancient reducing atmosphere is supported by rock samples drilled from different layers of Earth's crust. These rocks were deposited during ancient volcanic eruptions. These rock samples contain iron that would oxidize in the presence of oxygen to form rust. The samples show no sign of rust or oxidation. As a result, scientists speculate that there was no free oxygen in Earth's early atmosphere.

The existence of animal life on land is relatively recent. Fossils indicate that insects first came onto land around 440 million years ago, and vertebrate animals moved onto land about 417 million years ago (mya).

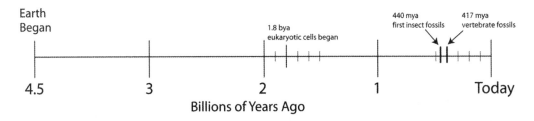

Figure 7.5 Timeline of Earth's Existence

Even though radiometric dating is called "absolute dating," it does not always produce undisputed ages of fossils. Using radiometric dating requires scientists to make several assumptions that may or may not be correct. First, radiometric dating assumes that the decay of radioactive elements is not affected by external environment. Second, it assumes the sample was isolated so that no parent or daughter isotopes were lost or added over time. Third, it assumes that the starting conditions are known. Scientists generally agree that the first assumption is valid, although some argue that certain types of decay do depend on the external environment. The second and third assumptions depend on unknown factors. Since there is no guarantee that the sample was isolated and there is no proof of the starting conditions of an ancient sample, the effect of these assumptions is not certain and may cause discrepancies in the dating process.

Section Review 2:   Fossils and the Fossil Record

A. Terms

fossil	absolute dating	radioactive parent	half-life
fossil record	radioactive decay	daughter product	reducing atmosphere
index fossils	radioactivity	radiometric dating	oxidizing atmosphere

B. Multiple Choice

1. A fossil recognized as unique to a certain time period is known as

    A. an index fossil.   C. a marker fossil.

    B. a distinct fossil.   D. a time marker fossil.

2. The Earth's oxidizing atmosphere developed as a result of

    A. a change in the gases emitted from volcanoes.

    B. the weathering of ancient rock formations.

    C. the development of oxygen-producing life forms.

    D. A and C only.

3. One event that ***does not*** lead to fossil formation is

    A. floods.   B. forest fires.   C. earthquakes.   D. mudslides.

4. When is it hypothesized that the first living organisms appeared on Earth?

    A. 3.8 billion years ago   C. 440 million years ago

    B. 1.8 billion years ago   D. 3.8 million years ago

5. It is difficult for fossils of cells to be found because

    A. none exist.

    B. humans cannot dig deep enough into the earth.

    C. no catastrophic events occurred in the ecosystems of the early Earth.

    D. they are rare because cells have no hard parts that will fossilize.

C. Short Answer

1. Explain the difference between relative dating and absolute dating.

2. Why would uranium-238 not be useful in determining the age of a mummy? What radioactive isotope would be best? Why?

3. A new rock cooling in a magma chamber contains a parent isotope with a half-life of 10 million years. If we begin with 10,000 atoms of a parent isotope, how many atoms of the parent isotope will be present after the third half-life? How much time will have passed since the magma cooled?

4. What conclusions can you draw about the completeness of the fossil record?

DEVELOPMENT OF EVOLUTIONARY THOUGHT

Scientists observe the natural world and come up with many questions. How can a rhea in South America, an ostrich in Africa and an emu in Australia look so much alike, but be different birds? How can the finches on the Galapagos Islands all have different beaks? How can sharks and dolphins have similar-looking structures when one is a fish and one is a mammal? The theory of evolution attempts to answer such questions and more.

Special creation is the belief that every organism is created by God and is not capable of undergoing change. Naturalists began to question the idea of special creation after traveling around the world and observing different plants and animals. Their observations led to new theories about how organisms may have evolved. The theory of evolution states that organisms go through a process of change over time and develop new species from preexisting ones. **Phylogeny** is the evolutionary history of one organism or a group of related organisms. Both theories of evolution and special creation continue to change as scientists study and record the phylogeny of various organisms. Most scientists, regardless of their belief in either evolution or special creation, now acknowledge that organisms have changed over time. The extent of that change is one of the differences between modern evolutionary theory and modern special creation theory. The following sections will show evidence, mechanisms and patterns of modern evolutionary theory.

DARWIN

Charles Darwin (1809–1882), who was born in England, attended Cambridge to train for the ministry after a short period of study at a medical school. While at Cambridge, he developed a passion for studying biology and geology. Through the efforts of his professors, he was able to get aboard a British science ship, the *Beagle*, bound on a five-year trip around the world.

During this trip, Darwin observed fossils on many different continents. Darwin observed and collected many different organisms from places all **Figure 7.6** Darwin around the globe. He took notes about every place he visited. One place that was of particular interest to Darwin was the Galapagos Islands off the coast of South America.

Figure 7.7 Evolution of Finches on the Galapagos Islands

Darwin noticed that all the organisms on this island looked very similar to the organisms on the South American continent, especially the finches. On the South American continent, finches only eat seeds and have very few species. Every bird Darwin saw on the Galapagos Islands was a type of modified finch. The finches were about the same size and all very similar in color. The only differences in the finches Darwin saw were their beaks and what they ate. There were finches that ate insects, seeds, plant matter, egg yolks and blood. The finches on the Galapagos Islands looked very similar to one type of finch on the South American continent, but none of the Galapagos Island types of finches were found on the South American mainland.

The types of finches seen were indeed very diverse. Darwin began to ask many questions, one of which began to plague him above all others: "How did one species change into a different species?" It is important to note that scientists in the 19th century did not know how a trait passes from one animal to its offspring; they did not know of the existence of DNA. After the trip on the *Beagle,* Darwin studied his collection of organisms as well as many different books and readings. He also talked with several domestic animal breeders.

After 20 years of study, Darwin published his book, *The Origin of Species*, in 1859. In this book, Darwin describes his theory of how one species changes into another species. According to Darwin, in all living populations of organisms there is some natural variation between individual organisms.

Darwin had repeatedly observed that environmental pressures can change how an organism interacts with its environment. He developed a theory based on these observations and called it the theory of natural selection.

Recall that the entire diet of the Galapagos finches changed in response to their isolated environment. That was a modification of behavior (eating habits) in response to environmental pressure (limited food resources). The existence of certain physical traits may also be modified over time. As the finches began to eat more varied food items, the actual function of their beaks began to change. Finches that began to eat insects needed longer beaks for digging beetles out of their burrows. Finches that ate seeds or nuts required stronger jaw muscles to crack the shells.

How did the population of finches change their beaks in response to these needs? Modern science now views the process of natural selection in this way: The finches' beaks did not change overnight, but rather over many, many generations. Among the population of beetle-eating finches, those that were born with longer, sharper beaks naturally had access to more beetles than those finches with blunter beaks. The sharp-beaked finches thrived, and had many offspring, while the blunt-beaked finches gradually died out. The sharp beak was a trait that was, in effect, *selected* by nature to thrive. The same thing happened in each finch population, until finches from a given population began to look similar to each other and different than other finches.

To be clear: the individual physical traits of a finch are not modified by the finch (his beak does not grow and change to suit his changing needs). Rather, the animals who already possess a trait that is favored by the current environmental pressures survive and pass that trait on to their offspring. This insures that, over time, the expression of the favored trait becomes more pronounced and other traits disappear. This is why Darwin's theory of natural selection is also called the **survival of the fittest**.

MODERN IDEAS

Darwin's ideas, along with Mendel's work and the work of others, have lead to modern ideas about evolution. Modern synthesis is the merging of Darwinian ideas with modern knowledge about genetics. Modern synthesis forms the foundation of ever-changing ideas about evolution. There are four important facets to know about modern evolutionary thought.

It recognizes:

1. There are several mechanisms responsible for the evolution of organisms. One of the most important is **genetic drift** (random change in genes), which occurs through natural selection, and which we will discuss in the next section.

2. Characteristics that are inherited are carried by genes, and natural variation within a population is the result of several alleles working together.

3. **Speciation** (formation of new species) is due to gradual genetic changes, and large scale evolution is the result of a lot of small scale evolution.

4. Microevolution is the process that is responsible for the variations that exist within a species, or a change in the allele frequency. The many breeds of dogs known today are good examples of microevolution. All dogs are of the genus and species *Canis lupus familious* and can therefore produce fertile offspring, with each other, but many variations are present among breeds. Consider golden retrievers and poodles. **Macroevolution** is evolution that occurs between species. The separation of a species to form two distinct species or the development of a new species from many small changes within an existing species are examples of macroevolution.

Most importantly, modern synthesis recognizes that evolution can be seen as the changes in gene frequencies of a population. Darwin saw evolution as changes in individual organisms of that population.

Section Review 3:   Development of Evolutionary Thought

A. Terms

phylogeny	genetic drift	micro evolution
survival of the fittest	speciation	macro evolution

B. Multiple Choice

1. Ideas about evolution

    A. have already been thought.

    B. are perfect and need no refinement.

    C. may change based on new data.

    D. only involve animals.

2. What is genetic drift?

    A. the random change in genes within a population

    B. the formation of new species

    C. the isolation of individual organisms of a population

    D. the ability of an organism to survive in its environment

C. Short Answer

1. Explain why natural selection is also called survival of the fittest.

2. An ecosystem is the interdependence of plants and animals and the physical environment in which they live. Suppose you had a miniature ecosystem that you could observe. Within your ecosystem, you could observe many generations of organisms. You could observe their phenotypes and their genotypes. Could you use your ecosystem to help support modern ideas about evolution? Explain.

SPECIATION

Speciation is the development of a new species. Two organisms are considered part of a different species when they can no longer breed and produce fertile offspring. Speciation can be allopatric or sympatric.

Allopatric speciation occurs when a population becomes geographically divided. Organisms can become physically isolated when a boundary such as an ocean, mountain or lake divides a population. Consequently, two gene pools exist in different environments. After several years, the genetic differences between the species become so great that new species are formed. For example, one frog species lived in a large area. Then the river they lived in was dammed, thereby creating a large lake with several islands. A new frog species developed on each of those islands.

Figure 7.8 Orchids Showing Sympatric Speciation

Sympatric speciation exists when differences in habitat, sexual reproduction or heredity isolate members of a population from one another. For example, several frog species live in the same area. One breeds in May, and the other breeds in July. These two species of frog are genetically isolated from each other because of their breeding patterns. Many rain forest orchids cannot interbreed because their flowers bloom at different times. Some animals will not breed until a characteristic behavior or scent is displayed.

MECHANISMS OF EVOLUTION

Mechanisms of evolution deal with how evolution occurs. Most scientists consider natural selection one of the most important mechanisms of evolution, but other mechanisms like mutations, gene flow and genetic drift are also significant.

NATURAL SELECTION

Naturalist Charles Darwin proposed the idea of natural selection in 1859. **Natural selection** states that organisms best suited to the environment are the ones most likely to survive and reproduce. A few important points Darwin made in his book, *The Origin of Species*, are:

- **Resources are limited in all environments**. The availability of food, water and shelter in an environment is limited. This leads to competition among organisms. **Competition** is the fight among living things to get what they need for survival. For example, moths must find food before other moths take all the food.

- **Most organisms have more offspring than the environment can support**. For example, a moth lays thousands of eggs or one tree produces millions of seeds. **There is natural variation within a population**. A **variation** is a difference in a trait between organisms within a population. Not all organisms are exactly alike. For example, not all moths are the exact same color. Another example of variation is that not all humans are the same height.

Figure 7.9 Natural Variation in Human Height

- **Natural selection is always taking place**. Organisms with traits that are the most desirable are selected to survive. Organisms in any environment have a specific fitness for that environment. **Fitness** is the ability of an organism to live, survive and reproduce in that environment. Not all of the individual animals within a population have the same fitness.

Figure 7.10 The Cheetah

Variation in physical characteristics make some organisms better suited, or more fit, to live in their environments. Much of this variation is inherited. For example, the fastest cheetah is better equipped to hunt than a slower cheetah. The faster cheetah will get more food. The most successful cheetah lives the longest and is, therefore, able to reproduce the most offspring. Scientists say that the fastest cheetahs are the most fit for their environment. This is where the idea of survival of the fittest comes from.

Inherited traits that are more versatile than others improve the chances of the organisms' survival and reproduction. For example, having long legs and a skinny body helps a cheetah stay cool. These adaptations also help the cheetah to run fast. These traits are beneficial for survival for more than one reason, making them highly likely to pass on to offspring.

An improved chance of survival allows organisms to produce offspring that will make up more of the next generation, while passing along their favorable traits. Unfavorable traits will eventually be lost since there is less reproduction among the individuals with such traits.

The slowest cheetahs will get the least amount of food and will, therefore, have a greater chance of dying. These slow cheetahs are said to be less fit, or unfit, for their environments. In many cases, the most successful traits are maintained and change very little over a long period of time. Sharks, turtles, crocodiles and ferns are examples of organisms that have successful traits that have remained virtually unchanged over millions of years.

ENVIRONMENT AND VARIATIONS

Environmental conditions also contribute to variations in traits among individuals of the same species. The size of house sparrows in North America varies depending on location. House sparrows living in colder climates are larger than those living in the warmer climates. As a general rule, the larger the body size of an animal, the more body heat it can trap or conserve.

The size of extremities, such as ears or legs in some animals, also demonstrates environmental differences. Since extremities give off heat to help cool the animals' bodies, mammals living in hot climates tend to have larger ears and longer legs than their cousins in cooler climates. An African elephant has much larger ears than an Asiatic elephant,

Figure 7.11 Desert and Temperate Rabbits

and a desert jackrabbit has much larger ears than a rabbit found in a temperate (cooler winter) climate.

Natural variation within a population allows for some individuals to survive over other individuals in a changing environment. This natural variation can eventually lead to the formation of new species, which is also called speciation.

MUTATIONS

Mutations are random changes in DNA that act as another mechanism for evolution. These changes result in a variation in traits, which then pass from one generation to the next. Mutations can be beneficial, neutral, or harmful to an organism. Mutations beneficial to the organism in a particular environment lead to furthering of the species. For example, a mutation can result in the production of an enzyme that breaks down a particular food product predominant in an area. Individuals with the expression of that gene have more food choices, giving them greater survival chances, and allowing them to be more successful. Another example could be a mutation in color pigments that leads to an individual that is a different color than the normal population.

GENE FLOW

Gene flow is the change in the occurrence of genes in a population. Population refers to the group of organisms of the same species in a given geographic area. Gene flow occurs when an individual leaves a population or a new individual joins a population. **Immigration** occurs when organisms enter into a new population, and **emigration** occurs when organisms leave a population. Gene flow tends to increase similarities of populations since individuals from different populations share their genes with

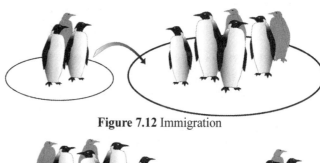

Figure 7.12 Immigration

Figure 7.13 Emigration

each other through reproduction. Emigration often leads to the formation of new species.

Gene flow happens easily in plants that have seeds carried by wind. The wind carries the seeds of a plant from one population to another population. When these new seeds grow into plants, the plants can cross-pollinate with the existing plants, and, therefore, genes from different populations are shared.

GENETIC DRIFT

Figure 7.14 Founder Birds

Genetic drift provides random changes in the occurrence of genes through chance events. These chance events can take place when a few individuals of a population break off from the original group and start their own population, also known as the **founder effect**. This is what happened with Darwin's finches. A few birds might have been blown to the Galapagos Islands during a storm. These "founder" birds remained on the island and reproduced, eventually developing into a distinct species.

Genetic drift can also occur if a large number of the population is killed because of disease, starvation, change in natural environment or a natural disaster. When this happens to a population, it is called **bottlenecking**. A large population is reduced to a few individuals, and the genes of subsequent generations become very similar.

Inbreeding between these few individuals leads to populations that have very few genetic differences. It is believed that African cheetahs went through two bottlenecks, one about 10,000 years ago and one about 100 years ago. All African cheetahs alive today are descendents of a few cheetahs, and possibly only three females. Because cheetahs are genetically similar, they have become very susceptible to diseases.

Figure 7.15 Bottleneck

PATTERNS OF EVOLUTION

The theory of evolution suggests that there is more than one way to evolve or change. These different patterns provide different paths to explain the degree of variation among organisms. Some ways that organisms evolve include convergent evolution, divergent evolution, adaptive radiation and co-evolution.

CONVERGENT EVOLUTION

Convergent evolution explains how unrelated species can develop similar characteristics. Convergent evolution is demonstrated through the porpoise and the shark. The porpoise is a mammal, and the shark is a fish. These two unrelated animals share characteristics that suit their environment: long, streamlined bodies and fins similar in both appearance and function. Another example is the bird and the butterfly. Both organisms have broad, flat wings for flying; thus, their wings are said to be **analogous**.

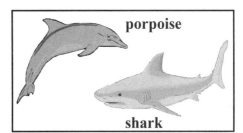

Figure 7.16 Convergent Evolution of Porpoise and Shark

Convergent evolution also occurs in the plant kingdom. Cacti and Euphorbs are both plants that look very similar and live in desert climates. They both have spines, small leaves and water storage tissues in large, fleshy stems. Cacti are found in North America and Euphorbs are found in Asia and Africa. Despite the similarity in characteristics, these plants have very different flowers and are not closely related. These organisms evolved similar characteristics to suit their specific environments.

DIVERGENT EVOLUTION

Divergent evolution suggests that many species develop from a common ancestor. The different species adapt to their particular environments. For instance, penguins and vultures are both birds. They both have wings, but the wings of a penguin are adapted to swimming, whereas the wings of the vulture are adapted to flying and gliding. The wings have the same basic form but have different functions. The vulture and the penguin *diverged* from a common ancestor.

ADAPTIVE RADIATION

Adaptive radiation is the belief that many species evolve from a single ancestral species after entering a new environment. Traits that were considered unfavorable in the old environment might now be favorable in the new one. The traits beneficial to the new environment pass on to the offspring.

An example of adaptive radiation is seen in the finches of the Galapagos Islands. Different species of finches have different beak styles based on their methods of obtaining food. Long beaks are useful for finches that dig for insects. Other finches have shorter beaks that are useful for crushing seeds (see Figure 7.5 on page 165). In the original finch population, the natural variations in beak length led to the development of several distinct finch species.

CO-EVOLUTION

Co-evolution occurs when two or more organisms in an ecosystem evolve in response to each other. Co-evolution is believed to occur frequently with flowers and their pollinators. Hummingbirds have long, narrow beaks, an attraction to the color red and a poor sense of smell. The fuchsia plant, whose flowers bloom in various shades of red, emit little fragrance and have long, narrow flowers. Fuchsias rely on hummingbirds as their pollinators. Over time, the red flowered fuchsias and the long beaked hummingbirds have had great success as partners in survival.

Section Review 4:   Mechanisms and Patterns of Evolution

A. Terms

natural selection	gene flow	founder effect	adaptive radiation
competition	immigration	bottlenecking	co-evolution
variation	emigration	convergent evolution	allopatric speciation
fitness		divergent evolution	sympatric speciation

B. Multiple Choice

1. What are the effects of genetic drift and gene flow?

    A. change in gene occurrences   C. change in DNA replication patterns

    B. change in vision acuity   D. change in organism size

2. Which of the following are patterns of evolution?

    A. structural replication, reproductive homology and special creation

    B. metabolic pathways, hormonal indicators and genetic studies

    C. modern creationism, fossil theory and punctuational model

    D. convergent evolution, co-evolution and adaptive radiation

3. If two organisms evolve in response to each other, which evolutionary pattern is demonstrated?

  A. natural selection   C. co-evolution

  B. gradualistic method   D. adaptive radiation

C. Short Answer

1. What is the difference between convergent and divergent evolution? Give an example of each.

2. Explain the theory of natural selection.

3. What is the difference between allopatric and sympatric speciation?

4. How is variation beneficial to an organism? How is it harmful?

ADAPTATIONS AND BEHAVIOR

ADAPTATION

Adaptations are structural and functional changes that make organisms better suited to their environments. Evolution suggests that plants and animals adapt in a variety of ways in an effort to protect themselves and better survive in their environment.

PLANT ADAPTATIONS

Figure 7.17 Animal Seed Dispersal

Plants cannot flee from predators, but they do have spines, thorns and leathery leaves to discourage herbivores from consuming them. Some plants manufacture chemicals that are poisonous or have a foul odor to keep animals away. Milkweed, tobacco and peyote cactus are three such plants. The Venus flytrap plant has adapted a

Figure 7.18 Wind Seed Dispersal

unique way to gather food by catching insects within its modified leaves. Many plants have also adapted means of dispersing their seeds. Plants such as the cocklebur contain seeds with small spines that adhere to the fur of passing animals. The seeds are carried away to drop and grow later. Other plants have adapted wind- or water-borne means to carry their seeds.

Mechanical stress such as wind, rain and animals have an effect on the growth of plants. Indoor plants will grow taller than outdoor plants of the same species because they are protected from the weather. Adaptations to mechanical stress include shorter, thicker stems, which helps outdoor plants withstand the stress and increases their survival chances, even if the plant's overall growth is inhibited.

ANIMAL ADAPTATIONS

Most animals have also developed some special processes of adaptation. Animals show physical, chemical and behavioral adaptations to increase their chances for survival and reproduction.

Figure 7.19 Giraffe

Physical adaptations help animals to survive and flourish in their environment. Many species living in cold weather climates grow thick fur during the winter and shed it during the summer months for a thinner coat. Camels, which typically reside in dry deserts, store large amounts of water in their bodies, particularly in their humps, for later use. Giraffes have adapted longer necks to reach high in the trees. Porcupines grow sharp quills for protection against predators. Turtles retreat inside their shells to hide. Many insects and animals have adapted **camouflage** either to hide from danger or to use in their function as a predator. For example, the praying mantis is able to blend into foliage because it looks like a green twig.

Adaptations can be easily seen by observing bird beaks. Observations about a bird's beak and/or talons can help determine the food source of that particular bird. A bird of prey like an eagle or owl has a specialized hooked beak. This type of beak is helpful in tearing flesh from bone. A fishing bird like a stork, egret or kingfisher has a long straight beak perfect for darting through the water to catch fish. A seed eating bird like a finch or a cardinal has a short, stubby, strong beak for breaking open seeds. Some birds like ducks or geese have soft, sensitive beaks for collecting food.

Chemical adaptations also help animals protect themselves and obtain food. The skunk and the bombardier beetle spray predators with irritating chemicals. Squids squirt ink to help them evade predators. Bees sting to protect their hives. Snakes use venom to immobilize prey and to protect themselves.

Some animals develop survival adaptations that **mimic** other animals. To mimic means to copy or imitate closely. Mimicry can be found visually, auditory, behaviorally or in any combination thereof. Some butterflies have large eyespots on their wings to mimic the appearance of eyes. Sometimes butterflies look like other distasteful insects. For example, the harmless Viceroy butterfly looks similar to the distasteful Monarch butterfly. Some flies mimic the coloration, shape and behavior of bees. The harmless scarlet king snake looks similar to the venomous coral snake. Some animals mimic the calls or displays of other animals to lure them into a trap. To catch prey, angler fish and alligator snapping turtles have adapted appendages that look similar to worms.

Animals use **behavioral adaptations** for survival and reproduction. Cats raise the hair on their backs and gorillas show their teeth to appear more intimidating. The opossum and some snakes play dead to avoid being eaten by predators. Territoriality is a behavioral adaptation that ensures adequate space and resources for reproduction. Courting behavior is a behavioral adaptation and helps ensure beneficial genes are passed along to offspring.

Behavioral adaptations also allow animals to communicate. Animals make sounds for a variety of reasons. Some species make noise to broadcast their locations for mating purposes. Other species make sounds to deter predators from coming close. People use sound as a way to communicate with others and transfer information.

BEHAVIOR OF PLANTS AND OTHER ORGANISMS

Response to internal and external stimuli by an organism is called **behavior**. Plants respond to stimuli in a variety of ways to increase their chances for survival.

TROPISMS

Tropisms are the growth of a plant in response to a stimulus. **Positive tropisms** are toward the stimulus, and **negative tropisms** are away from the stimulus.

Phototropism is the response to light. Light is extremely important to plants since they are photosynthetic. Photosynthetic structures, like leaves and stems, are positively phototropic. They will grow in a variety of directions to get the best possible light source. Roots are negatively phototropic. They grow away from the light source.

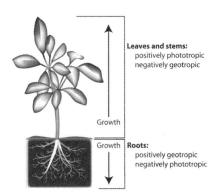

Leaves and stems: positively phototropic negatively geotropic

Growth

Growth **Roots:** positively geotropic negatively phototropic

Figure 7.20 Plant Tropisms

Geotropism is a plant's response to gravity. Roots are positively geotropic. They grow toward Earth in response to gravity. Stems and leaves are negatively geotropic.

Plants also respond to touch, called **thigmotropism**. Climbing plants, like grapevines, generally have weak stems and will wrap around another plant, a wall, a fence post or another structure for support. The tentacles of climbing plants respond to the touch of something else and wrap around the object.

OTHER PLANT BEHAVIORS

Nastic movements are the responses of plants to stimulus regardless of direction. Examples include flowers opening and closing in response to light, or mimosa leaves curling up when touched by an object or blown by wind. Carnivorous plants, like the Venus flytrap, will close in response to something touching the little hair-like structures inside their leaves, which helps them obtain food.

Plants also follow circadian rhythms. **Circadian rhythms** are behavior cycles that follow roughly 24-hour patterns of activity. Some plants fold their leaves and flowers during the night and open them during the day, to preserve water. For many plants, light stimulates growth hormones. Other plants have adapted to secreting perfumes and nectars at times when their pollinators are active, increasing chances of fertilization.

Plants can send communication signals to predators and other plants. They have the ability to secrete foul-tasting substances, so herbivores will avoid eating them. Even leaves damaged by an herbivore can secrete the chemical warning to other plants. The other plants then produce the chemical substance. The plants only secrete the protective substance when needed.

Flower blooming follows photoperiodism. **Photoperiodism** is the response of plant processes to the amount of daylight. Photoperiodism explains why plants bloom in different seasons. The amount of daylight in fall and winter is less than the amount of daylight in spring and summer. The photoperiods of various plants are summarized in Table 7.1.

Table 7.1 Photoperiods

Short-Day Plants	Flowers bloom in fall and winter. Includes ragweed, goldenrod and chrysanthemums.
Long-Day Plants	Flowers bloom in spring and summer. Includes spinach, clover and iris.
Day-Neutral Plants	Flowers bloom over a range of photoperiods. Examples include roses, tomatoes and beans.

BEHAVIORS OF UNICELLULAR ORGANISMS

Bacteria, amoeba and paramecia also have behaviors when they respond to light and chemical signals. Photosynthetic bacteria, cyanobacteria and protists gravitate toward light to ensure survival. Monerans and protists can detect chemical signals given off by food sources, ensuring their survival. Some bacteria even have magnetic crystals inside their bodies that direct their movements. One-celled organisms are also capable of avoiding negative stimuli, such as temperature and chemical changes in their environments.

ANIMAL BEHAVIOR

Ethology is the study of animal behavior. Scientists evaluate animal behavior to see how their responses relate to their goals—survival and reproduction. Behavior is broadly divided into innate behavior and learned behavior. Behavior is influenced by hormones and by the nervous system. Hormones direct certain behaviors, and the nervous system allows an animal to respond to stimuli.

INNATE BEHAVIOR

Innate behaviors are those that are under genetic control and are inherited like physical traits. Innate behaviors are animals' instincts and are performed perfectly without any learning. A baby is behaving on instinct when he or she sees a human face and smiles. Innate behavior causes a baby cuckoo bird to push an unhatched egg out of the nest so it does not have to share resources. Instinct allows a female

Figure 7.21 Geese

digger wasp to emerge from her pupa, make a nest, mate, hunt and lay eggs all within her short life span of only a few weeks.

Animals, like plants, follow circadian rhythms, which are innate behavior cycles. Some animals are active during the day. They are **diurnal** animals, like squirrels and blue jays. Animals active at night are **nocturnal**, like bats and racoons.

Figure 7.22 Bear

Some animals hibernate, estivate or migrate to escape extremes in weather. These activities are innate behaviors. **Hibernation** is a period of dormancy during cold months. When animals enter a period of **dormancy**, which is a period of biological rest or inactivity, food supplies are limited, and the animal lives off its fat stores. Metabolism, breathing and body temperature drop to conserve energy. Growth and development also cease during the dormant period. Bears hibernate in winter. **Estivation** is dormancy in hot climates. Lungfish estivate. Other animals **migrate**, or move to new locations in response to weather changes to stay close to food sources. These animals, like geese, usually follow the same routes every year.

Hormones organize and activate specific forms of innate behavior. Mating behavior in many animals and singing behavior in some birds are activated by hormones. For example, some animals, usually males, engage in elaborate rituals to lure a mate. Many male mammals fight with other males, and some birds will decorate nests, perform dances or puff up colorful feathers. The females generally select the males with the best traits, and those genes are passed along to offspring.

LEARNED BEHAVIOR

Learned behavior is a result of an animal's experiences. It allows animals to adapt, so survival chances are enhanced. There are several types of learned behaviors, and it is generally believed that only animals with complex nervous systems are capable of learning. Learned behaviors are related to life span and parental care. Animals with short life spans and little or no parental care have fewer learned behaviors. Table 7.2, summarizes these learned behaviors.

Table 7.2 Learned Behavior

Type of Learning	Description	Example
Imprinting	A rapid form of learning that occurs at a young age during a critical period of development. The animal identifies a moving object as a mother figure and follows the mother figure. The figure on which the young animal imprinted also affects which species a male will attempt to mate with.	Some birds use imprinting. If the original mother figure is not actually the bird's mother, the baby will still act as if it is. Later in life, males will try to mate with the same species of animal that he imprinted to. A rooster that imprinted to a duck will try to mate with a duck. If the rooster had been imprinted to its mother, he would have sought out hens to mate with.
Habituation	An animal learns not to respond to repeated stimulus.	Dogs stop barking at familiar people entering the house.
Reasoning or Insight	The ability to solve unfamiliar problems in a new situation. This type of learning is limited to humans and other primates.	A chimpanzee was placed in a room with bananas hanging from the ceiling and several boxes were on the floor. When he was unable to reach the bananas, he began to stack the boxes until he could reach the bananas.
Spatial or Latent	The ability of an animal to create a mental map of its environment.	Blue jays know where they have hidden food, even if food is stored in up to one hundred locations.
Classical Conditioning	An animal learns to associate a stimulus with a response that would not normally occur.	Dogs salivate when they are aware of food. The scientist Pavlov trained dogs to salivate at the sound of a bell by associating the stimulus with food. Sounds are not stimuli that normally stimulate salivation.
Operant Conditioning	An animal learns to associate an activity with a consequence.	Toads flick their tongues at flying insects, their food source. If they are stung by a bee, they learn to associate the sting with insects that have stripes, and they avoid them in the future.

Section Review 5: Animal Behavior

A. Terms

ethology   hibernation   adaptations   estivation   innate behavior
diurnal   migrate   nocturnal   learned behavior

B. Multiple Choice

1. Which of the following is true about the connection between parental care and learning?

    A. more parental care, more learned behaviors

    B. more parental care, fewer learned behaviors

    C. less parental care, more learned behaviors

    D. less parental care, all behavior is learned

2. A cat might raise the hair on its back to

    A. appear gentle.   C. attract a mate.

    B. appear intimidating.   D. conserve heat.

3. Milkweed, tobacco and peyote have adapted which type of measures to protect themselves?

    A. behavioral   B. physical   C. chemical   D. territorial

4. Why is it beneficial for some insects to be able to blend in with their surroundings?

    A. It protects them from predators.

    B. It allows them to regulate body temperature.

    C. It helps them find a mate.

    D. It protects their territory.

C. Read each statement and decide if it is a learned behavior or an innate behavior. Mark L for learned and I for innate.

1. _____ instincts

2. _____ toads avoid eating bees

3. _____ dogs no longer bark at familiar person

4. _____ migration

5. _____ baby smiling at human face

6. _____ conditioning

7. _____ imprinting

8. _____ blue jays know where to find their hidden food

D. Short Answer

1. Name two adaptations plants have developed to disperse their seeds.

2. What are some reasons that animals emit sounds?

CHAPTER 7 REVIEW

Choose the best answer.

1. Use the chart below to determine which element would be the BEST choice to determine the age of an object suspected to be less than 40,000 years old.

Radioactive Parent	Daughter Product	Half-Life
Uranium - 238	Lead-206	4.5 billion years
Krypton - 79	Bromine - 79	35.040hours
Radium - 228	Actinium - 228	6 - 7 years
Carbon - 14	Nitrogen - 14	5,730 years

   A. Uranium-238   C. Radium - 228

   B. Krypton - 79   D. Carbon-14

2. The time required for half of a parent isotope to decay into a daughter product is known as

   A. half-life.   C. parent-to-daughter reduction.

   B. measurable rate.   D. isotopic enumeration.

3. Radioactive elements change into other elements by

   A. molecular collision.   C. combustion.

   B. decay.   D. reduction.

4. Radioactive decay

   A. occurs at a predictable rate.   C. slows when pressure is added.

   B. speeds up when temperature rises.   D. occurs only in the sun.

5. Evidence of evolution includes

   A. cave drawings, ancient stories and ceremonial rites.

   B. homologous structures, DNA, and embryonic evidence.

   C. eukaryotes, symbiosis and competition.

   D. nephrons, antibodies and homeostasis.

6. Two different organisms have anatomically similar structures that are believed to have originated from a common ancestor. The functions of the structures are different as a result of the environments in which the organisms live. These anatomically similar structures are

   A. vestigial.   B. mutations.   C. homologous.   D. tropisms.

7. Natural selection states that individuals

   A. with adaptive traits are more likely to survive.

   B. on the bottom level of a hierarchy have the greatest reproductive success.

   C. demonstrating altruistic behavior are the ones with the most mutations.

   D. remain unchanged over a period of time.

8. A mountain, ocean or ravine divides a population. After many years, the organisms show genetic differences from the original population. Which of the following explains how this change occurred?

   A. sympatric speciation

   B. natural selection

   C. co-evolution

   D. allopatric speciation

9. Humans have an appendix, a thin tube connected to the large intestine that serves no purpose and is a threat to human health and life if it becomes infected and/or inflamed. It is believed that the appendix once had a function as part of the human digestive system. The human appendix, therefore, is

   A. a homologous structure.

   B. a vestigial organ.

   C. a vital organ.

   D. a mutation.

10. Biochemical similarities exist among organisms and indicate relationships. These biochemical characteristics are studied using

   A. observations of plant and animal behavior.

   B. fossil records.

   C. observations of various cells under a microscope.

   D. DNA sequences.

11. The evolution of brown bears and polar bears is an example of

   A. co-evolution.

   B. convergent evolution.

   C. divergent evolution.

   D. parallel evolution.

12. Certain insects and plants evolving in tandem is an example of

   A. co-evolution.

   B. convergent evolution.

   C. divergent evolution.

   D. parallel evolution.

13. Sharks and whales are an example of

   A. co-evolution.

   B. convergent evolution.

   C. divergent evolution.

   D. parallel evolution.

14. Increased use of antibiotics has killed off bacterial populations that were most susceptible to antibiotic treatment. Consequently, many strains of bacteria are resistant to prescription drugs. What is the mechanism by which these resistant bacteria have been allowed to thrive?

    A. natural selection

    B. mutation

    C. speciation

    D. germination

15. Mixing of gene pools

    A. promotes diversity.

    B. increases the number of organisms.

    C. reduces the number of organisms.

    D. reduces diversity.

16. Mechanisms of evolution include

    A. natural selection, mutations, genetic drift and gene flow.

    B. gradualistic model and punctuational model.

    C. adaptive radiation, co-evolution, convergent evolution and divergent evolution.

    D. sympatric speciation and allopatric speciation.

17. A copperhead snake is tan, orange and yellow. The pattern and coloration of this snake helps the snake to blend in perfectly with the forest color. What type of adaptation does the copperhead have?

    A. migration   B. hibernation   C. camouflage   D. mimicry

Examine the pictures below.

Eastern coral snake

Scarlet king snake

18. The coral snake is highly venomous. The Scarlet king snake is harmless. These two snakes share similar coloration and territories. What type of adaptation is shown by these two snakes?

    A. migration   B. hibernation   C. camouflage   D. mimicry

19. What statement BEST describes hibernation?

    A. when a large population of animals annually moves from one area to another

    B. when an organism develops a physical adaptation to help it blend into its environment

    C. when an organism develops a structure or behavior that aids in its survival

    D. when an organism goes through a dormant period during the winter

20. What statement BEST describes migration?

   A. when a large population of animals annually moves from one area to another

   B. when an organism develops physical adaptation to help it blend into its environment

   C. when an organism develops a structure or behavior that aids in its survival

   D. when an organism goes through a dormant period during the winter

Answer the following questions.

21. What type of bird foot below is adapted to swimming?

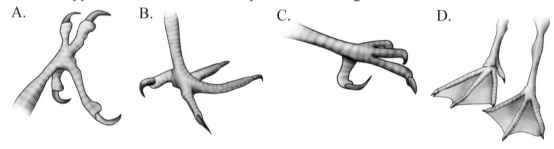

A.   B.   C.   D.

22. What feature of the bird foot led you to believe it helped the bird to swim?

23. Look at the features of the other three bird feet. Which do you think would be best adapted to climbing up the side of a tree and hanging on tightly?

24. What was one of the most important life forms to bring about a change in the Earth's atmosphere? How did the atmosphere change? How did the life form bring about the change?

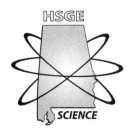

Chapter 8
Interactions in the Environment

ALABAMA HSGT IN SCIENCE STANDARDS COVERED IN THIS CHAPTER INCLUDE:

13	Trace the flow of energy as it decreases through the tropic levels from producers to the quaternary level in food chains, food webs and energy pyramids.
13a	Describing the interdependence of biotic and abiotic factors in an ecosystem.
13b	Contrasting autotrophs and heterotrophs.
13c	Describing the niche of decomposers.
13d	Using the ten percent law to explain the decreasing availability of energy trough the trophic levels.
14	Trace biogeochemical cycles through the environment, including water, carbon, oxygen and nitrogen.
14b	Describing the process of ecological succession.
15	Identify biomes based on environmental factors and native organisms.
16	Identify density-dependent and density-independent limiting factors that affect population in an ecosystem.
16a	Discriminating among symbiotic relationships, including mutualism, commensalism and parasitism.
5	Identify cells, tissues, organs, organ systems, organisms, populations, communities and ecosystems as levels of organization in the biosphere.

EARTH'S MAJOR ECOLOGICAL SYSTEMS

HOW CLIMATE RELATES TO BIOME

Plants comprise the ecological foundation for most ecosystems. Plants are the main pathway by which energy enters ecosystems. Because plants are generally stationary organisms, they cannot respond to rapidly changing environmental conditions. If the amount of rainfall or sunlight received in an area changed suddenly and permanently, most plant species would become extinct. The general climate found in an area determines the plant species that will grow under those conditions. A hot, humid and rainy climate will be favorable to jungle-like plants. The plant types found in an area will determine the animal species that live there. There are six major terrestrial ecological systems and three major aquatic ecological systems.

TERRESTRIAL ECOSYSTEMS

Large land areas characterized by a dominant form of plant life and climate type that make up large ecosystems are called **biomes**. Organisms living in biomes have adapted to the climate of the geographic region. Distinct boundaries between biomes are not apparent; instead, one area gradually merges into the next. The six major biomes are shown in Figure 8.1.

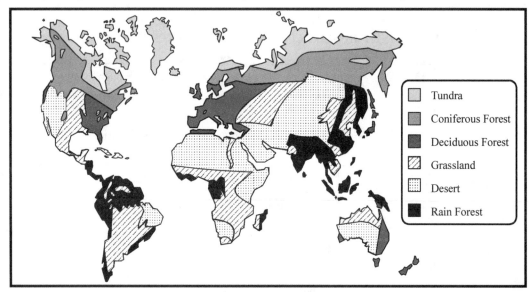

Legend:
- Tundra
- Coniferous Forest
- Deciduous Forest
- Grassland
- Desert
- Rain Forest

Figure 8.1 Biomes of Earth

Figure 8.2 Tundra Biome

The **tundra** biome is located near the north and south poles. Rainfall is light and summer temperatures average only 1° C (34°F). The land in the tundra has gently rolling plains with subsoil that is permanently frozen. There are many lakes, ponds and bogs. Grasses are present, but only a very few small trees grow there. The small plants mostly consist of mosses, lichens and reindeer moss. Examples of animals found in tundra areas are *reindeer, caribou, polar bears, arctic wolves, foxes, hares, lemmings, birds* and *insects*.

The **coniferous forest** biomes are found above 60°N latitude. Rainfall is medium and the average summer temperature is around 12°C (54°F). In the coniferous forest, the subsoil thaws for a few weeks in summer. The land is dotted with lakes, ponds and bogs. The trees are mostly coniferous, such as spruce and fir. There are only a few deciduous trees, which shed or lose their leaves at the end of the growing season. Examples of animals living in coniferous forest areas are *moose, black bears, wolves, lynx, wolverines, martens, porcupines* and *birds*.

The **deciduous forest** biomes are found in the middle latitudes between 20° and 60°N latitude. The deciduous forest has variations in rainfall but, in general, the rainfall is medium. The average summer temperature is around 24°C (75°F). The deciduous forest has trees that are broad-leaved with foliage that changes color in autumn. The animals consist mostly of *squirrels*, *deer*, *foxes* and *bears*. The state of Alabama falls into this biome.

Figure 8.3 Deciduous Forest Biome

Figure 8.4 The Grasslands

The **grasslands** are located in mid-continent areas of middle latitudes. They are found in regions that have warm and cold cycles as well as in the tropic regions on the savannas with wet and dry cycles. In general, the rainfall is low, and the average summer temperature is 20°C (68°F). There are large herbivores on the savannas such as *bison*, *pronghorn antelope* and *zebras*, as well as smaller ones such as *burrowing rodents* and *prairie dogs*.

Tropical rain forest biomes are found near the equator and near mountain ranges. They have abundant rainfall and are very humid. The average summer temperature is 25°C (77°F). The trees are very tall with dense canopies. The floor of the tropical rain forest does not get much sunlight, but it does keep a fairly constant temperature. There is a great diversity of species of both the plants and animals.

The **deserts** are found on either side of the equator between 0° and 20° latitudes. They get little rain and have extreme temperature fluctuations. The average summer temperature is 30°C (86°F). There is not much grass in the desert, but what is there is very drought resistant. Other plants, like *sage- brush*, *mesquite* and *cacti*, have also adapted to desert conditions. Animals common to the desert are the *kangaroo rat*, *snakes*, *lizards*, *insects*, *spiders* and some *birds*.

Figure 8.5 Desert

Activity

Make a travel brochure or comic strip about a particular biome. Be sure to include at least five facts.

AQUATIC ECOSYSTEMS

Aquatic ecosystems depend on a number of different factors such as amount of light, oxygen and the **salinity** (salt) level of the water. The amount of salt in the water is the most important factor in determining the type of organisms in the ecosystem. Light and oxygen are important for photosynthesis. Temperature is less important in aquatic systems since water temperatures do not fluctuate a great deal. Aquatic ecosystems include **marine areas**, **freshwater areas** and **estuaries**, all of which are determined by the salinity of the water.

Freshwater ecosystems consist of streams, rivers, lakes, marshes and swamps. All have a low salinity level. Fresh water has a salinity of less than 0.5 ppt. This means that each liter of fresh water contains 0.5 grams of salt or less. Fresh water is important in recycling the earth's water supply through the water cycle. Freshwater ecosystems are found in areas with differing temperatures and support a wide variety of animal and plant life.

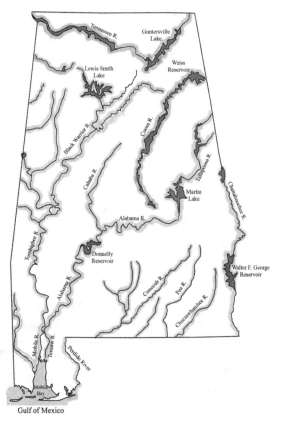

Figure 8.6 Freshwater Ecosystem of Alabama

Marine ecosystems are divided into the intertidal, pelagic and benthic zones. All have a high salinity level. In general, sea water has a salinity of 3.5% or 35,000 ppt or higher. Each liter of sea water contains 35 grams of salt or more.

The intertidal zone is the area of shore that can be seen between low and high tides. It is the most biologically active area in a marine ecosystem, with a high level of light and nutrients. Because of the high tides and shifting sand, this area is also under the most stress. Animals like sand crabs often move to find protection. Rocky shores provide good places for *kelp* and *invertebrates* to

Figure 8.7 Marine Ecosystem

attach themselves, but these organisms also have to deal with changing water levels.

The largest ocean area is the **pelagic** zone, which is further divided into two areas. The more shallow area is closer to shore and has a maximum depth of 200 meters (600 feet). There is good light for photosynthetic organisms in this relatively shallow area. Many types of fish like *tuna*, *herring*, *sardines*, *sharks* and *rays* live in this area along with whales and porpoises. The deeper part of the pelagic zone comprises most of the oceans in the world. This area is deeper than 200 meters. It receives little light, has cold water temperatures, and high pressure. Many different organisms are adapted to the various characteristics of the ocean depths. Some fish have no eyes or have developed luminescent organs. *Lantern fish*, *eels* and *grenadier fish* live in this area.

The **benthic** zone is the ocean floor. Animals like *worms*, *clams*, *hagfish* and *crabs* can be found in deep benthic areas, in addition to bacteria. In deep benthic areas, hydrothermal vents can form the basis of a complex food web supporting a variety of animals. Coral reefs are commonly found in warm, shallow benthic areas. The reefs prevent erosion and provide habitats for many organisms like *sea stars*, *plankton*, *sponges* and a *variety of fish*.

Figure 8.8 An Estuary

An **estuary** is where fresh and salt water meet in a coastal area. The salinity level in an estuary fluctuates, but is generally not as high as in the ocean ecosystems. The salinity in estuaries varies depending on time of year. Increased river discharge in spring lowers salinity levels, while increased evaporation in summer raises salinity levels. In general, the brackish waters of an estuary fluctuate between 0.5 ppt and 35 ppt. This means that each liter of water contains between 0.5 grams and 35 grams of salt. The water is partly surrounded by land with access to open ocean and rivers. Estuaries contain salt marshes and swampy areas and are among the most biologically diverse locations on Earth. The diversity is attributed to the large amount of nutrients, the tides that circulate the nutrients and remove waste, and the abundance of different types of plants.

Section Review 1: Earth's Major Ecological Systems

A. Terms

biome	grasslands	freshwater ecosystem	pelagic zone
tundra	tropical rain forest	estuary	benthic zone
coniferous forest	desert	marine ecosystems	
deciduous forest	salinity	intertidal zone	

B. Multiple Choice

1. Tundra biomes generally occur near which latitudes?

   A. equatorial   B. mid-continent   C. middle   D. polar

2. The eastern United States is predominately a

   A. grassland biome.   C. coniferous biome.

   B. desert biome.   D. deciduous biome.

3. Tropical rain forests

   A. have little to no rainfall.

   B. have a diversity of species.

   C. fluctuate greatly in yearly temperatures.

   D. are found between the 0° and 20° latitudes.

C. Short Answer

1. Compare and contrast marine and freshwater biomes.

2. Why is climate important to biotic factors in a biome?

ORGANIZATION OF ECOSYSTEMS

ECOSYSTEM

An **ecosystem** is the interdependence of plant and animal communities and the physical environment in which they live. The **biosphere** is the zone around the earth that contains self-sustaining ecosystems composed of biotic and abiotic factors. **Biotic** factors include all living things, such as birds, insects, trees and flowers. **Abiotic** factors are those components of the ecosystem that are not living, but are integral in determining the number and types of organisms that are present. Examples of abiotic factors include soil, water, temperature and amount of light. In order for an ecosystem to succeed, its biotic factors must obtain and store energy. In addition, the biotic and abiotic factors of the ecosystem must recycle water, oxygen, carbon and nitrogen.

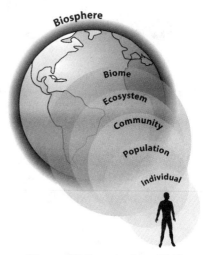

Figure 8.9 Organization of Life

COMMUNITY

A **community** is a collection of the different biotic factors in a particular ecosystem. Communities include many different species of plants and animals that live in close proximity to one another. For example, in a marine ecosystem a coral reef supports a large community of organisms. In this example, the community of fish, shrimp, mammals, algae, sharks, coral, urchins, sea stars and clams all live together and interact with one another. A community might have very different types of plants and animals living in one area. The members of a community interrelate with each other. Deer

Figure 8.10 A Forest Community

grazing in a clearing in the forest may be alert to the activity or movement of birds that warn them of approaching danger. In turn, the birds may depend on the deer grazing in a clearing to disturb insects hiding in the grass, thus causing them to become visible.

Each member of a community has its own **habitat**. A habitat is the dwelling place where an organism seeks food and shelter. A woodpecker lives in a hole in a tree. It eats the insects that live in the bark of the tree. A robin builds its nest and raises its young in the same tree. A mouse lives in a burrow at the base of the tree. An owl sleeps on a branch of the same tree. The tree supports a whole community of organisms and becomes their habitat. The habitat provides food and shelter for the members of the community. In turn, each species of the tree community has its own **niche**. A niche is the role that an organism plays in its community, such as what it eats, what eats it and where it nests.

POPULATION

A community of living things is composed of populations. **Populations** are made up of the individual species in a community. For example, in a forest community ecosystem, there are populations of various plant and animal species such as deer, squirrels, birds, insects and trees.

Figure 8.11 A Population of Deer

SPECIES

A species is a group of similar organisms that can breed with one another to produce fertile offspring. Organisms of the same species share similar characteristics common to all organisms within the population. For example, all domestic cats can breed to produce kittens. All domestic cats have whiskers, retractable claws, canine teeth, eat meat and can land on their feet; these characteristics are common to all cats.

Some natural variation exists within all members of a species. Not all cats have whiskers of the same length or bodies of the same size. However, all domestic cats can breed to produce offspring.

Two organisms are part of a different species when they cannot breed and produce fertile offspring. A horse and a donkey can breed, but they produce a mule, which is infertile. Therefore, a horse and a donkey are different species.

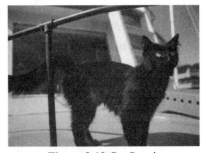

Figure 8.12 Cat Species

Section Review 2: Organization of Ecosystems

A. Terms

ecosystem	biotic	community	niche
biosphere	abiotic	habitat	population

B. Multiple Choice

The area in which certain types of plants or animals can be found living in close proximity to each other is called a

    A. habitat.   B. community.   C. niche.   D. kingdom.

C. Short Answer

Name four abiotic conditions that might determine the kind of ecosystem in an area.

RELATIONSHIPS AMONG ORGANISMS

Each organism in an ecosystem interrelates with the other members. These relationships fall into one of three categories: **symbiosis**, **competition** or **predation**.

SYMBIOSIS

A **symbiotic relationship** is a long-term association between two members of a community in which one or both parties benefit. There are three types of symbiotic relationships: commensalism, mutualism and parasitism.

- **Commensalism** is a symbiotic relationship in which one member benefits, and the other is unaffected. Hermit crabs that live in snail shells are one example of this type of relationship. Some argue that one member in most commensalistic relationships is harmed in some way by the relationship. For example, orchids are a type of epiphytic plant that grows on top of the branches of rainforest trees. Having a *few* orchids in its branches does not harm the tree. However, the accumulation of many epiphytic plants could cause the tree to loose limbs, sunlight or nutrients. For this reason, true commensalistic relationships are rare in nature.

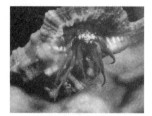

Figure 8.13
A Commensalistic Relationship

- **Mutualism** is a symbiotic relationship that is beneficial to both organisms. In South America, the tree *Acacia cornigera* and a species of ant (*Pseudomyrmex ferruginea*) are one example of mutualism. The acacia tree provides a home for the ants by growing specialized hollow thorns. The tree also provides food for the ants in the form of a protein-lipid and a carbohydrate-rich nectar from structures on the leaf stalk called nodules. The ants, in turn, protect the tree from predators by biting or stinging them and other plant competitors by killing all plant life that comes into contact with the branches. There are many examples of mutualism in nature including: remoras and sharks and clown fish and sea anemones.

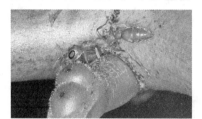

Figure 8.14 A Mutualistic Relationship

- **Parasitism** is a symbiotic relationship that benefits one organism (the parasite), but harms the other (the host). For example, heartworms in dogs (and humans) are parasites. The heartworm benefits by getting its nutrition from the bloodstream of its animal host. The host, however, is harmed because blood flow is restricted and nutrients are lost to the parasite.

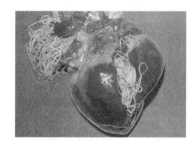

Figure 8.15 A Parasitic Relationship

COMPETITION

When two or more organisms seek the same resource that is in limited supply, they **compete** with each other. A **resource** could be food, water, light, ground space or nesting space. Competition can be intraspecific or interspecific. **Intraspecific competition** occurs between members of the same species, whereas **interspecific competition** occurs between members of different species.

PREDATION

Predators and prey help maintain an ecological balance within their ecosystem. This balance benefits the community as a whole, but can be helpful or harmful to the members that make up the community, depending upon whether they are the predator or the prey. A **predator** is an organism that feeds on other living things. The organism it feeds on is the **prey**. For instance, wild dogs will hunt down and kill zebra, separating out weak and sick animals from the herd. The predator/prey relationship is the way energy passes up the food chain of the ecosystem, and is the main driving force behind natural selection.

Figure 8.16 Predator-Prey Relationship Between a Wild Dog and Zebra

Section Review 3:   Relationships among Organisms

A. Terms

symbiotic relationship	parasite	interspecific competition
commensalism	host	predation
mutualism	competition	predator
parasitism	intraspecific competition	prey

B. Multiple Choice

The relationship between two members of a community in which one member harms another by its presence is

A. parasitism.

C. mutualism.

B. commensalism.

D. dependency.

C. Do the following exercise.

Compare mutualism and parasitism.

POPULATION DYNAMICS

A population is a group of organisms of the same species living in the same geographic area. Important characteristics of populations include the growth rate, density and distribution of a population. The study of these characteristics is called population dynamics.

GROWTH

The **growth rate** of a population is the change in population size per unit time. Growth rates are typically reported as the increase in the number of organisms per unit time per number of organisms present. The size of a population depends on the number of organisms entering and exiting it. Recall that organisms can enter the population through birth or immigration. Also remember that organisms can leave the population by death or emigration. Immigration occurs when organisms move into a population. Emigration occurs when organisms move out of a population. If a population has more births than deaths and immigration and emigration rates are equal, then the population will grow. Ecologists observe the growth rate of a population over a number of hours, years or decades. It can be zero, positive or negative. Growth rate graphs often plot the number of individuals against time.

A population will grow exponentially if the birth and death rates are constant and the birth rate is greater than the death rate. **Exponential growth** occurs when the population growth starts out slowly and then increases rapidly as the number of reproducing individuals increase. Exponential growth is also sometimes called a **J-shaped curve**. In most cases, the population cannot continue to grow exponentially without reaching some environmental limit such as lack of nutrients, energy, living space and other resources. These environmental limits will cause the population size to stabilize, which we will discuss shortly.

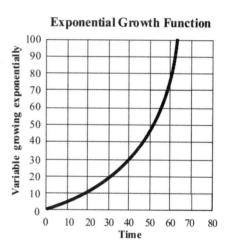

Figure 8.17 Exponential Growth Function

DENSITY AND DISTRIBUTION

The **density** of a population refers to the number of organisms per unit area. For example, there could be an average distribution of 100 maple trees per square kilometer in the eastern United States. However, population density does not reveal how organisms are distributed in that space.

The **distribution** of a population refers to the pattern of where the organisms live. The areas in which populations are found can range in size from a few millimeters in the case of bacteria cells, to a few thousand kilometers in the case of African wildebeests. Organisms within the population can have random, clumped, or even distribution within the ecosystem.

Several factors, including the location of resources and the social behavior of animals, affect the dispersion of a population. A **random distribution** is one in which there is no set pattern of individuals within the ecosystem. This pattern is rare in nature. A **clumped distribution** is one in which individuals are found in close-knit groups, usually located near a resource.

Clumped distributions frequently form among highly social animals like baboons. This distribution pattern is common in nature. **Even distribution** is a set pattern or even spacing between individuals. This distribution sometimes occurs with highly territorial animals. However, even distribution, like random distribution, is also rare in nature. Dispersion patterns can vary seasonally or throughout the life cycle.

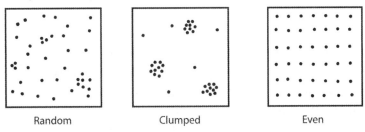

Random   Clumped   Even

Figure 8.18 Possible Population Distributions

CARRYING CAPACITY

As the population uses up available resources, the overall growth of the population will slow or stop. Population growth will slow or decrease when the birth rate decreases or the death rate increases. Eventually, the number of births will equal the number of deaths. The **carrying capacity** is the number of individuals the environment can support in a given area. The population size will eventually fluctuate around the carrying capacity. When the population size exceeds the carrying capacity, the number of births will *decrease* and the number of deaths will *increase*, thus bringing the population back down to the carrying capacity. This type of growth curve is known as **logistic growth**. Logistic growth is sometimes called an **S-shaped curve** because it levels out at a certain point

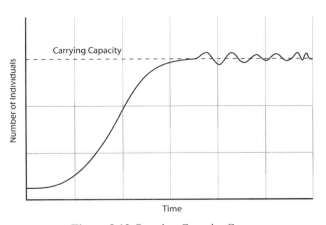

Figure 8.19 Carrying Capacity Curve

For example, a specific pond has a carrying capacity of 40 frogs. If more than 40 frogs are in the pond, then food and space become limited, and some frogs will likely move to another pond or die. If fewer than 40 frogs are present in the pond, then some frogs may move into the pond or more offspring will survive.

A decrease in environmental quality will decrease the carrying capacity of that environment. In the example above, if the pond becomes polluted, it will likely not be able to support 40 frogs; instead, it will support an amount lower than 40.

An increase in the environmental quality will increase the environmental carrying capacity. For instance, if the pond is cleared of some or all of its pollution, it will be able to support more than 40 frogs.

REGULATION OF POPULATION SIZE

Availability of resources is not the only factor that limits population growth. A **limiting factor** is anything in a population that restricts the population size. Remember that resources in an ecosystem are limited, and the availability of matter, space, and energy is finite. There are two main categories of limiting factors: **density-dependent factors** and **density-independent factors**. Density-independent factors are limiting, no matter the size of the population, and include unusual weather, natural disasters and seasonal cycles. Density-dependent factors are *phenomenon*, such as competition, disease and predation, which only become limiting when a population in a given area reaches a certain size. Density-dependent factors usually only affect large, dense populations.

SUCCESSION

Over time, an ecosystem goes through a series of changes known as **ecological succession**. Succession occurs when one community slowly replaces another as the environment changes. There are two types of succession: primary succession and secondary succession.

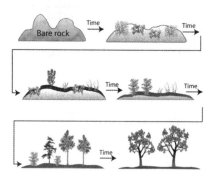

Figure 8.20 Primary Succession

Primary succession occurs in areas that are barren of life because of a complete lack of soil. Examples are new volcanic islands and areas of lava flows such as those on the islands of Hawaii. Areas of rock left behind by retreating glaciers are another site for primary succession. In these areas, there is a natural reintroduction of progressively more complex organisms. Usually, lichens are the first organisms to begin to grow in the barren area. Lichens hold onto moisture and help to erode rock into soil components. The second group of organisms to move into an area — bacteria, protists, mosses and fungi — continue the erosion process. Once there is a sufficient number of organisms to support them, the insects and other arthropods inhabit the area. Grasses, herbs and weeds begin to grow once there is a sufficient amount of soil; eventually, trees and shrubs can be supported by the newly formed soil.

In habitats where the community of living things has been partially or completely destroyed, **secondary succession** occurs. In these areas, soil and seeds are already present. For example, at one time prairie grasslands were cleared and crops planted. When those farmlands were abandoned, they once again became inhabited by the native plants. Trees grew where there were once roads. Animals returned to the area and reclaimed their natural living spaces. Eventually, there was very little evidence that farms ever existed in those parts of the prairies.

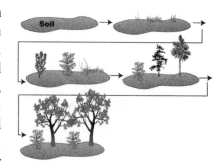

Figure 8.21 Secondary Succession

Section Review 4: Population Dynamics

A. Terms

growth rate	carrying capacity	density-independent factor
immigration	logistic growth	ecological succession
emigration	limiting factor	primary succession
exponential growth	density-dependent factor	secondary succession

B. Multiple Choice

1. A density-dependent factor

    A. limits a population in a given area regardless of size.

    B. limits the population when the population reaches a certain size.

    C. may include weather or a natural disaster.

    D. often affects small, sparse populations.

2. Anything that restricts a population is called a

    A. bad omen.   B. restricting factor.   C. predator.   D. limiting factor.

3. A population will tend to grow if

    A. it has no environmental limitations.

    B. the number of births exceeds the number of deaths.

    C. the immigration rate exceeds the emigration rate.

    D. all of the above.

4. An active volcano under the ocean erupts, and the build-up of cooled lava eventually forms a new island. What type of succession will immediately occur on the newly formed island?

    A. primary succession   C. both primary and secondary succession

    B. secondary succession   D. no succession

C. Short Answer

1. How is the carrying capacity of a population determined?

2. Why do you think it is important for a population to have limiting factors?

ENERGY FLOW THROUGH THE ECOSYSTEM

Matter within an ecosystem is constantly recycled over and over again. Earth has the same amount of abiotic matter today as it did one hundred years ago. Elements, chemical compounds and other sources of matter pass from one state to another through the ecosystem.

As a deer eats grass, the nutrients contained in the grass are broken down into their chemical components and then rearranged to become living deer tissues. Waste products are produced in the deer's digestive system and pass from the deer's body back into the ecosystem. Organisms break down this waste into simpler chemical components. The grass growing close by is able to take up those components and rearrange them back into grass tissues. Then, the energy cycle begins again.

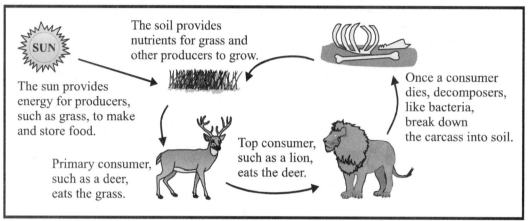

Figure 8.22 Energy Cycle

Energy can be added, stored, transferred and lost throughout an ecosystem. **Energy flow** is the transfer of energy within an ecosystem. Inorganic nutrients are recycled through the ecosystem, but energy cannot be recycled. Ultimately, energy is lost as heat. Remember, however, that energy cannot be destroyed; although it may be lost from one system as heat, it is gained somewhere else. In this way, energy is conserved.

FOOD CHAINS AND FOOD WEBS

The producers, consumers and decomposers of each ecosystem make up a **food chain**. Energy flow through an ecosystem occurs in food chains, with energy passing from one organism to another. There can be many food chains in an ecosystem.

The **producers** of an ecosystem use abiotic (not living) factors to obtain and store energy for themselves or the consumers that eat the producers. In a forest ecosystem, the producers are trees, bushes, shrubs, small plants, grass and moss.

The **consumers** are members of the ecosystem that depend on other members for food. Each time a plant or animal consumes another organism, energy transfers to the consumer. Deer, foxes, rabbits, raccoons, owls, hawks, snakes, mice, spiders and insects are examples of consumers in a forest ecosystem. There are three types of consumers: **herbivores**, **carnivores** and **omnivores**. Table 8.1 lists characteristics of the three different types of consumers.

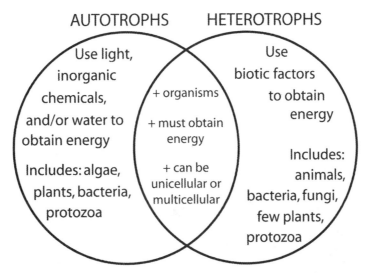

AUTOTROPHS

Use light, inorganic chemicals, and/or water to obtain energy

Includes: algae, plants, bacteria, protozoa

+ organisms

+ must obtain energy

+ can be unicellular or multicellular

HETEROTROPHS

Use biotic factors to obtain energy

Includes: animals, bacteria, fungi, few plants, protozoa

Figure 8.23 VENN Diagram Autotrophs vs. Heterotrophs

Autotrophs are organisms that get their own energy from abiotic factors in the environment. Autotrophs use sunlight, and/or inorganic chemicals to capture energy. Autotrophs are also sometimes called producers. **Heterotrophs** are organisms that get their energy from biotic factors in the environment. Heterotrophs are also sometimes called consumers.

The **decomposers** are members of the ecosystem that live on dead or decaying organisms and reduce them to their simplest forms. They use the decomposition products as a source of energy. Decomposers include fungi and bacteria. They are also called **saprophytes**.

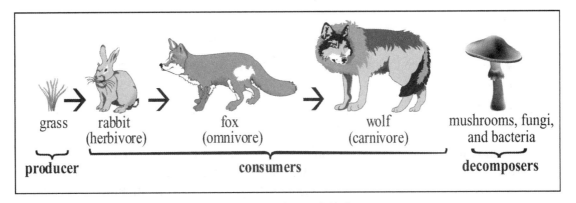

grass → rabbit (herbivore) → fox (omnivore) → wolf (carnivore) → mushrooms, fungi, and bacteria

producer   consumers   decomposers

Figure 8.24 Food Chain

Table 8.1 Types of Consumers

Consumer	Food Supply
Herbivore	animals that eat only plants
Omnivore	animals that eat both plants and other animals
Carnivore	animals that eat only other animals
Saprophytes	organisms that obtain food from dead organisms or from the waste products of living organisms

Practice 1: Food Chains

Assemble two food chains, choosing your own plants and animals.
Use at least four organisms in each of your food chains.

The interaction of many food chains is a **food web**. Most producers and consumers interact with many others forming a complex food web out of several simple food chains. Figure 8.25 shows the more complex food web.

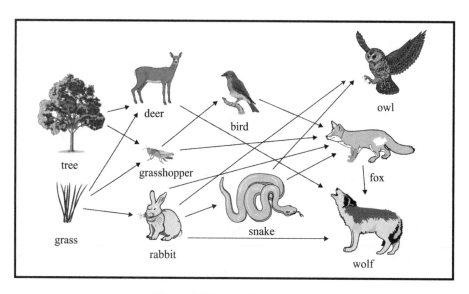

Figure 8.25 A Food Web

Activity

Select a biome from the list below and construct a food web using organisms found only in the biome.

tundra, coniferous forest, deciduous forest, grassland, desert or rain forest

A **trophic level** is the position occupied by an organism in a food chain. Organisms that share a trophic level get their energy from the same source. Producers are found at the base of the energy pyramid and comprise the first trophic level of the food chain. Producers capture energy as sunlight and convert it into usable forms. Above them are the primary consumers that make up the second trophic level. Above the primary consumers are the secondary consumers that occupy the third trophic level. Finally, there are the tertiary consumers at the top trophic level. This group is often called the "top" of the food chain. They are generally omnivores, like humans, or carnivores, like lions. Different ecosystems will have different tertiary consumers. Figure 8.26 shows an energy pyramid where the organisms at different tropic levels are arranged in a pyramid shape.

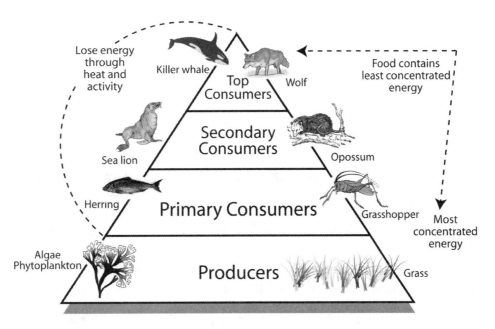

Figure 8.26 Energy Pyramid

Ecologists sometimes consider energy in terms of **biomass**, the mass of all the organisms and organic material in an area. A pyramid of biomass is a representation of the biomass at each trophic level of a food chain, as shown in Figure 8.27. The word "pyramid" is a bit deceiving when discussing biomass. It is possible for a level with a smaller biomass to sit under a level with a greater biomass. Such is the case in some aquatic environments where the producers reproduce so quickly that the biomass of the first trophic level at any one time is less than that of the trophic level above it.

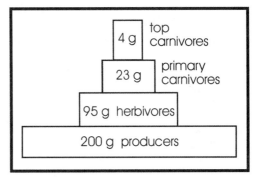

Figure 8.27 Biomass Pyramid

Activity

Now, use your food web from the previous activity to create your own energy pyramid, like the one in Figure 8.26.

TEN PERCENT LAW

As organisms trap and use energy, it constantly changes form. The amount of energy available to producers in the first trophic level is much greater than the amount available to consumers at the top trophic level. As energy is transferred from one trophic level to the next some is lost. The **ten percent law** states that the amount of energy available to organisms at a particular trophic level is ten percent of what it was at the previous level. For example, sunlight energy strikes the Earth's surface. Grass traps some of that energy and some of that energy is lost to the environment. Some energy is stored in the form of carbohydrates and some is lost due to respiration and new tissue growth. A rabbit eats the grass. Some of the energy from the grass is stored in the tissues of the rabbit and some is used for metabolism, locomotion, reproduction and homeostasis. A fox eats the rabbit. Some of the energy is stored in the fox's tissues and some is used for metabolism, locomotion, reproduction, and homeostasis. Each time the energy is transformed from one state to another, some is lost. Energy is expressed in the SI unit called the **joule** (J).

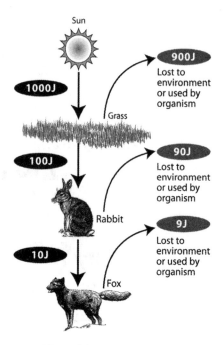

Figure 8.28 Ten Percent Law

The ten percent law does not mean to imply an *exact* amount of energy lost at each level. It is instead, intended to be used as a general rule to remember the inefficiency of natural systems.

Section Review 5: Food Chains and Food Webs

A. Terms

food chain	decomposer	carnivore	trophic level	omnivore
producer	herbivore	food web	consumer	energy cycle

B. Multiple Choice

1. Organisms that share a trophic level are

    A. elephants and lions.

    B. cheetahs and giraffes.

    C. chipmunks and squirrels.

    D. wolves and sparrows.

2. The owl is a nocturnal hunter of small mammals, insects and other birds. An owl is an example of a/an

    A. producer.   B. omnivore.   C. carnivore.   D. decomposer.

C. Fill in the blanks.

1. Animals that eat both plants and other animals are called _____.

2. Organisms that obtain food from dead organisms or waste material are called _____.

D. Do the following exercises.

1. Give a complete example of a food chain.

2. Give a complete example of a food web.

THE NUTRIENT CYCLES

The process of recycling substances necessary for life is called the **nutrient cycle**. Nutrient cycles include the **carbon cycle**, the **nitrogen cycle**, the **phosphorous cycle** and the **water cycle**. When examining these cycles, it is important to remember that the elements are cycled in the real world. The nutrients shown in these images are not cycled as solo elements but rather, they often combine with other elements during their cycle. That is to say, when carbon, nitrogen and phosphorous cycle through the lithosphere, atmosphere or hydrosphere, they often carry other nutrients, like hydrogen or oxygen, along with them as ions that form salts. The images here show the cycles as stand-alone nutrient cycles for your learning benefit only.

CARBON CYCLE

The **carbon cycle** is the cycling of carbon between carbon dioxide and organic molecules. Inorganic carbon makes up 0.03% of the atmosphere as carbon dioxide. The main component of organic molecules is carbon. Plants use carbon dioxide and energy from the sun to perform photosynthesis. When animals eat plants, carbon passes into their tissues. Through food chains, carbon passes from one organism to another, as shown in Figure 8.29. It returns to earth through respiration, excretion or decomposition after death. Some animals do not decompose after death; instead, their bodies become buried and compressed underground. Over long periods of time, fossil fuels such as coal, oil and gas develop from decomposing organic matter. When fossil fuels burn, carbon dioxide returns to the atmosphere.

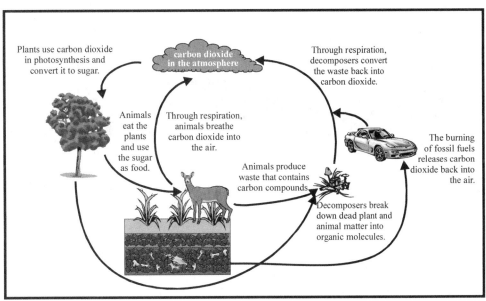

Figure 8.29 The Carbon Cycle

NITROGEN CYCLE

Nitrogen is the most abundant atmospheric gas, comprising 78% of the earth's atmosphere. This element is a component of proteins and nucleic acids. However, nitrogen gas is not in a form that is usable by most organisms. The **nitrogen cycle** transforms nitrogen into ammonia, nitrite and finally nitrate, so that it is usable by plants and animals. Refer to Figure 8.30 to see the nitrogen cycle.

Nitrogen fixation is the conversion of nitrogen gas into nitrate by several types of bacteria. Nitrogen fixation occurs in three major steps. First, nitrogen is converted into ammonia (NH_3) by bacteria called **nitrogen fixers**. Some plants can use ammonia directly, but most require nitrate. **Nitrifying bacteria** convert ammonia into nitrite (NO_2^-) and finally into nitrate (NO_3^-). The nitrogen-fixing bacteria live on the roots of legumes (pea and bean plants). This process increases the amount of usable nitrogen in soil. The plants use the nitrogen, in the form of nitrate, to synthesize nucleic acids and proteins. The nitrogen passes along through food chains. Decomposers release ammonia as they break down plant and animal remains, which may then undergo the conversion into nitrite and nitrate by nitrifying bacteria. Other types of bacteria convert nitrate and nitrite into nitrogen gas that then returns to the atmosphere. The nitrogen cycle keeps the level of usable nitrogen in the soil fairly constant. A small amount of nitrate cycles through the atmosphere; this is created when lightning converts atmospheric nitrogen into nitrate.

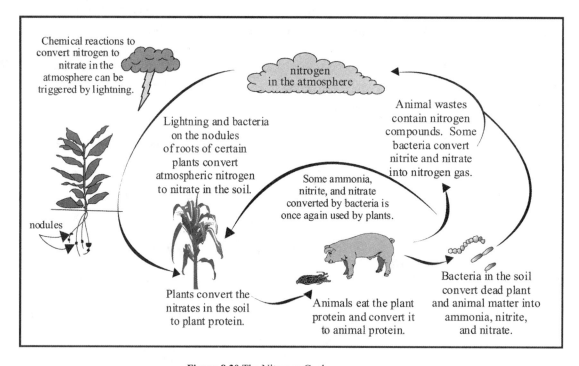

Figure 8.30 The Nitrogen Cycle

PHOSPHOROUS CYCLE

Phosphorous is an element that is essential to life, as it is a component of such important biomolecules as **DNA** and **RNA**. Phosphorous is also essential in the transfer of energy through organisms in the form of **ATP** and **ADP**. Unlike nitrogen and carbon, phosphorous is not found in the atmosphere. Phosphorous exists only as part of an organism, dissolved in water or as an element in rock. Phosphorous, like nitrogen, is a water pollutant in excess quantities. The **phosphorous cycle** begins with the introduction of phosphates (PO_4) into the soil from weathering, or breakdown, of sedimentary rocks. Plants then absorb phosphate ions from the soil, which introduces phosphorous into living ecosystems. Fungi can also directly absorb phosphates from the soil. All other organisms obtain phosphorous through the consumption of fungi or plant producers. Phosphorous then passes to the consumers of the plants before returning to the soil as waste or decomposed material. Figure 8.31 diagrams the phosphorous cycle.

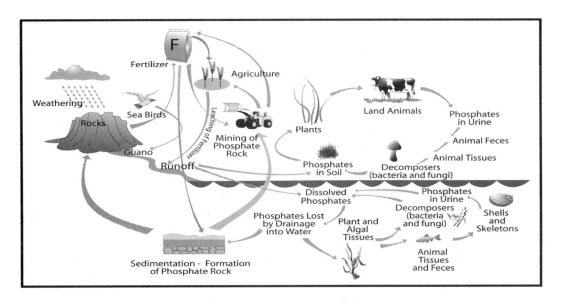

Figure 8.31 Phosphorous Cycle

WATER CYCLE

The **water cycle** circulates fresh water between the atmosphere and the earth as seen in Figure 8.32 on the following page. Even though water covers the majority of Earth, about 95% of it is saltwater. Most fresh water is in the form of glaciers, leaving a very small amount of fresh water available for land organisms. Fresh water is vital for carrying out metabolic processes; the water cycle ensures that the supply is replenished. Precipitation in the form of rain, ice, snow, hail or dew falls to the earth and ends up in lakes, rivers and oceans through the precipitation itself or through runoff. The sun provides energy in the form of heat, thus driving evaporation that sends water vapor into the atmosphere from bodies of water. Energy from the sun also powers winds and ocean currents. Respiration from people and animals and transpiration from plants also send water vapor to the atmosphere. The water vapor cools to form clouds. The clouds cool, become saturated and form precipitation. Without this cycle of precipitation, runoff and evaporation, a fresh water supply would not be available.

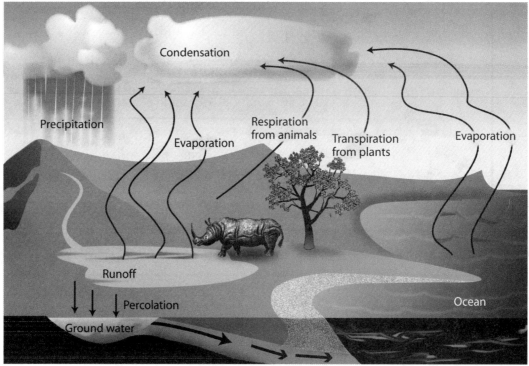

Figure 8.32 The Water Cycle

OXYGEN CYCLE

The **oxygen cycle** is the movement of oxygen between the atmosphere, lithosphere and the biosphere. Oxygen is found stored in the rocks of the earth as oxide minerals. Oxygen is also found floating freely in the atmosphere in the form of oxygen and ozone. Oxygen is found in the biosphere when it is exchanged between plants and animals during photosynthesis and cellular respiration. Plants and algae produce the main source of oxygen on the earth. Oxygen

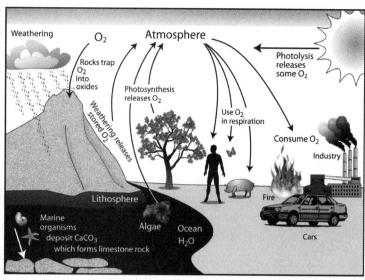

Figure 8.33 Oxygen Cycle

is consumed during rock weathering processes where oxides are produced like iron oxide (rust). Oxygen is also consumed during the combustion process. About 99.5% of the Earth's oxygen is contained in the lithosphere, 0.49% in the atmosphere and 0.01% in the biosphere.

Section Review 6: The Nutrient Cycles

A. Terms

nutrient cycle	nitrogen cycle	nitrogen fixers	phosphorous cycle
carbon cycle	nitrogen fixation	nitrifying bacteria	water cycle

B. Multiple Choice

1. In the nitrogen cycle, bacteria

    A. convert nitrogen to ammonia. C. cause lightning strikes.

    B. convert nitrogen to animal protein. D. convert nitrogen to plant protein.

2. All metabolic processes are dependent on the presence of

    A. fungi. B. lysosomes. C. fresh water. D. lipids.

3. The main component of organic molecules is

    A. phosphorous. B. carbon. C. nitrogen. D. carbon dioxide.

4. Plants use nitrogen to

    A. make sugar. C. make proteins and nucleic acids.

    B. attract pollinators. D. transport water to their leaves.

CHAPTER 8 REVIEW

A. Choose the best answer.

CHAPTER
REVIEW

1. What are biotic factors?

   A. living

   B. lipids

   C. non-living

   D. always unicellular

2. What are abiotic factors?

   A. decomposers

   B. living

   C. non-living

   D. photosynthetic

3. The place where a member of a community lives and finds food is called its

   A. pond.   B. biome.   C. habitat.   D. residence.

4. Brim fish in a pond are _____ of that community.

   A. producers

   B. a population

   C. unnecessary elements

   D. a habitat

5. What do the interactions of plants, animals and microorganisms with each other and with their environment constitutes?

   A. food chain

   B. ecosystem

   C. trophic level

   D. symbiotic relationship

6. Unusual weather will

   A. affect all individuals within a population.

   B. only affect small populations of organisms.

   C. only affect large populations of organisms.

   D. have no affect on populations.

7. Which terrestrial ecological system has the greatest diversity of plants and animals?

   A. tundra

   B. grassland

   C. rain forest

   D. deciduous forest

8. What type of ecological system can include rivers, lakes and streams?

   A. freshwater   B. estuary   C. marine   D. ocean

9. Lions are carnivores and are considered a _____ in the energy cycle.

   A. primary consumer

   B. top consumer

   C. provider

   D. decomposer

10. Photosynthesis is performed by

    A. omnivores.   C. secondary consumers.

    B. producers.   D. primary consumers.

11. Which of the following most likely would be a part of the first community on a newly formed volcanic island?

    A. pine trees   B. oak trees   C. lichen   D. sea gulls

12. Many types of bacteria obtain their nutrition from dead plants and animals and, in turn, recycle elements such as carbon and nitrogen. These bacteria are

    A. decomposers.   C. carnivores.

    B. producers.   D. viruses.

13. In the nutrient cycle, producers use carbon dioxide in the process of

    A. respiration.   C. decomposition.

    B. recycling.   D. photosynthesis.

14. Nitrogen makes up _____ of the atmosphere.

    A. 25%   B. 33%   C. 78%   D. 92%

15. During the nitrogen cycle, a plant converts the nitrates in the soil to

    A. plant protein.   C. fertilizer.

    B. fat.   D. carbohydrates.

16. Decomposers are a group of organisms that are very efficient at utilizing all available energy. Which statement below BEST explains why this is so?

    A. Decomposers are the producers in ecosystems and must trap all available energy for an ecosystem to be successful.

    B. Decomposers are tertiary consumers at the top of the food chain and receive the smallest amount of available energy.

    C. Decomposers receive the smallest amount of energy from all other organisms.

    D. Decomposers receive the smallest amount of energy from the sun.

17. When organisms produce carbon dioxide from cellular respiration, which molecule provides the carbon?

    A. glucose   B. water   C. carbon dioxide   D. enzyme

B. For questions 18 – 21 examine the diagram below.

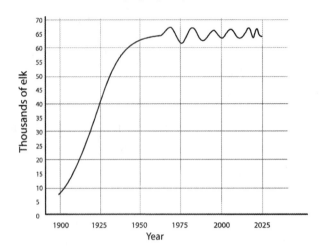

Carrying Capacity of Elk in Alaska

18. This graph shows _____ growth for the population.

  A. exponential   C. logistic

  B. J-shaped   D. M-shaped

19. The carrying capacity for elk in this environment is around

  A. 65.   C. 75,000.

  B. 6,500.   D. 65,000.

20. If a large oil company enters this environment and begins drilling for oil, building structures, and polluting the land, what will probably happen to the carrying capacity of the elk?

  A. It will be more than 65,000.

  B. It will be less than 65,000.

  C. Nothing; it will remain the same.

  D. The elk will all leave and move into a new environment.

21. The United States government established this ecosystem as a native tribal reserve. Hunting is not permitted on native lands by anyone other than the native peoples. Based on the graph above, at what time was this ecosystem likely to have become a protected land?

  A. 1962   B. 1950   C. 1925   D. 1890

22. A symbiotic relationship means

  A. no energy cycle is involved.   C. a relationship that symbolizes a trend.

  B. no one benefits.   D. one or both parties benefit.

23. Red foxes are nocturnal and live in meadows and forest edges. They are predators to small mammals, amphibians and insects. The scraps that red foxes leave behind provide food for scavengers and decomposers. The preceding sentences describe the red foxes

    A. community.   B. prey.   C. niche.   D. food web.

24. Man-of-war fish cluster around the venomous tentacles of jellyfish to escape larger predators. The presence of the man-of-war fish does not harm or benefit the jellyfish. This type of relationship is called

    A. parasitism.   C. succession.

    B. commensalism.   D. mutualism.

25. In nature, why might organisms have the distribution shown below?

    A. They are greedy and like to compete for space.

    B. They want to be located near a resource.

    C. An organism secretes a hormone that causes individuals close by to move away.

    D. They want to learn to live in close knit communal groups.

26. Which organism is a tertiary consumer receiving the least amount of energy?

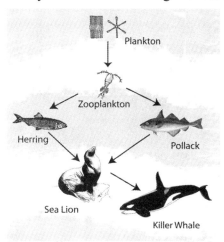

    A. plankton   B. sea lion   C. pollack   D. killer whale

27. Which organism listed below is an example of a producer receiving the MOST amount of available energy?

    A. cougar   B. grass   C. human   D. rainbow trout

28. Examine the image. Ultimately, what is the driving force behind this cycle?

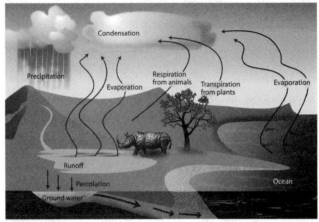

A. energy from the Sun

B. waste from organisms

C. heat from fossil fuels

D. fertilizer from agriculture

29. Examine the picture. What type of species interaction is shown in this picture?

A. competition

B. predator/prey

C. mutualism

D. parasitism

30. Which organism is the producer in this food web?

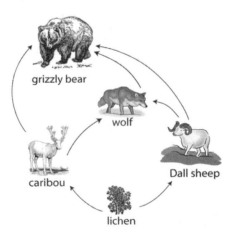

A. lichen   B. Dall sheep   C. wolf   D. bear

Chapter 9
Environmental Awareness

ALABAMA **HSGT** IN SCIENCE STANDARDS COVERED IN THIS CHAPTER INCLUDE:

14a	Relating natural disasters, climate changes, nonnative species and human activity to the dynamic equilibrium of ecosystems.

BEGINNINGS OF ENVIRONMENTAL AWARENESS

Several events during the 20th century brought the attention of society to the way we interact with the world around us.

One event was the national recognition of the decline of the bald eagle (*Haliaeetus leucocephalus*), the national symbol of the United States. Bald eagles were once abundant in the U.S, with perhaps 500,000 birds inhabiting 45 of the lower 48 states. As settlers arrived in North America and human populations grew, the habitat of the bald eagle was gradually compromised. By the late 1800s their numbers had noticeably dwindled, inspiring the passage of the **Bald Eagle Protection Act of 1940**.

Figure 9.1 Bald Eagle

No longer harassed by human hunters, the bald eagle began to make a comeback. But the beginning of widespread usage of DDT and other pesticides instigated another period of decline. These pesticides were sprayed directly on plants, but made their way through the environment through water runoff and other avenues. Sometimes the birds were poisoned outright, but the long-term damage occurred from a secondary effect of the pesticides; they weakened the eagles production of egg shell material within the bird. Often, the eggs were not strong enough to be laid; if they were, they cracked during incubation. Bald eagles essentially stopped producing babies.

They were officially placed on the Endangered Species list in 1967, through legislation that preceded the currently enforced **Endangered Species Act of 1973**. Through this Act, and the banning of DDT and other environmental toxins, bald eagles received the targeted attention and care that the species needed to recover. It is currently estimated that wild populations of the bald eagle number between 70,000 and 100,000 birds. They are no longer considered endangered, having been downgraded to a threatened species.

The state of Alabama has 18 plants and 71 animals on its endangered and threatened species list — including the American bald eagle. Current information on endangered and threatened species can be found at www.pfmt.org/wildlife/endangered/default.htm.

Public scrutiny of DDT and water-borne pesticides increased. Runoff from fertilizers and manure, as well as direct chemical dumping, resulted in the decline of freshwater ecosystems across the country. Evidence of harm came in two forms: rampant algal blooms and widespread fish kills. Algal blooms are usually the result of agricultural runoff, which loads water with extra nutrients, essentially overfeeding the native algae. The spread of algae reduces the available oxygen in the water, suffocating other native species like fish. The directly toxic effects of chemical dumping also contributed to environmental decline.

Growing public awareness of these environmental catastrophes and demand for remediation, resulted in legislation that came to be called the **Clean Water Act**. This piece of environmental legislation joined the **Clean Air Act** and was followed by the **Resource Conservation and Recovery Act (RCRA)**. These laws enforced by the federal government's **Environmental Protection Agency** have reduced air, water and soil pollution in this country. However, there is still work to be done. In the following sections, we will look at various types of pollution and their sources.

AIR POLLUTION

Air pollutants are substances present in the air at sufficient quantities to cause harm. These substances can be gases, liquids or solids. The two main categories of air pollutants are primary and secondary. The classification of air pollutants depends on their origin. **Primary air pollutants** are harmful substances that enter the atmosphere directly from their source of origin. Some examples include carbon monoxide, nitric oxide, volatile organic chemicals, dust, ash and salt particles produced from vehicle emissions and industrial combustion processes. **Secondary air pollutants** are compounds that form in the atmosphere after chemically or photochemically reacting with other compounds that have also been released. Some examples include sulfuric acid, nitrogen dioxide and ozone. Secondary air pollutants often form smog.

Air pollution negatively impacts the environment and living organisms. It can reduce visibility in the atmosphere. It can cause corrosion of materials such as metals and plastics. It can affect regional temperatures. Air pollution can also diminish crop production. Air pollution can bring about droughts. Sometimes air pollutants can become trapped in rainwater and enter the hydrosphere. These pollutants can stress the local plant and animal life. Air pollution's most serious threat is to the health of living things, as it is responsible for a variety of health problems in animals and plants. Respiratory and cardiovascular problems in humans are health issues that pollution can cause or worsen. On a global scale, air pollution has contributed to global temperature changes and depletion of the ozone layer.

Table 9.1 Six Major Sources of Air Pollution

Origin	Primary or Secondary
Particulate (dust, lead, etc.)	Primary
Nitrogen oxides	Secondary
Sulfur oxides	Primary
Sulfuric acid	Secondary
Carbon oxides	Primary
Hydrocarbons	Primary
Ozone	Secondary

WATER POLLUTION

Water pollutants are substances present in water in levels sufficient to cause harm. Water pollutants are divided into several categories as summarized in Table 9.2. In general, water pollution threatens both animals and plants. Water pollution can spoil food sources and destroy living tissues. Some types of water pollution can enter and remain in living tissues for some time.

Table 9.2 Water Pollutants

Source	Use	Some Effects
Dioxins (TCDD)	Chemical Contaminants	May cause cancer. May harm reproductive, immune and nervous systems
Aldicarb	Pesticide	Attacks nervous system
Benzene	Solvent	Can cause leukemia and blood disorders
Carbon tetrachloride	Solvent	May cause liver damage, cancer and attack kidneys and vision
Chloroform	Solvent	Causes cancer
Ethylene dibromide (EDB)	Fumigant	Causes cancer and attacks liver and kidneys
Polychlorinated biphenyls (PCBs)	Various	Attacks liver and kidneys. May cause cancer
Trichloroethylene (TCE)	Solvent	Caused liver cancer in mice
Vinyl chloride	Plastics Industry	Causes cancer

SOIL POLLUTION

Soil pollutants are substances present in the soil in sufficient quantities to cause harm. Many of the pollutants found in water originate as soil pollutants and migrate into the water over time. Many soil pollutants have the same sources and health consequences as the water pollutants. One notable pollutant in soils is the concentration of mineral salts, which kills plant life by robbing the roots of water. The mineral salts create a hypertonic solution around the roots, causing the water to move out of the roots and into the surrounding soil.

Section Review 1: Pollution

A. Terms

pollution   primary air pollutant   water pollutant

air pollutant   secondary air pollutant   soil pollutant

B. Multiple Choice

1. Pollution comes in the form of

   A. gases.   B. liquids.   C. solids.   D. all of these

2. Secondary air pollution is

   A. not harmful to humans.

   B. pollution that has reacted with something in the atmosphere to become less harmful.

   C. pollution that has reacted chemically or photochemically while in the atmosphere.

   D. only a risk to human health.

3. Where do you find pollution?

   A. water   B. air   C. soil   D. all of these

C. Short Answer

1. Name two sources of natural pollution.

2. What are two health problems in people caused or made worse by air pollution?

PROTECTING THE ENVIRONMENT

Most people are aware of the damage society can inflict on the environment, and acknowledge that this harms people, other animals and plants. As a result, for every action humans take, they are more likely to investigate how it will affect the environment. Humans must evaluate if the actions are worth the risk they pose to the surroundings. There are several factors for people to consider when undertaking new ventures. These factors help people promote sustainable development, fulfilling our current needs while also protecting the planet for future generations. Often conservation efforts increase biodiversity and overall ecosystem health.

ECOLOGICAL FACTORS

In recent years, growing environmental concerns have led people to evaluate the effects of their decisions on the **ecological health** of the planet. Countries have laws aimed at protecting ecosystems from the potential threat of human activities. In many areas of the United States, studies must be completed prior to permitting any new construction or disturbance of the land, water, or air. The purpose of these studies is to determine if any endangered or sensitive life forms and habitats are present on the proposed construction site. If sensitive or endangered life forms exist in the area, the disruption is not allowed. Businesses, industries and households are regulated for such things as soil erosion, water management, waste discharge, air and noise pollution, as well as other types of environmental concerns. The focus of the environmental movement has been on preserving the planet's ecosystems and reducing the amount of pollution and waste.

HEALTH FACTORS

Human health and well being is of paramount importance when making environmental decisions. Foremost in the decision making process is balancing how much pollution is acceptable versus what level causes serious health concerns. If the overall health of the planet is good, that is, if the air and water are clean (unpolluted), humans will be healthier. When people live in areas of unclean air and polluted water, statistics show that more disease and sickness are present.

Humans pollute as part of their culture. It has become increasingly apparent in the last century that, in many instances, people create pollution faster than the planet's ecosystems can absorb and remove the waste products. Scientists have struggled to find answers as to how much pollution is acceptable, to both people and other organisms in the environment before the damage becomes irreparable. Many of the questions regarding how much pollution is acceptable are still unanswered.

Figure 9.2 Landfill

SOCIAL FACTORS

One of the looming challenges facing the human species today is the **population growth rate**. Since the Industrial Revolution changed the face of both industry and agriculture, the world population has been able to expand at an increasing rate. The British economist **Thomas Malthus** (1766 – 1834), predicted that the human species, growing exponentially, and the food supply, growing linearly, would lead to massive starvation worldwide at some future point. Over the centuries since, however, the opposite has proved to be the case: increases in agricultural efficiency and overall food supply has, since the industrial revolution, far exceeded the growth in population worldwide. However, certain problems remain between population and food supply. For example, food is not distributed evenly worldwide. While food is abundant in the U.S., the food supply is below the needs of the people in Somalia. These situations lead to famines, especially when wars and lack of infrastructure such as roads do not allow food to reach these populations in crisis.

A new problem, related to belief in the theories of Malthus, has occurred in population changes. Because many world governments believed Malthus was correct, they aggressively encouraged population control methods, both voluntary (Western nations) and forced (China's One Child policy) among their people. However, this has led to an emerging problem, particularly in Europe at this point: underpopulation, especially of the youth. As a result of falling birthrates, an aging and retiring workforce has fewer youth and working age populations to support the elderly in the population. European governments are finding it increasingly difficult to support the masses of elderly, given the current workforce available.

The United Nations (UN) currently projects the population to grow to 9.1 billion by 2050, but also shows the growth in population as declining. Both government promotion of population control and voluntary changes on an individual basis have changed the level of the growth, for better or worse. For example, as people gain education and socioeconomic status, they often wait until they have completed their education and establish their careers before starting a family, which reduces the number of children possible for a family. Projections of worldwide populations have been revised downward every decade since the UN began tracking growth rates. This is a very complicated issue. You should research the topic objectively before determining your position.

RESOURCE USE

As stated earlier in the book, matter cannot be created or destroyed. This is also true concerning the earth's resources. There are a finite amount of natural resources available on the planet. **Natural resources** are raw materials used by humans to live. A natural resource can be considered renewable or non-renewable. **Non-**

Figure 9.3 Logging Operation

renewable resources like coal, oil and natural gas are replaced only after long periods of time and under certain conditions. **Renewable resources** can be replaced within the human lifetime. Renewable resources are things like timber, water and solar energy. However, it is important to remember that even renewable resources can be depleted. Too much logging can lead to timber shortages, and excessive water use can deplete the supply of fresh water. Strategies that help prevent depletion include sustainable use practices, reducing the amount of raw materials used, reusing products and recycling.

Natural resources are not evenly dispersed throughout the world. Nonrenewable resources form or accumulate over a long period of time, so that our present supply is considered a fixed amount. **Nonrenewable resources** were deposited in different locations on the planet as the earth's crust evolved. For example, mineral deposits like aluminum and tin were moved as a result of plate tectonics. Earth processes, like erosion, concentrate the minerals in different areas of the earth. When minerals are concentrated, they can be mined.

Renewable resources, like bodies of water and forests, can be replenished over a short period of time. Renewable resources are also unevenly distributed. Most of Earth's surface is covered by oceans, a water source that is mostly unusable to people because of its high salt content. The land areas of earth have varying climates. Different climates determine the type of vegetation and water bodies that exist. Humans tend to live in areas where resources like fresh water, rich soil and forests are available. These areas of the planet also have warmer temperatures.

Humans use both renewable and nonrenewable resources inefficiently, thus depleting much of the supply. As the human population grows larger, the need to plan for the future and to protect resources becomes apparent. However, ideas and opinions about how resources should be used differ. In developing nations, resources required for survival are generally small per person. In wealthier nations, individuals perceive that their requirements are far above what is necessary for survival. Developed nations, like the United States, have "throwaway" lifestyles, and thus, overuse resources. A baby born in the United States consumes about as much as 12 babies born in a developing nation in Africa.

Highly developed nations have the economic ability to purchase resources that aren't available in their own country. For example, the United States buys oil from countries in the Middle East. Most people in the United States live in urban areas and purchase food grown in other parts of the country or in other nations. Wood and minerals can be transported to areas that can afford to pay for such materials. This economic prosperity is not an option for many developing nations.

If increasing development in the world is the solution to many problems, the development needs to be sustainable. Our planet cannot support a total population that consumes resources at the rate of developed nations, even if a lower overall population is achieved. A more conservative-minded approach to resource use includes using less of a particular resource and recycling wastes. The United States has implemented several practices to help conserve and recycle. For example, soil conservation and timber replacement measures have been implemented. Reducing water consumption by installing showers and toilets that use less water and limiting water use for landscape activities have been mandated in many places. Research into using alternative energy sources will also help reduce the amount of fossil fuels used and may help find renewable energy sources.

SUSTAINABLE PRACTICE

Sustainable practice is using the natural resources in a way that does not deplete them. This type of practice applies to agriculture, fishing, power usage and land development. **Sustainable agriculture** is increasingly important as our population continues to grow.

Sustainable agriculture encourages several practices among farmers. Farmers should select species and varieties of plants and animals that are well suited to the area and to conditions on the farm. Farmers are also

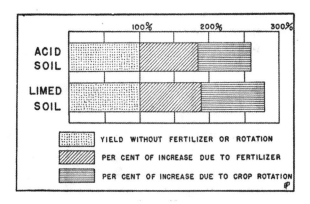

Figure 9.4 Percent Increase with Sustainable Practice

encouraged to diversify crops and livestock to enhance the biological and economic stability of the farm. They are taught how to manage the soil to enhance and protect soil quality. One way to improve soil quality is through legume crop rotation. **Legume crop rotation** is the practice of alternating a planting of regular crops with legumes. Planting legumes, or beans, traps atmospheric nitrogen in the soil, thus reducing the need for chemical fertilizers. Finally, farmers should use lesser amounts of chemically applied substances. Instead, they are taught how to use beneficial insects and plants to help control pests, fungi and encourage plant growth.

NON-SUSTAINABLE PRACTICE

A **non-sustainable practice** uses natural resources in a way that is often harmful to the environment. These practices often use up natural resources and degrade the natural environment.

Non-sustainable agriculture has been in use for many years in human populations. This type of agriculture often strips the topsoil and increases soil erosion. Non-sustainable agriculture often leads to **desertification**, a process where once fertile, productive land becomes non-productive and desert-like. The dust bowl of the 1930s in the United States was a result of non-sustainable methods. Also, the addition of many pesticides to crops is unhealthy to the ecosystem, killing all insects, including the beneficial insects. The surviving insects are resistant to the chemicals. The resistant insects then reproduce making more insects that are resistant. Soon, the need arises for stronger pesticides.

The addition of fertilizers can lead to disasters in local watersheds. Fertilizers can wash large amounts of unused nutrients into the watershed. This increase in the amount of nutrients can create an algal bloom, where algae grows to excessively large amounts often covering the entire surface of the water. These blooms frequently kill entire aquatic ecosystems.

Clearly, how humans choose to use natural resources affects the quality of life for all organisms within the community.

ECONOMIC FACTORS

Economics is the study of how people use Earth's limited resources as they attempt to fulfill their own needs. As the human population has grown, its demand on the planet's resources has put stress on the earth's environment. Continued advancement of industry has added to this demand. Figure 9.5 below shows how the natural environment and economics affect one another.

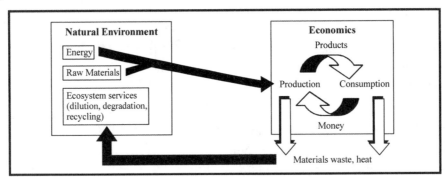

Figure 9.5 Relationship Between Environment and Economics

The **rate of depletion** is the speed at which a given resource is consumed. Usually, this rate is measured in years, and it can vary as changes in consumption rate or discovery of new resources change the availability of the resource. For example, during the early 1970s, scientists projected that the world supplies of oil would be depleted by the end of the 1990s. However, as scientists discover new fields and more efficient technologies are developed, the depletion figure is revised. Today, the depletion date is projected somewhere around 2050.

TECHNOLOGICAL DEVELOPMENT

After realizing the damaging effect of technological development, humans now attempt to direct new technological developments towards improving the health of the planet. **Technological developments** have been instrumental in all areas of the environmental movement Technological development has decreased air emissions by decreasing gasoline consumption in automobiles and has cut pollutants from vehicles and factories by installing filters. Barriers that absorb sound have been installed on highways and around appliances as well. Energy efficient appliances have been created, reducing the amount of water, electricity or natural gas required to operate the machines.

INSTITUTIONAL CHANGE

An **institution** may be a company or a government. Institutions working together are the most prudent way to ensure the overall health of the human species. At one time, each country was content to work by itself for the express interests of its citizens. For centuries, the world has been plagued by isolation and war as countries have vied to satisfy their own interests. During the 1990s, this emphasis shifted to a global community, where countries shared information and resources in spite of their differences. The idea of a **global community** increases the exchange of technology and allows countries to focus on major problems of concern to the planet. The free exchange of information across the face of the globe has increased cooperation between nations, prevented major epidemics, decreased pollution and protected the major ecosystems of the world. In many cases, when a country is found to work against ideals held by the global community, they find themselves facing global embargoes, or other such measures.

THE INTERACTION BETWEEN SOCIETAL FACTORS: RECYCLING

In past years, recycling was an activity encouraged by many, but actually done by very few. Some state governments, like Michigan, actively encouraged recycling through bottle return programs. Returning glass bottles paid 5 cents each; even more was paid for aluminum cans, which are very expensive to manufacture. Over time, the program grew to include paper products, styrofoam and steel.

Figure 9.6 Recycle

You may think that this is entirely reasonable, that a returned glass bottle is actually worth 5 cents. It is not. This is what is called a **subsidized program,** which means a program aided by public money. The point of the program was to establish the habit of recycling, because recycling is only economically worthwhile if a great number of people recycle.

It is clear that there are environmental benefits to recycling. The practice decreases landfill waste as well as the use of raw materials; therefore, many governments felt that it was a habit worth enforcing. New Jersey, for instance, was an early enforcer of mandatory garbage sorting and residential roadside pickup of recyclables. This situation occurred in great part because the state's small size and lack of landfill space. Recycling was not just environmentally attractive, but nearly imperative.

More recently, technological advances in the area of recycling have enabled recycled products, most especially aluminum, to become increasingly competitive with similar products made from new raw materials. Further, the ongoing work of various institutions, including state and local governments and environmental groups, has increasingly encouraged the practice of recycling within residential communities. Recycling is an excellent example of economic, technological and institutional factors working together to gradually produce the desired goal of environmental improvement.

Section Review 2: Protecting the Environment

A. Terms

nonrenewable resources	legume crop rotation	economics
renewable resources	non-sustainable practice	rate of depletion
sustainable practice		

B. Multiple Choice

1. Businesses that follow principles of sustainable development
   - A. only think about money.
   - B. think only about the present.
   - C. think about present and future needs.
   - D. don't care about a healthy planet.

2. How does the amount of resources used by a developed nation compare to the amount of resources used by an underdeveloped nation?
   - A. developed nations use a lot more
   - B. resource use is about the same
   - C. developed nations use a lot less
   - D. underdeveloped nations use a lot more

3. If the environment is healthy, then
   - A. people are healthier.
   - B. there are more diseases.
   - C. there are fewer plants on earth.
   - D. there is less development.

4. Using natural resources in a way that is harmful to the environment is also called a
   - A. sustainable practice.
   - B. non-sustainable practice.
   - C. maintaining practice.
   - D. current practice.

5. If a farmer alternates the planting of soybeans with his regular crop, he is probably
   - A. using legume crop rotation.
   - B. using sustainable practices.
   - C. using non-sustainable practices.
   - D. A and B only

6. Using sustainable practice techniques is important because
   - A. humans are the most important organism on the planet.
   - B. ecosystems are nice to look at.
   - C. as human beings it is our job to keep the planet going for future generations.
   - D. as the human population increases so does the demand on natural resources.

7. Practices that will help prevent the depletion of natural resources are

   A. sustainable use by reducing, reusing and recycling products.

   B. using only natural renewable resources.

   C. increasing consumption of renewable resources.

   D. returning to subsistence lifestyles.

C. Short Answer

Why is sustainable development important?

ALTERATIONS TO THE ENVIRONMENT

ALTERATION OF NUTRIENT CYCLES

Recall that elements and nutrients cycle through the biogeochemical pathways in natural processes. Humans impact many of these processes in harmful ways.

THE CARBON CYCLE

The activities of humans have greatly impacted the carbon cycle. The carbon cycle examined earlier in Chapter 8 was somewhat incomplete. There is another component to the cycle. The long-term carbon cycle relies on processes of the earth that take hundreds, thousands or even millions of years to complete. Humans alter this cycle by digging up stored carbon, in the form of oil and coal, from the earth and then burning it. This releases the carbon into the atmosphere millions of years before it would have happened naturally. Scientists speculate that if humans stopped burning and drilling all carbon, the cycle would stabilize in about 300 years.

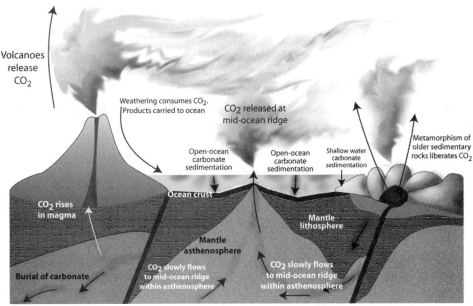

Figure 9.7 The Long-Term Carbon Cycle

THE NITROGEN CYCLE

Human activities have also impacted the nitrogen cycle. Humans have doubled the rate of land based nitrogen released into the environment through the use of fertilizers and pesticides. This has affected natural systems in many ways. Nitrogen is key to controlling plant diversity and productivity. Large amounts of nitrogen can become a pollutant in land and water systems. Nitrogen can acidify watersheds and coastal waters, as well as cause soil to lose nutrients like calcium and potassium. This can create a loss of biodiversity and cause declines in coastal fisheries. Increased nitrogen has also been linked to increased concentrations of nitrous oxide, which is an air pollutant. Humans can reduce the amount of nitrogen entering the ecosystem through sustainable agriculture.

THE PHOSPHOROUS CYCLE

Humans have also altered the phosphorous cycle. Mining of phosphorous from sedimentary rock accelerates the phosphorous cycle. Humans mine phosphorous to produce fertilizers and detergents. Excess phosphorous is added to aquatic ecosystems by runoff, improper disposal of animal wastes and discharge from municipal sewage.

THE WATER CYCLE

Humans, like most other living things, need a constant supply of water to survive. As a result, most humans live near water or bring water to where they live. Humans dam rivers to create lakes. This increases the rate at which water evaporates, thereby speeding up the water cycle. This increases rainfall amounts, which, in turn, increases weathering and soil erosion.

ALTERATION OF THE BIOSPHERE

Usually food webs and energy pyramids exist in a state of natural balance. If one component of the system becomes unbalanced, other parts of the system react to compensate. Humans alter food webs in many ways. Humans destroy habitats for crop production and housing. Humans cut down timber, which disrupts millions of acres of land a year. Humans kill many top predators like wolves, puma and bears. By destroying the top predator, other predators in the ecosystem must attempt to assume the role of the top predator. However, this strategy is not usually successful, as other animals are not adapted to fill that niche. Often, overpopulation of prey species becomes a serious problem, and many animals starve to death. By creating disruptions within the system, humans usually reduce biodiversity.

Humans sometimes alter the Earth's systems. The following are examples of activities that upset the balance of nature:

- Carelessness with a campfire can destroy a forest community.
- The building of a dam across a river can affect the animals in the area by changing the food supply.
- In-ground mining will disturb the plants and animals in the area.
- The dumping of harmful chemicals in a river will affect the quality of the water and the plants and fish in the river.
- Acid rain, a result of air pollution, can damage trees and lakes over a large area.
- Waste products from factory smokestacks pollute the air.

NON-NATIVE SPECIES INTRODUCTION

Normally all ecosystems exist in a natural state of equilibrium. Predator-prey interactions maintain the population of most species at a constant level. Humans often alter this balance by introducing non-native species into an ecosystem. In this new ecosystem, the introduced species often has very little predatory control and can quickly take over an ecosystem. There are many examples of this throughout the world. One example is the red imported fire ant (RIFA). This type of fire ant is native to South America. It was accidentally brought to the U.S. on Brazilian cargo ships, landing in Mobile, AL in the 1930s. Since that time, the RIFA has spread through the southern U.S. and across the world. Another example is kudzu. In America, from 1935 to the early 1950s, farmers were encouraged to plant kudzu to decrease soil erosion. Kudzu is native to Japan. When introduced to the United States, it grew vigorously. A kudzu vine can grow as much as 30 cm (12 in) per day. Kudzu covers all surfaces and kills many native plant species. Non-native species introduction is a serious threat to ecosystems.

Figure 9.8 Kudzu

ATMOSPHERIC ALTERATIONS

The Sun provides solar energy to the planet. Heat energy travels to the surface of the Earth from the Sun. The planet absorbs some of this solar energy, and some reflects back into the atmosphere. Gases present in the atmosphere trap reflected heat energy. These gases include water vapor, carbon dioxide, methane and chlorofluorocarbons (CFCs). Without the trapping of this heat, the average temperature of Earth would be approximately –20°C. This trapping of heat within the Earth's surface is called the **greenhouse effect**. Burning fossil fuels and rain forests is increasing the amount of carbon dioxide released into the atmosphere and, consequently, may lead to an overall increase in the Earth's temperature. Some scientists predict that a doubling of carbon dioxide will lead to a temperature increase of 1°C to 5°C. A slow global warming trend will affect the oceans, land surfaces and living things.

Global warming is an issue that many scientists believe will raise the Earth's overall temperature several degrees. The changes humans have made to the carbon, nitrogen, phosphorus and water cycles are theorized to have catastrophic effects on the human population. It is believed that the polar ice sheets will melt, which will raise sea levels. Storms may become more frequent and intense. Some climatologists believe that the melting of the polar ice sheets will slow the ocean currents. This could have a cooling effect on the planet. No one really knows the true effects of human disruptions to the global climate. The fact remains, the overall temperature of the Earth has risen 1°C since 1950.

Humans can control acid rain, water pollution, air pollution, land pollution and thermal pollution. We must recognize the signs of pollution and devise methods to control it.

The following are ways that pollution levels are being reduced:

- Emission controls issued by the state and federal government are being enforced by law. Automobiles are required to pass emission tests each year.

- Sewage plants process raw waste by adding oxygen to it and by introducing enzymes into it which digest the harmful wastes.

- Pesticides control insects but cause environmental pollution. The animals that feed on these insects ingest the poisonous chemicals stored in the bodies of the insects. Ways to farm organically, without chemicals, are being used in many places.

- Waste heat is heat that is discharged from power plants and other industries, usually in the form of hot water. This hot water is dumped into rivers, lakes and oceans and causes unhealthy plant growth, kills fish and has even changed the weather in some cities. Federal and local governments are more carefully monitoring this kind of thermal pollution, and industries are finding ways to use and minimize waste heat.

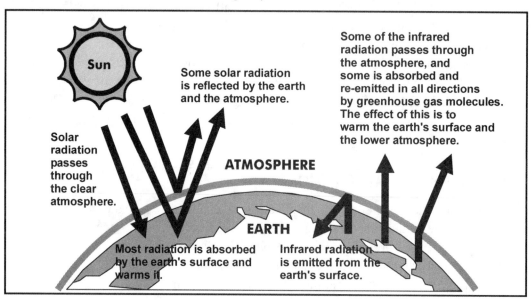

Figure 9.9 The Greenhouse Effect

Section Review 3: Alterations to the Environment

A. Terms

greenhouse effect   global warming

B. Multiple Choice

1. Humans have altered or interrupted

   A. the carbon cycle.   C. the water cycle.

   B. the nitrogen cycle.   D. all of the nutrient cycles.

2. Humans have interrupted the nitrogen cycle by

   A. digging up the stored nutrient resources and combusting them during industrial processes.

   B. damming rivers and lakes.

   C. increasing the rate at which land-based nitrogen is released into the environment.

   D. all of the above

3. Humans have altered the water cycle by
   A. digging up the stored nutrient resources and combusting them during industrial processes.
   B. damming rivers and lakes.
   C. increasing the rate at which land based nitrogen is released into the environment.
   D. all of the above

4. Humans have altered the carbon cycle by
   A. digging up the stored nutrient resources and combusting them during industrial processes.
   B. damming rivers and lakes.
   C. increasing the rate at which land based nitrogen is released into the environment.
   D. all of the above

5. When the top predator of an ecosystem is eradicated,
   A. other animals attempt to fill the niche unsuccessfully.
   B. the ecosystem continues to function normally.
   C. humans are pleased.
   D. the entire ecosystem crashes and is incapable of ever recovering.

6. Air pollution is being reduced through
   A. automobiles having emissions controls.
   B. salting of clouds.
   C. collecting methane produced by cattle.
   D. slower driving speeds on roads.

7. What natural process causes global warming?
   A. greenhouse effect
   B. non-native species introduction
   C. combustion of carbon dioxide
   D. sewage plant effluence

8. Why do non-native species, like Asian Carp, quickly take over new ecosystems?
   A. They like to travel.
   B. They enjoy the company of humans.
   C. They lack predatory controls.
   D. They enjoy warmer temperatures.

9. Which nutrient is released by humans into the environment in excess quantities through fertilizers and detergents?
   A. phosphorous   B. carbon   C. water   D. oxygen

C. Short Answer

1. Can you think of other ways to control human pollution?

2. Is the greenhouse effect necessary for life on Earth?

CHAPTER 9 REVIEW

A. Choose the best answer.

1. Which statement is true concerning the Earth's natural resources?

   A. They are evenly distributed.

   B. They are all in the poles.

   C. They are concentrated in different areas.

   D. They are all along the equator.

2. Most water pollutants originate as

   A. soil pollutants.

   B. air pollutants.

   C. primary pollutants.

   D. secondary pollutants.

3. Which disease listed below is MOST LIKELY caused by water pollution?

   A. heart attacks   B. diabetes   C. osteoporosis   D. cancer

4. How can people reduce the amount of resources they use?

   A. Write to their congressional representative to ask for more landfills.

   B. Make sure that products use extra packaging materials so it is easier for people to use.

   C. Use water, electricity and gas efficiently and recycle metal, paper and glass.

   D. Think only about what you need right now and not about the big picture.

5. The benefits of international discussions about the environment are that

   A. the blame can be placed on the greatest polluter, and that country pays for clean-up.

   B. pollution controls are implemented because of the increased dialogue and understanding.

   C. wars can be started on those countries that don't follow environmental laws.

   D. the country with the most money can pay for pollution clean-up.

6. Humans have interrupted the carbon cycle by

   A. allowing more rock surfaces to weather.

   B. drilling and using fossil fuels.

   C. polluting the ocean, so that carbon can no longer be naturally stored there.

   D. living longer, thereby storing more carbon in their tissues.

7. Changes in the amount of greenhouse gases in the air may cause

   A. global warming.

   B. thermal pollution.

   C. photosynthesis.

   D. clear cutting of rain forests.

8. Humans sometimes use chemical fertilizers to help agricultural crops grow faster. These fertilizers usually contain large quantities of nitrogen and phosphorous. The use of these substances are harmful because

   A. the manufacture of these chemicals creates more nitrogen and phosphorous on the Earth.

   B. only plants in or near an agricultural area can benefit from the addition of fertilizers.

   C. the addition of these chemicals alters the natural nitrogen and phosphorous cycle, causing an increase in plant matter in the ecosystem and the local watershed.

   D. the addition of chemical fertilizers contributes to an increase in greenhouse gases found in the atmosphere.

9. Which statement below is true regarding global warming?

   A. It is an immediate threat to human existence.

   B. It is not completely understood.

   C. It is a fully tested theory.

   D. It is not really a problem.

10. The human population growth

    A. will stop at a reasonable number.

    B. is in the middle of an exponential growth curve.

    C. will never stop or slow down.

    D. will not strain the planet's natural resources.

11. If a farmer planted varieties well-suited to his area, what type of agriculture is he practicing?

    A. legume crop rotation   C. non-sustainable agriculture

    B. sustainable agriculture   D. subsidized agriculture

12. Benzene is a solvent that can cause leukemia and blood disorders. Where is benzene often found as a pollutant?

    A. water   B. air   C. animal tissues   D. clouds

13. In America, termites destroy millions of dollars in property. Termites have no natural predators in North America. How did termites most likely arrive in North America?

    A. They were brought by humans.

    B. They crossed a land bridge.

    C. Their eggs floated across the ocean.

    D. They were parasites inside animals.

Examine the charts below.

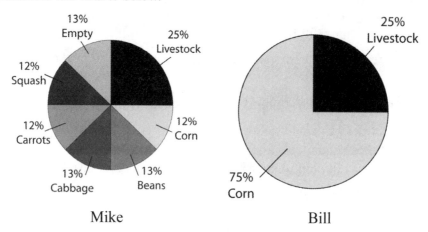

Mike   Bill

14. Who is using sustainable practices?
    A. Bill   C. both Bill and Mike
    B. Mike   D. neither Bill nor Mike

15. Who is MORE LIKELY to use fertilizers and pesticides?
    A. Bill   C. both Bill and Mike
    B. Mike   D. neither Bill nor Mike

16. Who is MORE LIKELY to use legume crop rotation?
    A. Bill   C. both Bill and Mike
    B. Mike   D. neither Bill nor Mike

B. Answer the following questions.

17. What is responsible for the global shift of mineral resources throughout history?

18. How does the human population affect natural resources?

19. Of the three arguments to solve world hunger, which do you think is the best? Explain.

20. How has technology helped prevent pollution?

Use the list to answer question 1.

> • found at latitudes between 20° and 60° N
>
> • medium rainfall amounts
>
> • average summer temperature around 24°C
>
> • contains plants that loose their leaves in the fall

1 Which biome is described in the list?   15

    A tundra   **C** deciduous forest

    B coniferous forest   **D** grassland

2 What is the control center of the cell is known as?   4

    A vacuole   **C** nucleus

    B ribosome   **D** mitochondria

3 After fertilization, an embryo develops into a zygote through many cell   6b
divisions. If the sperm and egg each contain 8 chromosomes, how many
chromosomes are contained within the zygote?

    A 4   **B** 8   **C** 16   **D** 24

4 Sewage treatment facilities sometimes allow tons of untreated sewage to flow   14a
into the Alabama river systems. Which of the following is an appropriate
method for dealing with this situation?

    A build dams along the river to catch the sewage

    B put up pollution warning signs

    C process the untreated sewage by adding oxygen and sewage-eating bacteria

    D ask farmers in the area to use some untreatable sewage for fertilizer

5 If rice is covered with water in a pan and left overnight, what will happen?   2b

  A The rice will reproduce itself through fission.

  B The rice will become dehydrated.

  C The rice will undergo plasmolysis.

  D The rice will swell through osmosis.

6 An adaptation known as camouflage may aide in some salamanders'   12

  A mutations.

  B geographic isolation.

  C convergent evolution.

  D survival.

7 Which biome below has low average rainfall but usually maintains large herds of herbivores?   15

  A tropical rain forest

  B tundra

  C coniferous forest

  D grassland

8 Which of the following categories of classification is MOST specific?   9a

  A kingdom   **C** class

  B order   **D** genus

9 What is the correct conversion of 5.32 m to km?   1d

  A 0.0532 km

  B 5320 km

  C 0.00532 km

  D 532 km

10 Animals that cannot make their own food are   13b

  A omnivores.   **C** autotrophs.

  B heterotrophs.   **D** producers.

Use the diagram to help you answer question 11.

11 What is the inheritance pattern for color in pansies?   7

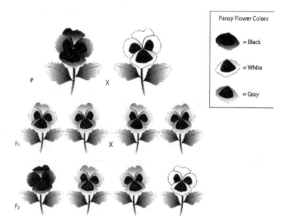

Pansy Flower Colors
= Black
= White
= Gray

  A simple dominant/recessive

  B sex-linked

  C incomplete dominant

  D co-dominant

12 The transfer of characteristic traits from parent to offspring is known as   7a

  A genetics.   **C** replication.

  B mutation.   **D** heredity.

13 In the energy pyramid, the level with the MOST stored energy is   13

  A the top consumer.

  B the secondary consumer.

  C the producers.

  D the primary consumer.

14 Which of the examples does NOT complete the following sentence? Carbon dioxide can be found as a gas in

A the atmosphere.

B a carbonated drink.

C the respiration process.

D dry ice.

15 Latasha opened some canned peaches. The expiration date on the can was 12 years ago. They gave off a pungent odor and had tiny bubbles rising to the top. Which of the following processes has taken place in the can of peaches?

A sublimation   C cohesion

B fermentation   D corrosion

16 What are long tubelike structures which carry water, minerals and sugar throughout the plant?

A stems   C stomata

B roots   D vascular tissue

17 A cell which results from the process of fertilization is a(n)

A gamete.   C haploid cell.

B egg.   D zygote.

18 Which organism in the food chain has the GREATEST amount of available energy?

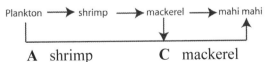

A shrimp   C mackerel

B plankton   D mahi mahi

19 Your teacher reminds you to "Be sure to wear eye protection at all times in the lab." This is known as a(n)

A safety procedure.

B step in the scientific method.

C observation.

D laboratory theory.

20 The process in which a plant makes food from water and carbon dioxide using energy from the Sun is known as

A respiration.

B absorption.

C reproduction.

D photosynthesis.

21 How does passive transport differ from endocytosis?

A In passive transport, substances are moved into and out of cells without the use of energy, while endocytosis is a type of active transport.

B Passive transport is the movement of water into a cell with the help of ATP, while endocytosis is a type of active transport.

C In passive transport, substances are moved into and out of cells without the use of energy, while endocytosis moves molecules by diffusion and osmosis.

D In passive transport, molecules move from areas of lower concentration to higher concentration. In endocytosis, water is diffused through the cell membrane.

22 Where does respiration take place?   4

   A in the nucleus of the cell

   B in the mitochondria of the cell

   C in the Earth's crust

   D in the atmosphere

23 Four groups of rats are tested in a lab. Group 1 is given a special hormone for muscle growth. Group 2 is given a special multivitamin diet. Group 3 receives both the hormone treatment and the multivitamin diet. Group 4 does not receive any extra treatment or special diet. Which of the following groups is the control group for this experiment?   1b

   A Group 4

   B Group 2

   C Group 3

   D Group 1

24 Which of the following is the BEST example of maintaining homeostasis?   2

   A a horse sweating after a long ride

   B frog croaking to attract a mate

   C a lizard changing color to match its background

   D worker ants protecting the queen

25 The eukaryotic cell is composed of small structures called   5

   A carbon and oxygen.

   B organelles.

   C DNA.

   D cell walls.

26 What native plants and animals are found in a tropical rain forest?   15

Native Plants		Native Animals	
1	pine, spruce and fur	1	bison, antelope and prairie dogs
2	reindeer moss and lichens	2	monkeys, poison dart frogs, tapir and jaguar
3	sagebrush, mosquito and tumbleweed	3	polychaete worms, hagfish, sunfish, tuna and herring
4	broad leaf trees, vines, ferns, mosses and orchids	4	kangaroo rat, scorpion and rattlesnake

   A native plant 1 and native animal 2

   B native plant 4 and native animal 3

   C native plant 4 and native animal 2

   D native plant 2 and native animal 1

27 Which type of bird foot is BEST adapted to walking on the ground?   12

A 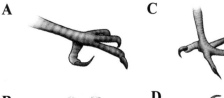   **C**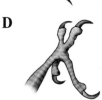

B    **D**

28 What level of biological organization is shown in the picture?   5

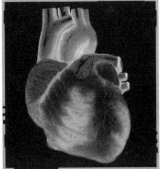

A organ   C organism

B organ system   D tissue

29 The wing of a bird and the arm of a man are considered   12a

A homologous structures.

B evidence of evolution of man from birds.

C vestigial structures.

D variable structures.

30 The process of male and female gametes uniting is known as   6b

A germination.

B pollination.

C fertilization.

D transcription.

31 A large volcano erupts, spewing millions of tons of ash and dust into the atmosphere. These particles block sunlight, hindering which vital biological process?   3

A cellular respiration

B reproduction

C photosynthesis

D carbon dioxide and water

32 The gene for Tay-Sachs is a recessive trait. This disorder causes fatty acids to build up in the nerve tissues eventually leading to death. If a couple marries who are both carriers of the disease, what are the chances that their first child will have the disease?   8e

A one in two

B The child will definitely have the disease.

C one in three

D one in four

33 The offspring of the hydra start to grow while still attached to the outside of the parent organism. When they grow large enough to survive on their own, they break away from the parent. This type of reproduction is known as   11

A sending off spores.

B budding.

C vegetative propagation.

D binary fission.

34 As a result of meiosis in humans,   6

A a cell divides into two new cells.

B pairs of identical alleles are joined.

C six daughter cells are produced.

D each egg and sperm cell have a haploid (23) number of chromosomes.

35 What nutrient cycle is depicted   14
in the diagram?

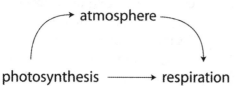

A water   **C** nitrogen

B oxygen   **D** phosphorous

36 Which of the following is the   1b
purpose of an experimental
group?

A Experimental groups are designed
with variable conditions to test the
hypothesis.

B An experimental group is designed
to yield observations under carefully controlled conditions.

C An experimental group is a judg-
ment or decision based on experimentation.

D Experimental groups are the results
of an investigation or experiment.

37 Which biogeochemcial cycle is   14
disrupted when humans remove
and combust fossil fuels form the
lithosphere?

A water

B carbon

C nitrogen

D phosphorous

Examine the list.

- kelp forest
- kelp
- sunlight, sea water, protists, marine organisms
- kelp forests, sea urchins, otters

38 Which entry represents a   5
population?

A kelp

B kelp forest

C sunlight, sea water, protists, marine
organisms

D kelp forest, sea urchins, otter

39 The feeding habits of vultures,   13c
whose diet consists exclusively
of dead and rotting things, are similar
to the feeding habits of decomposers.
What is the name of the kingdom of
decomposers?

A Protista   **C** Fungi

B Plantae   **D** Animalia

40 Plants give herbivores, such as   13
deer, energy. What abiotic factor
gives energy to plants?

A sunlight   **C** water

B oxygen   **D** rock

41 Protozoa living in the small   16a
intestine of a human gain
nutrients from undigested food. At the
same time, the protozoa aid the small
intestine in digestion. This in an
example of a

A commensalistic relationship.

B mutualistic relationship.

C parasitic relationship.

D predator/prey relationship.

42 How should a meniscus be read in a graduated cylinder filled with water?   1

   A The meniscus should be read with a magnifying glass.

   B The meniscus should be read from the top of the curve.

   C The meniscus should be read from left to right.

   D The meniscus should be read from the bottom of the curve.

43 A chemical pesticide kills 75% of the locust population in a localized area. The remaining percentage is unaffected by the chemical. What is likely to be the consequence of this pesticide on the environment?   14, 14a

   A The remaining locusts will leave the area immediately.

   B The remaining locusts will change their digestive system to use the chemical as food.

   C The remaining locusts will reproduce generations of locusts that are also resistant to this chemical.

   D Half of the locusts will remain in the area and die. The other half will leave and live.

A biologist studying in Alabama collected the following information on three aquatic reaches.

Coosa River		Tallapoosa River		Corn Creek	
Cajun dwarf crayfish	4	Boxclaw crayfish	2	Painted devil crayfish	14
Boxclaw crayfish	7	Speckled madtom catfish	10	Mapleleaf mussel	63
White warteyback mussels	31	Banded darter fish	9	Three ridge mussel	21
Banded darter fish	6	Mapleleaf mussel	43	Hogsucker fish	3
Three ridge mussel	47	White wartyback mussels	69	Yellow spotted salamander	2

44 How many communities did the biologist study?   5

   A 6   **B** 5   **C** 4   **D** 3

45 Tammy made a study of the pine trees in Shannon Park. She noticed not all the trees had cones on them. But beneath the trees with cones were many seeds with small wing-like structures attached. These pine trees could be classified as   10

   A non-vascular.

   B spore-bearing.

   C gymnosperms.

   D angiosperms.

46 What is the cellular component indicated below?   4

   A cilia   **C** cell membrane

   B flagellum   **D** pili

47 The chemical energy supply for all   3
living cells is contained in a
specific molecule. When broken
down, this molecule releases the
energy so it may be used for activities
such as muscle contractions,
photosynthesis and locomotion. What
is the molecule that is a storehouse of
energy called?

A ATP   **C** DNA

B ADP   **D** RNA

48 Which situation below is   16
density-dependent for the
communities living on a coral reef?

A human polluting the oceans

B spread of parasites

C warming of ocean temperatures

D seasonal typhoons

49 An animal cell is placed in a   2b
solution of distilled water. If left
overnight, this cell will

A swell and burst.

B shrivel and die.

C undergo chemosysthesis.

D remain the same, since it has a cell
wall to protect it.

50 A salamander raised away from   12
water until long after its siblings
begin swimming successfully will
swim every bit as well the very first
time it is placed in the water. What is
this called?

A learned behavior

B innate behavior

C diurnal behavior

D reflex behavior

51 During meiosis, only one   6, 6a
chromosome from each
homologue is passed on to the
offspring. This helps increase

A genetic variation.

B genetic mutations.

C fertilization rates.

D the rate of evolution.

52 What is the name of   1
the laboratory
instrument shown at
the right?

A thermometer

B beaker

C Bunsen burner

D graduated cylinder

53 The following illustration BEST   13
shows

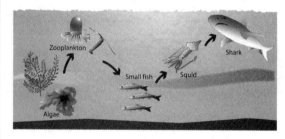

A the flow of energy from one
organism to the next in an
ecosystem.

B how much food a shark needs to
eat in order to survive.

C the diversity of biomass in the
ocean.

D the types of food a shark likes to
eat.

54 An organism that is endothermic,   11
has hair, produces milk for its
young and gives birth to live young
belongs to which class of vertebrates?

A Mammalia   **C** Reptilia

B Aves   **D** Amphibia

55 Which process converts large   3
quantities of ADP to ATP during
the electron transport chain?

A photosynthesis

B aerobic respiration

C anaerobic respiration

D bicellular respiration

56 The DNA code eventually direct   8
the cell to manufacture

A protein.

B amino acids.

C hydrogen bonds.

D sugars.

57 Which nutrient cycle is MOST   14
directly impacted by the
pervasive use of fertilizers in modern
agricultural practice?

A the carbon cycle

B the nitrogen cycle

C the phosphorous cycle

D the water cycle

The diagram below shows the classification of four organisms.

Organism	 1	 2	 3	 4
Common Name	Goats–beard	Serviceberry	Prostrate Bluets	Purple Bluets
Phylum	Anthophyta	Anthophyta	Anthophyta	Anthophyta
Family	Rose	Rose	Madder	Madder
Genus	*Aruncus*	*Amelanchier*	*Houstonia*	*Houstonia*
Species	*dioicus*	*laevis*	*serpyllifolia*	*purpurea*

58 According to the diagram, which two organisms are the MOST related?   9a, 9b

A organisms 1 &2

B organisms 2 & 3

C organisms 3 & 4

D organisms 2 & 4

59 To what phylum do worms belong? 11

    A *Platyhelminthes*

    B *Cnidaria*

    C *Porifera*

    D *Echinodermata*

60 Quin and Roseanna collected various samples of the flora in their backyard. Of the three samples shown below, which is/are non-vascular plants? 10, 10a

Sample 1	Sample 2	Sample 3
Magnolia	Norway Spruce	Moss

    A sample 1

    B sample 2

    C samples 1 & 2

    D sample 3

61 Cystic fibrosis is a recessive genetic disease that causes the body to produce a thick mucus. If both parents are carriers for this disease, what is the probability of a child being born WITHOUT the disease? 8e

    A 25%   **C** 75%

    B 50%   **D** 100%

62 A parent has four children. Three of the children have a widow's peak and one child has no widow's peak. The allele that controls have a widow's peak is MOST LIKELY a 7a

    A dominant.   **C** co-dominant.

    B recessive.   **D** mutating.

63 Which correctly shows the biological organization from LEAST complex to MOST complex? 5

    A ecosystem → population → species → tissue

    B species → organism → organ → tissue

    C tissue → organ → organism → species

    D cell → organ system → organ → ecosystem

64 In 2007, a severe drought struck the southeastern United States. Lake levels fell by 10 ft or more and many crops failed. Drought is an example of what type of limiting factor? 16

    A density-independent

    B density-dependent

    C carrying capacity

    D succession

65 A stand of sugar maple in the Buck's Pocket State Park can be classified as what level of organization? 5

    A ecosystem

    B population

    C community

    D species

66 Name the two classes of endothermic vertebrates. 9

    A Osteichthyes and Amphibia

    B Amphibia and Aves

    C Aves and Mammalia

    D Aves and Osteichthyes

67 The development of   10, 10a, 10b
seeds allows plants to
reproduce

   A asexually.

   B in a wide variety of ecosystems.

   C only in water.

   D only on land.

68 In orchids, the flower color   7, 7b, 7c
and fragrance are two
genetic traits. Each trait is located on a
separate chromosome. In orchids, the
allele for producing blue flowers (B) is
dominant to the allele for producing
white flowers (b). The allele for
producing strong fragrance (F) is
dominant to the allele for producing
little fragrance (f). Two orchids that
have blue flowers and strong fragrance
(BbFf) were crossed. Use the
completed Punnett square below to
determine the probability of offspring
that have blue flowers and strong
fragrance.

	BF	Bf	bF	bf
BF	BBFF	BBFf	BbFF	BbFf
Bf	BBFf	BBff	BbFf	Bbff
bF	BbFF	BbFf	bbFF	bbFf
bf	BbFf	Bbff	bbFf	bbff

   A 1/16

   B 3/16

   C 6/16

   D 9/16

69 The DNA strand below is one   8, 8a
half of a complementary pair.

ATGGGTAAGCTA

Which of the following complementary DNA
strands has a duplication mutation?

   A TACCCATTCGATGAT

   B TACCCATTCGAT

   C UACCCAUUCGAU

   D ATGGGTAAGCTA

70 What can you conclude from the general S-shaped curve in the graph below?

16

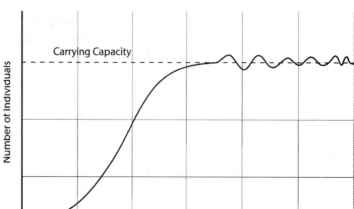

A   As resources become less available, the population growth slows or stops.

B   The number of births in the population continues to increase.

C   Abundant resources will continue to support the population.

D   The population is no longer living.

71 Which student correctly identified the density-dependent situations?

16

Student	Outbreak of viral infection	Starvation of deer in an over populated National Park	Humans hunting African elephants almost to extinction	Eruption of volcano causing global cooling
1		X	X	
2	X			X
3	X	X		
4			X	X

A   student 4

B   student 3

C   student 2

D   student 1

72 Which of the following is NOT   10a
a function of roots

   A to keep the plant anchored in place

   B to store sugar in the form of starch

   C to conduct respiration

   D to take up water and nutrients

73 Sexual reproduction encourages   8c
genetic variation in three ways.
Which of the following is NOT a
feature of sexual reproduction that
promotes new genetic combinations?

   A crossing over with genetic
recombination

   B independent assortment at the time
of meiosis

   C increasing the cell population by
mitosis

   D combination of parental genetic
backgrounds at fertilization.

The following image is of a salt water sponge.

74 Which type of body symmetry   11
does this sponge have?

   A asymmetry

   B bilateral

   C radial

   D incomplete

75 The graph below shows changes in two populations, the arctic rabbit and the arctic fox. After analyzing the data displayed in the graph, decide which of the following statements is a valid conclusion.   16

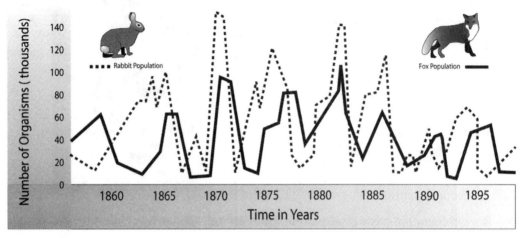

A The presence of foxes stimulates reproduction in the rabbit population.

B The fox and the rabbit have a predator-prey relationship.

C Foxes and rabbits have a symbiotic relationship.

D There is no correlation between the rabbit and the fox populations.

76 One octopus unscrews a jar lid and receives a food reward. Another octopus observes this occurrence and upon receiving a jar proceeds to quickly unscrew the lid. This is an example of   11

A innate behavior.

B learned behavior.

C diurnal behavior.

D territorial behavior.

77 A plant has a thick waxy cuticle to prevent moisture loss. The interior of the plant is hollow and is used to store large quantities of water. The leaves of the plant have evolved into sharp spines, which protect the flesh of the plant from water seeking animals. Which environment is MOST suited to this organism?   15

78 Which organelle indicated below is responsible for making food for the plant from sunlight?   4

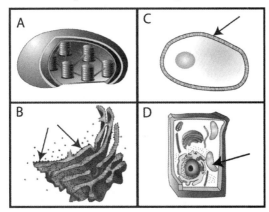

79 Which would a breeder use to produce cows which give more milk?   7a, 7b

A artificial selection

B natural selection

C gene mutation

D acquired characteristics

80 When lipids are immersed in a water-based system, like a cell, the long chains of carbon group together to separate themselves from the aqueous solvent. They may form one of two different lipid orientations, as shown in the diagram: a lipid bilayer (1) or a spherical arrangement   2a

called a micelle (2). Which statement explains this behavior?

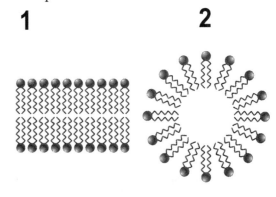

A The heads of the lipid are non-polar and the tails are polar.

B The heads of the lipid are polar and the tails are nonpolar.

C Both the heads and the tails consist of non-polar carbon.

D Both the heads and the tails consist of polar oxygen.

81 A free-living unicellular organism reproduces asexually through binary fission. If the parent cell contains 28 chromosomes, how many chromosomes are contained within the daughter cell?   6

A 7

B 14

C 28

D 56

82 Which limiting factor is density-dependent for the Ring-necked snake?   16

A flooding

B scale mites

C humans building a dam

D volcanic eruption

83 Which aquatic ecosystem contains organisms that MUST have a salinity of less that 0.5 ppm in order to thrive?   15

   A marine

   B estuary

   C intertidal

   D fresh water

84 Invertebrates are defined as animals without   11

   A exoskeletons.

   B backbones.

   C mammary glands.

   D specialization.

85 The equation below summarizes what biological process?   3

Light energy + $6H_2O + 6CO_2 \rightarrow$
$C_6H_{12}O_6 + 6O_2 + ATP$

   A chemophotosynthesis

   B fermentation

   C photosynthesis

   D cellular respiration

86 The diagram below shows DNA fingerprints from several people

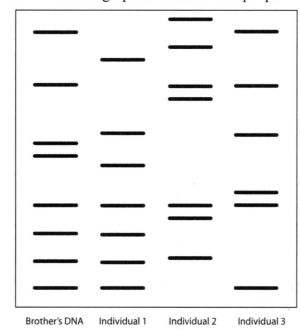

Brother's DNA   Individual 1   Individual 2   Individual 3

A mother and father die in a car accident and a brother and two sisters are placed in foster homes. Many years later the brother begins looking for his younger sisters. After a long and exhaustive search, three women claim that they are his sisters. Use the DNA fingerprints below to determine which two individuals are MOST likely his sisters?

A Individuals 1 and 2 are his sisters.

B Individuals 1 and 3 are his sisters.

C Individual 2 and 3 are his sisters.

D None of the individuals is a sibling.

87 In aspen trees, the allele for having round leaves (R) is dominant to the allele for having oval leaves (r). Use the Punnett square to determine the probability of parent trees of the following genotype having offspring with round leaves.

7c

	R	**r**
R		
r		

A 75%   **C** 50%

B 25%   **D** 0%

88 The Alabama state bird is the 12
Colaptes auratus, also called the
Yellowhammer. The Yellowhammer
has zygodactyl feet. These type of feet
have two toes pointing in each
direction, and are useful for clinging to
vertical surfaces. The Yellowhammer
also has a chisel-like beak and an
extremely long tongue, useful for
extracting insects from trees. What
type of adaptations do these represent?

A chemical

B behavioral

C physical

D cosmetic

89 The spines of a cactus are 12a, 12b
modified leaves. The thorn
of a rose is a modified branch. What
does this suggest about the evolution
of these two families of plants?

A The spine and the thorn are
homologous structures, so we can
conclude that the cactus and the
rose evolved from a common
ancestor.

B The spine and the thorn are vestigial structures, so we can conclude
that the cactus and the rose
evolved from a common ancestor.

C The spine and the thorn have similar functions, but did not evolve
from a common ancestor.

D The spine and the thorn have similar appearances, so we can conclude that they evolved from a
common ancestor.

90 An environment has cold harsh 15
winters with temperatures often
far below freezing and cool summers
with temperatures just above 45°F.
This environment receives a moderate
amount of precipitation. Which
organism would MOST likely live in
this environment?

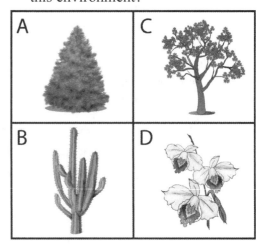

Alabama HSGT in Science
Post Test 2

1 The noting or recording of facts and events for scientific study is known as   1a

   A observation.   **C** speculation.

   B theorizing.   **D** hypothesizing.

2 DNA is made up of   8

   A sugars and phosphates.   **C** bacteria.

   B nitrogen and salt.   **D** water and oxygen.

3 Which organelle is the site of protein synthesis?   4

   A ribosome   **C** cell membrane

   B nucleus   **D** mitochondria

Use the following scenario to answer Question 4.

Researchers collected information on pond size preference for several different frog species found in southern Alabama. Each frog species has a unique preference for a particular pond size. Within each pond, the number of frogs of each species was counted and a dominant frog species was determined. The graph at right shows how pond size related to percentages of one native species, the burrowing mudhen.

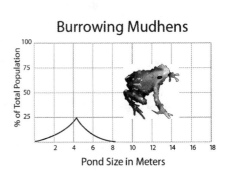

Burrowing Mudhens

4 What biological force is acting upon the burrowing mudhen population?   12a, 12b

   A natural selection

   B selective breeding

   C extinction

   D the founder effect

5 Judy knows that increased motion leads to increased temperature. She predicts that roads that are frequently traveled have a higher temperature than roads in the same area which are rarely traveled. This is an example of   1a

   A inductive reasoning.

   B street smarts.

   C the last step of scientific research.

   D deductive reasoning.

6 A single strand of DNA with the base pairing sequence C-G-A-T-T-G is compatible only with the sequence   8

   A T-A-G-C-C-T.

   B G-C-T-A-A-G.

   C G-C-T-A-A-C.

   D C-G-A-T-T-G.

7 A(n) _____ states how or why something happened based on research and testing.   1a

   A hypothesis   **C** experiment

   B observation   **D** theory

8 Turgor pressure   2d

   A is the result of a population that has succeeded its carrying capacity.

   B allows mammals to stand upright.

   C is what happens when divers ascend too rapidly causing bubbles to form in the blood and tissues.

   D is the internal pressure inside a plant cell swollen with large water vacuoles.

9 Which type of body symmetry does a stingray have?   11

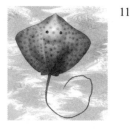

   A asymmetry   **C** radial

   B bilateral   **D** complete

10 Freckles are a dominant trait. A mother homozygous for the presence of freckles and a father heterozygous for freckles have a child. What is the chance that the child will be homozygous recessive for freckles?   7a, 7c

   A 0%   **C** 50%

   B 25%   **D** 75%

11 Which of the following contains a food chain in the correct order?   13

   A mouse - grass - hawk - snake - deer

   B snake - mouse - fox - eagle - vulture

   C birds - seeds - vulture - deer - grasshopper

   D grass - beetle - bird - bobcat - vulture

12 Which statement below BEST describes a density-independent situation?   16

   A hurricane Katrina striking the Gulf Coast.

   B the Ebola outbreak in Africa during 1976

   C the Kanyanja lion pride hunting immature elephants

   D two fish species competing to consume aquatic invertebrates

Use the following diagram to answer question 13.

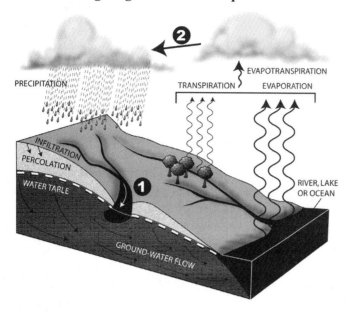

13 Two important processes are missing in this depiction of the water cycle. What   14
    are they?

    A Condensation is depicted by arrow (1). Sublimation is depicted by arrow (2).

    B Runoff is depicted by arrow (1). Sublimation is depicted by arrow (2).

    C Runoff is depicted by arrow (1). Condensation is depicted by arrow (2).

    D Condensation is depicted by arrow (1). Evaporation is depicted by arrow (2).

14 Which of the following   13, 13b, 13c
    describes the correct
    energy flow in an ecosystem?

    A Energy flows from heterotrophs to
        autotrophs to decomposers.

    B Energy flows from decomposer to
        consumers to producers.

    C Energy flows from producers to
        consumers to decomposers.

    D Energy flows from producers to
        decomposers to consumers.

15 What are the reactants in the   3
    process of respiration?

    A carbon dioxide, water and energy

    B carbon dioxide, energy and oxygen

    C oxygen and glucose

    D oxygen, glucose and water

16 "During phase two, 3-carbon   3
    sugars and oxygen enter the
    mitochondria to begin the citric acid
    cycle." This is a description of

    A anaerobic respiration.

    B aerobic respiration.

    C alcoholic respiration.

    D ATP respiration.

17 In which aquatic system would you find an ecosystem where Archaebacteria are producers for a complex food web located around hydrothermal vents? 15

A estuary

B marine benthic zone

C marine pelagic zone

D grassland

18 Somatic cells are body cells produced by 6

A meiosis.

B mitosis.

C reduction of chromosomes.

D interkinesis.

19 Microscopic organisms that live on the roots of legumes trap the atmospheric form of a nutrient, making it available to plants. What nutrient cycle is involved in this process? 14

A oxygen

B carbon

C water

D nitrogen

20 Coral reefs require warm, relatively shallow waters to grow and survive. Depending on the species, most coral require the temperature of the water to be between 18°C and 30°C. What do you suppose would happen to the coral if the average temperature changed in their ecosystem? 13a

A The coral would evolve into cold climate coral overnight.

B The coral would move to a more suitable habitat.

C Some of the coral would die.

D The coral would immediately begin to develop temperature adaptations.

21 Which statement BEST describes why the actions of humans are considered density-independent? 16

A The actions of humans only impact one or two species with a ecosystem like with artificial selection.

B The action of humans affect all populations with a particular ecosystem such as with pollution or habitat destruction.

C The actions of humans only impact the target species like with hunting of caribou.

D Humans cause global climate change affecting only densely populated species.

22 Which terrestrial biome is described by the graph? 15

Summer Abiotic Conditions

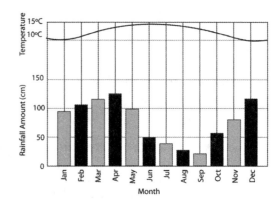

A rain forest

B tundra

C carboniferous forest

D desert

250

23 A botanist is attempting to identify an unfamiliar plant collected from a local 9b state park. Use the dichotomous key below to determine the genus and species of the following organism.

1. a. Flower pods located at the end of the stalk ....go to 2.
   b. Flower pods located along the bottom edge of the stalk....................go to 3.

    2. a. Small flowers located close together..............................*Smilacina racemosa*

  b. Large flowers located far apart..*Trillium undulatum*

    3. a. Hairs located on the underside of its leaf..................*Polygonatum pubescens*

  b. Surface of leaf is smooth... *Polygonatum biflorum*

    A *Smilacina racemosa*

    B *Trillium undulatum*

    C *Polygonatum pubescen*s

    D *Polygonatum biflorum*

24 Which two plants in the 9a, 9e previous question are *MOST* related?

    A *Polygonatum pubescens* and *Polygonatum biflorum*

    B *Smilacina racemosa* and *Trillium undulatum*

    C all the flowers are equally unre-lated

    D all the flowers are equally related

25 Which phylum of invertebrates 11 uses nematocysts to capture and kill prey?

    A Platyhelminthes

    B Cnidaria

    C Annelida

    D Arthropoda

26 What do prophase, metaphase, anaphase and telophase have in common?   6

A They are phases of protein synthesis.

B They are phases of cellular mitosis.

C They are phases of cytokinesis.

D They are phases of cellular respiration.

27 Which of the following are non-vascular plants?   10

A maple trees

B ferns

C mosses and liverworts

D gymnosperms and angiosperms

28 In the metric system, the prefix "centi" (as in centimeter) means   1d

A 1/1000   **C** 1/100

B 1000   **D** 100

29 Dicots are plants which have   10

A fibrous root systems.

B two seed leaves.

C naked seeds.

D parallel veins.

30 In biological terms, succession means   14b

A a descendent of animal breeding.

B the result when one species is more successful than another.

C the gradual change of dominant species present in an ecosystem.

D exceeding the carrying capacity of a population.

31 The life cycle shown below belongs to which plant?   10, 10a

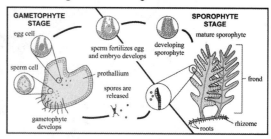

A moss   **C** deciduous tree

B fern   **D** conifer

32 Producers, consumers and decomposers make up the food chain. Which of the following statements is true about a food chain?   13

A There is more stored energy available with less producers.

B Top consumers have the most stored energy.

C Decomposers produce the most energy.

D The longer the food chain becomes, the less energy is available for consumers.

33 A molecule of K+ attaches to a carrier protein located on a cell membrane. A molecule of ATP attaches to the interior of the same carrier protein. The protein changes shape and allows the molecule of K+ to enter the cell. This process is generally known as   2

A passive transport.

B active transport.

C osmosis.

D mitosis.

34 When recovering from injury,   6b
blood platelets that cover the
wound are slowly replaced by newly-
formed skin cells. Old skin cells, with
46 chromosomes, divide to form new
skin cells with 46 chromosomes. This
is classified as what sort of
reproductive process?

  A sexual   **C** haploid

  B asexual   **D** genetic

35 Plants convert carbon dioxide   14
from the atmosphere into sugars
during photosynthesis. This action is a
major part of which nutrient cycle?

  A the phosphorous cycle

  B the carbon cycle

  C the nitrogen cycle

  D the water cycle

36 Some forms of a gene or trait   7a
mask the expression of other
forms. This statement summarizes the
principal of

  A segregation.

  B dominance.

  C independent assortment.

  D true breeders.

37 Deciduous trees like the tulip,   10b
poplar or maple tree have broad
flat leaves. This adaptation allows the
seedlings of deciduous trees to

  A survive and grow with little
sunlight on the forest floor, out-
competing pine seedlings.

  B reduce water loss due to transpiration common in forest environ-
ments.

  C grow taller faster and live for
longer periods of time.

  D produce more waste than other
types of trees making them a valuable member of the ecosystem.

38 Which of the following animals   11
uses external fertilization to
reproduce?

  A kangaroo   **C** salmon

  B potatoes   **D** chicken

39 A chameleon changes color to   12
match its environment. This
action promotes the survival of the
reptile by

  A hiding the reptile from potential
predators.

  B informing the other chameleons
that it is time to mate.

  C allowing the chameleon to find
more food.

  D informing other chameleons that
there is danger nearby.

40 UV light breaks down hydrogen bonds that hold the DNA strand together. Special enzymes act to correct the damage. As the organism ages, the corrective enzymes can no longer function at peak capacity. What will most likely happen to the DNA strand after intensive, repeated exposure to UV light?   8d

A evolution

B mutation

C translocation

D crossing over

41 How is a community different from an ecosystem?   5

A A community is the interaction of the plants and animals in an area whereas an ecosystem is the interaction of the plants and animals and the physical environment.

B A community is the interaction of the plants and animals and the physical environment whereas an ecosystem is the interaction of the plants and animals only.

C A community is the interaction of specific populations of plants whereas an ecosystem is the interaction of all the organisms in a particular area.

D An ecosystem is the interdependence of the plants and animals and the physical environment in which they live whereas a community describes a single type of organism found in a particular area.

42 After fertilization, an embryo goes through many mitotic cell divisions, eventually developing into a zygote. If the embryonic cell contains 32 chromosomes, how many chromosomes are contained within the cells of the zygote?   6a

A 4   **B** 16   **C** 32   **D** 64

43 The animals in the food web shown MOST LIKELY belong to which biome?   15

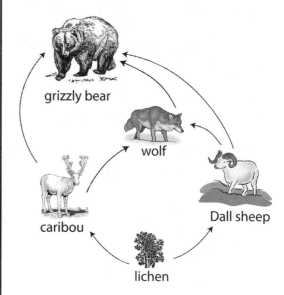

A tundra

B grassland

C desert

D deciduous forest

44 A horse breeder must confirm the lineage of a new foal in order to submit its pedigree. The diagram below shows DNA fingerprinting from the foal and its assumed father, Steeplechase. Which conclusions can you draw?

8b

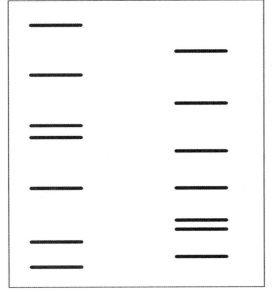

Foal's DNA   Steeplechase's DNA

A The foal definitely was not sired by Steeplechase.

B The foal definitely was sired by Steeplechase.

C Steeplechase is probably not the foal's sire; further testing is needed.

D The lack of matches indicates that the test is corrupted; a new test will have to be performed.

Use the following scenario to answer question 45.

In rabbits, the fur color and ear position are two genetic traits. Each trait is located on a separate chromosome. The allele for producing brown fur (B) is dominant to the allele for producing white fur (b). The allele for producing straight ears (E) is dominant to the allele for producing floppy ears (e).

45 Two rabbits that have the phenotype brown fur and straight ears and the genotype (BbEe) were crossed. Use the completed Punnett square below to determine the probability of offspring that have white fur and floppy ears.

7

	BE	Be	bE	be
BE	BBEE	BBEe	BbEE	BbEe
Be	BBEe	BBee	BbEe	Bbee
bE	BbEE	BbEe	bbEE	bbEe
be	BbEe	Bbee	bbEe	bbee

A 1/16

B 3/16

C 4/16

D 8/16

46 Use the illustration below to determine which of the following best describes   13
what can happen to a food chain when the top predator is removed.

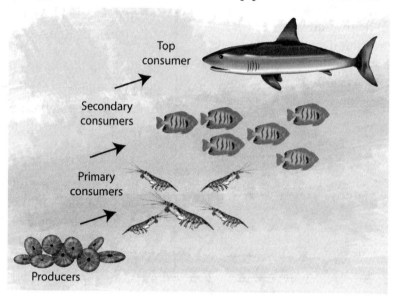

A Another predator will come in to take the place of the previous predator.

B A decrease in the predator's primary prey and an increase in plankton will occur.

C An increase in the predator's primary prey will cause an increase in primary consumers.

D An increase in the predator's primary prey will cause a decrease in primary consumers.

47 The beak and claws of a bird can   12
indicate:

A what type of food they eat and the habitat in which they live.

B the age of the bird.

C the temperament of the bird.

D the gender of the bird.

48 An organism that is well adapted   11
to life in water, uses gills to
breathe and has a bony endoskeleton
belongs to which class of vertebrates?

A *Amphibia*

B *Chondroichtyes*

C *Osteichthyes*

D *Mammalia*

49 Divergent evolution is the   12a, 12b
process whereby

A individuals which are better suited to their environment will survive.

B unrelated species develop similar characteristics.

C different species develop from a common ancestor.

D body parts or organs are similar in structure.

50 The labeled parts in the diagram   5
below collectively comprise a(n)

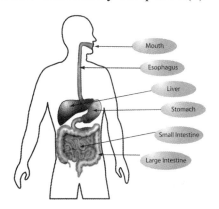

A organ system.

B tissue.

C cell colony.

D multicellular organism.

51 Some groups of chimpanzees   12, 12a
use grass like a spoon, to obtain
and eat termites. Other groups of
chimpanzees use rocks to break into
termite mounds. The way chimpanzees
eat termites is considered a

A learned behavior.

B innate behavior.

C diurnal behavior.

D nocturnal behavior.

52 Angiosperms are classified   10
according to

A their type of flower.

B their type of fruit.

C the difference in their cotyledons.

D the difference in their epidermis.

53 An organism has short arms, legs and ears. This animal is covered with fur   15
that is several layers thick. The animal is white with blue eyes. Which
Environment is most suited to this organism?

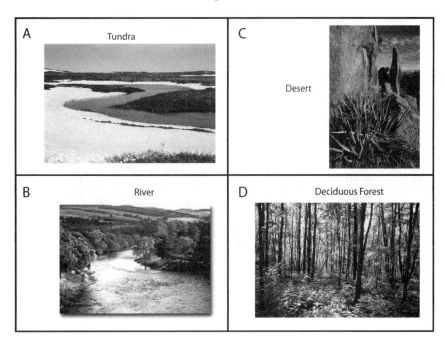

54 To learn how species are related, scientists can compare structures found in   12a
both species to observe similarities. The tail feathers of four different kinds
of birds are shown below. Which two birds are the most closely related?

| Penguin | Peacock | Koklass | Common Pheasant |

A penguin and peacock

B penguin and koklass

C koklass and common pheasant

D peacock and common pheasant

55 Which of the following   14a
statements best describes the
impact humans have had on wetlands
in the United States?

A Humans have not had any major
impacts on wetlands. Very few
wetlands have been drained due to
human activities.

B Humans have drained millions of
acres of wetlands across the United
States, causing increased flooding,
decreased habitat and decreased
water quality.

C Humans have drained millions of
acres of wetlands with no adverse
effects on habitats, water quality or
flooding.

D Human activity has lead to an
increase in wetlands throughout the
United States.

56 When the population of a given   16
area begins to approach the
area's carrying capacity, the
population

A quickly drops.

B begins to fluctuate wildly.

C increases exponentially.

D decrease linearly.

57 When Reynaldo examines a   1a
heart specimen in the
laboratory, he finds it contains three
chambers. Based on his findings, what
is the best conclusion?

A The heart probably belongs to a
bird.

B The heart most likely belongs to a
frog.

C The heart probably belongs to a
worm.

D The heart most likely belongs to a
fish.

58 A severe hurricane hits the Gulf   16
Coast and destroys a national
park. What facts would you select to
show that this situation is an example
of a density-independent limiting
factor?

A This storm only affected large,
dense populations of individuals.

B This natural phenomenon was a
result of the densely populated natural park and would have affected
individuals differently in the wild.

C This storm only affected individuals of a sparse population.

D This storm affected all individuals
of all populations equally regardless of population size.

59 The correct order for the stages of   6
mitosis is

A prophase - metaphase - anaphase -
telophase.

B anaphase - prophase - metaphase -
telophase.

C telophase - prophase - metaphase -
anaphase.

D metaphase - anaphase - telophase -
prophase.

60 All the biotic and abiotic   5
components seen in the picture
represent what level of organization?

A organism   **C** community

B population   **D** ecosystem

61 An example of sexual   6a
reproduction is

A seed fertilization.

B vegetative propagation.

C budding.

D spore formation.

62 Which phylum of invertebrates   11
has a water-vascular system and
tube feet?

A Arthropoda

B Mollusca

C Annelida

D Echinodermata

63 Stomata is/are   10a

A a waxy substance that
surrounds the leaves.

B a tissue that transports water
throughout the plant.

C a layer of plant tissue inside the
stem that protects the plant.

D tiny openings in the leaves that
allow for the exchange of gasses.

64 What type of aquatic system supports brim, bass and trout and ALWAYS has a salinity level lower than 0.5 ppm?   15

   A estuary   **C** pelagic

   B intertidal zone   **D** lake

65 Which of the following statements is NOT true?   3

   A Photosynthesis and respiration convert energy from one form to another.

   B In plants, the products of photosynthesis are used as reactants in respiration, and the products of respiration are used to fuel photosynthesis.

   C Plants carrying out photosynthesis provide a source of oxygen for animals, and respiration provides a source of carbon dioxide for plants.

   D Plant and animal cells perform both respiration and photosynthesis.

66 Which of the following is the function of Golgi bodies?   4

   A packaging and distribution of materials in a cell

   B chemical conversion of fats to carbohydrates in a cell

   C site of protein synthesis in a cell

   D digestion, storage and elimination in the cell

67 Based on the diagram shown below, which of the following statements is true?   14

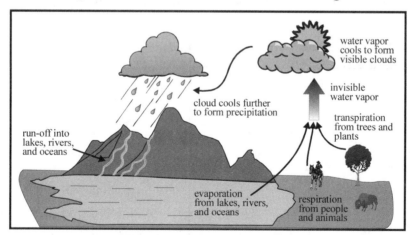

   A The effects of acid rain can be experienced far from their original source of air pollutants.

   B The effects of acid rain are only experienced if acid rain fell directly on the body of water.

   C The effects of acid rain would stop immediately if all air pollution was halted.

   D The effects of acid rain only affect small, localized areas.

68 Identify the density-dependant limiting factor for pronghorn sheep.   16

   A debilitating intestinal parasites

   B a four year drought

   C humans drilling for oil

   D severe flooding that destroys habitat

69 What type of natural ecosystem would you expect to find at a latitude between 30° and 55° N and S that has an average rainfall of 81 cm (32 in) and a temperature range of 31°C (56°F)?   15

   A deciduous forest

   B tropical rain forest

   C polar

   D coniferous forest

70 Solution G has a salt concentration of 2.36 g/mL and it is placed in one side of a U-shaped tube. Solution H has a salt concentration of 0.236 g/mL and is placed on the other side of the U-shaped tube. The semi-permeable membrane separating the two solutions will not allow passage of solute. Predict the outcome of this experiment.   2

   A Water will not move through the membrane, because both sides contain salt.

   B Water will move through the membrane from solution H to solution G.

   C Water will move through the membrane from solution G to solution H.

   D Solute will accumulate at the membrane barrier and clog the passage of solvent.

71 A molecule that is found on the surface of most cells is responsible for communication between the cells. This molecule is made up of long chains of amino acids and is specific to each cell type. This molecule is most likely a   2

   A lipid.   **C** DNA.

   B carbohydrate.   **D** protein.

72 According to the ten percent law, if 10,000 J of sunlight energy reached the Earth's surface approximately how much energy would be lost to the environment or used by an organism at the first trophic level?   13

   A 1000 J   **C** 100 J

   B 9000 J   **D** about 10%

73 Three groups of plants are
grown in the same conditions,
and their growths are compared. The
hypothesis is that exposure to music
changes the growth rate of plants.
Group 1 has plants that are exposed to
heavy metal music for 3 hours per day.
Group 2 is composed of plants that are
exposed to love songs for 3 hours per
day. Group 3 is not exposed to any
music. Which of the groups discussed
above is/are the experimental group(s)
and why?

1b

A All three groups are experimental
groups, since they will demonstrate
that exposure to music can affect
growth rates of plants.

B Group 1 is the experimental group
because it will show a different
growth rate.

C Groups 1 and 2 are the experimental groups because they will test the
variable components of the hypothesis.

D Group 3 is the experimental group
because it does not actively partici-
pate in the variable that supports
the hypothesis.

74 A green pigment called
chlorophyll is responsible for
capturing sunlight needed for
photosynthesis. Identify the cell
organelle that contains cholorphyll.

4

A chloroplast

B nucleus

C endoplasmic reticulum

D mitochondria

75 Red blood cells contain a high
concentration of solutes,
including salts and protein. When the
cells are placed in a hypotonic
solution, water rushes to the area of
high solute concentration, bursting the
cell. This is an example of

2

A diffusion.

B facilitated diffusion.

C osmosis.

D a mutation.

76 Mollusks use a muscular
_____ for locomotion and
_____ for scraping food from an
object.

11

A visceral mass, radula

B radula, coelom

C foot, radula

D foot, visceral mass

77 In the desert, the saguaro cactus
provides shelter for many native
birds and rodents. The flowers of this
plant provide food for nectar-seeking
insects, birds and bats alike. The fruit
of this cactus provides for a wide
variety of organisms including
reptiles, mammals and insects. What
level of biological organization is
described in the preceding sentences?

5

A organism

B population

C community

D ecosystem

78 The main function of lipids within a cell is to   2a

   A provide the main structural components of the cell membrane.

   B provide energy storage within the cell.

   C provide cellular energy.

   D store cellular information.

79 Ostriches and gazelles feed next   16a to each other. They both watch for predators and alert each other to danger. The visual abilities of the two species are different, so that together they can identify threats that the individual animal would not readily see. This is an example of

   A commensalism.   **C** predation.

   B mutualism.   **D** parasitism.

80 Why is plankton important to   9c humans?

   A It is made up of algae.

   B It produces ¾ of the oxygen on Earth.

   C It causes many human diseases every year.

   D It becomes a pollutant in high concentrations.

81 Examine the equations below.   3 What are the reactants in the process of respiration?

$$6\,CO_2 + 6\,H_2O + \text{light energy} \rightarrow C_6H_{12}O_6 \text{ (glucose)} + 6\,O_2$$

$$C_6H_{12}O_6 \text{ (glucose)} + 6\,O_2 \rightarrow 6\,CO_2 + 6\,H_2O + \text{energy}$$

   A carbon dioxide, water and energy

   B carbon dioxide, energy and oxygen

   C oxygen and glucose

   D oxygen, glucose and water

82 Xylem and phloem are groups of   5 specialized cells found in plants, what level of biological organization are xylem and phloem?

   A cells   **C** organs

   B tissues   **D** organisms

83 How is transcription different   8 from translation?

   A In transcription, mRNA is converted into a sequence of amino acids. In translation, a strand of mRNA is created along a strand of DNA.

   B In translation, mRNA is translated in DNA. In transcription, the DNA is then replicated inside the nucleus.

   C In transcription, a strand of mRNA is created along a strand of DNA. In translation, tRNA carries amino acids to mRNA.

   D In translation, DNA is broken apart and assembled in the mitochondria. Transcription then takes place. The pieces of DNA recombine in a vacuole, creating a nucleus.

84 Anaerobic respiration is where   3 sugars are broken down in the absence of oxygen to release energy for cells. Use your knowledge of photosynthesis and respiration to determine which type of organism below CANNOT conduct anaerobic respiration.

   A yeast

   B bacteria

   C tree

   D human

85 Amino acids are linked by peptide bonds to make proteins during the process of

8, 8a

   A translation.

   B transcription.

   C replication.

   D complimentary stranding.

Use the following scenario to answer question 86.

In rabbits, the fur color and ear position are two genetic traits. Each trait is located on a separate chromosome. The allele for producing brown fur (B) is dominant to the allele for producing white fur (b). The allele for producing straight ears (E) is dominant to the allele for producing floppy ears (e).

86 What are the possible genotypes for a rabbit with brown fur and floppy ears?

7, 7b, 7c

   A Bbee, BBee

   B Bbee, BbEe, BBee and BBEe

   C BBee and BBEE

   D BbEe, BBEe, BbEE and BBEE

87 What is the probability that two parents, both with a genotype Bb, will have a child who has brown eyes? B = brown eyes (dominant) b = blue eyes (recessive).

7c

   A 25%

   B 50%

   C 75%

   D 100%

88 Which gas is a product of photosynthesis?

3

   A CO_2

   B H_2O

   C O_3

   D O_2

89 In humans, blood type O is recessive to blood types A and B. Blood type A is co-dominant to blood type B. A mother with blood type BB has a child with blood type AB. Which of the following possible men could be the father to this child?

7a

   A Man 1 with blood type OO

   B Man 2 with blood type BO

   C Man 3 with blood type AO

   D Man 4 with blood type BB

90 The image represents which level of organization?

5

   A cell

   B tissue

   C organ

   D organism

A

absolute dating, 162
absorption, 49
acid, 76
activation energy, 74
active transport, 60
adaptation, 47, 48, 158
    types of, 174
adaptive radiation, 172
adenine, 87, 88
adenosine diphosphate, ADP, 74
adenosine triphosphate, ATP, 74
ADP, 74, 203
aerobic respiration, 79
agricultural biotechnology, 113
air pollutant
    types of, 212
alcoholic fermentation, 80
alcoholic formation, 80
algae, 127
    types of, 127
allele, 101, 104, 107, 166
allopatric speciation, 167
alternation of generation, 131
amino acid monomer, 70
amino acids, 89
amoeba, 128
anaerobic, 124
anaerobic respiration, 79, 80
anaphase, 93
angiosperm, 133
animal cell, 52
animal safety, 26
animalia, 122
anther, 134
antibiotic, 125, 129
anticodon, 89
aquatic ecosystems, 186
archaebacteria, 122, 124
asexual reproduction, 48, 93
atmosphere, 162
ATP, 72, 74, 203
autotroph, 124

B

bacteria, 52, 81, 125
base, 76
behavior, 174
behavioral adaptation, 174
benthic zone, 187
binary fission, 125
binomial nomenclature, 123
biochemical similarity, 159
biodiversity, 157, 222

biome, 183
    types of, 184
biomolecule, 68, 203
biosphere, 188
biosynthesis, 49
biotechnology, 112, 125
birth rate, 192, 193
bond strength, 73
bottlenecking, 171
brown algae, 127
bryophyte, 131
budding, 130

C

Calvin cycle, 78
cambium, 133
capsid, 124
carbon, 67
carbon cycle, 201, 221
carbon dating, 162
carbon fixation reaction, 79
carbon-14, 162
carnivore, 196, 197
carrier, 106
catalyst, 74
cell, 47, 48, 50
    animal, 52
    animal, parts of, 53
    cycle, 92
    daughter, 93
    differentiation, 96
    division, 92, 93
    eukaryotic, 51
    membrane, 125
    parts of, 51, 53
    plant, 52
    plant, parts of, 53
    prokaryotic, 51
    reproductive, 92
    somatic, 92, 93
    system, 96
    types of, 53
    wall, 125
cell division, 109
cell membrane, 51, 53, 57
cell theory, 50
cell wall, 53
cellular biomolecule
    classes of, 68
cellular respiration, 73, 81, 82
Celsius, 36
centriole, 53, 93
centromere, 93
chematroph, 124

migrate, 176
milliliter, 34
mitochondria, 53, 79
mitosis, 93, 125
    stages of, 93
modern synthesis, 166
mold
    types of, 128
molecule, 73
moneran, 124
monoclonal antibody, 114
monocot, 133
monohybrid cross, 102
monomers, 68
monosaccharide, 68
moss, 131
mRNA, 89
multicellular, 55
mutagen, 110
mutation, 109, 170
    types of, 109
mycorrhizae, 129

N
NAD, 75, 79
NADH, 79
nastic movement, 175
natural phenomenon, 37
natural resource, 216
natural selection, 168
natural variation, 169, 172, 189
negative tropism, 175
neutral, 76
newton, 34
niche, 189
nicotinamide adenine dinucleotide phosphate, NADP, 75
nicotinamide adenine dinucleotide, NAD, 75
nitrifying bacteria, 202
nitrogen, 67
nitrogen cycle, 201, 202, 222
nitrogen fixation, 202
nitrogen fixers, 202
nitrogenous base, 87
nocturnal, 176
nondisjunction, 111
nonpolar, 73
non-renewable resource, 216
non-sustainable practice, 218
nonvascular plant, 131
nucleic acid
    characteristics of, 70
nucleolus, 53
nucleotide, 70

nucleus, 52, 53
nutrient cycle, 201
nutrition, 49
nutritional strategy, 159

O
observation, 37
Occupational Safety and Health Administration (OSHA), 27
oligosaccharide, 68
omnivore, 196, 197
order, 121
organ, 55
organ system, 55
organelles, 50, 51, 52, 55
organic molecule, 68, 201
organism
    characteristics of, 47
Origin of Species, 165, 168
osmosis, 58, 59
ovary, 134
ovule, 134
oxidizing atmosphere, 162
oxygen, 67

P
paramecium, 53, 128
parasite, 128
parental generation, 104
passive transport, 58
pelagic zone, 186
pH, 75
phenotype, 102, 103
phenylketonuria (PKU), 111
phloem, 132
phosphate group, 87
phosphate groups, 57
phospholipid bilayer, 57
phospholipids, 57
phosphorous, 67
phosphorous cycle, 201, 203, 222
photoperiodism, 175
photosynthesis, 49, 78, 81, 82, 133, 186
phylogeny, 164
phylum, 121
physical adaptation, 174
Pi, 74
pigment, 78
pili, 125
pistil, 134
plankton, 128
plant cell, 52
plant kingdom, 131
plantae, 122
plasmids, 112

plasmolysis, 60
plastid, 53
plastids, 78
polar, 73
polar body, 94
pollen tube, 134
pollinate, 103
polygenic trait, 107
polymer, 68
polypeptide, 70
polysaccharide, 68
population, 189
positive tropism, 175
pound, 34
predation, 191
predator, 191
pressure, 61
prey, 191
primary air pollutant, 212
primary consumer, 198
primary succession, 194
producer, 196
prokaryote, 122
prokaryotic, 52, 53
prokaryotic organism, 124
proper dress, 27
prophase, 93
protein
    types of, 70
protein synthesis, 88, 112
protista, 122
protozoa, 127
pseudopod, 128
Punnett Square, 102, 106

R

radioactive decay, 162
radioactive parents, 162
radioactivity, 162
radiometric dating, 162
random distribution, 192
rate of depletion, 218
recessive gene, 101
recessive traits, 104
recombinant DNA technology, 112
red algae, 127
red tide, 127
renewable resource, 216
replication, 92, 109
reproduction, 47, 49
    types of, 48
reproductive cell, 92
resource, 190, 194
Resource Conservation and Recovery Act,

RCRA, 212
respiration, 49
response, 48, 49
restriction enzyme, 112
result, 40
rhizome, 132
ribose, 88
ribosome, 89
RNA, 71, 88, 203
    types of, 88, 89
root, 133
    cap, 133
    hair, 133
rRNA (ribosomal RNA), 88, 89

S

safety procedures, 25, 26, 27
salinity, 186
saprophyte, 129, 197
scanning election microscope, 52
Schleiden, Matthias, 50
Schwann, Theodor, 50
SCID, severe combined immunodeficiency, 115
science, definition, 36
scientific experiment, 38
scientific method, 36
scientific process, 37
secondary air pollutant, 212
secondary consumer, 198
secondary succession, 194
secretion, 49
segregation, principle of, 104
self pollination, 134
self-pollinate, 103
semi-permeable membrane, 57, 59
sensitivity, 47, 48
sex cell, 104
sex chromosome, 106
sexual reproduction, 48, 94
sharp instrument safety, 26
SI unit, 32
sickle-cell anemia, 110
silica,, 127
slime mold, 128
solute, 57
solution, 57
solvent, 57
somatic cell, 92, 93
speciation, 166, 167, 169
    sympatric, 168
species, 121, 122, 123, 157, 189
    diversity, 157
sperm, 94, 131
sperm cell, 94

NOTES

NOTES

NOTES

NOTES